To Steve & Rhona

with love & appreciation.

Susan Sperling Brock

The Promised Land

How Doing Your Homework in Your Wilderness Leads to Healthy, Lasting Relationships

Susan Sperling Brock

WESTBOW
PRESS
A DIVISION OF THOMAS NELSON
& ZONDERVAN

WestBow Press books may be ordered through booksellers or by contacting:

WestBow Press
A Division of Thomas Nelson & Zondervan
1663 Liberty Drive
Bloomington, IN 47403
www.westbowpress.com
1 (866) 928-1240

ISBN: 978-1-4908-5619-3 (sc)
ISBN: 978-1-4908-5620-9 (hc)
ISBN: 978-1-4908-5621-6 (e)

Library of Congress Control Number: 2014919911

Printed in the United States of America.

WestBow Press rev. date: 11/25/2014

My two life verses:

"And above all things have fervent love among yourselves; for love shall cover a multitude of sins."
(1 Peter 4:8, KJV)

"As we have therefore opportunity, let us do good unto all men, especially unto them who are of the household of faith."
(Galatians 6:10, KJV)

This book is dedicated in loving memory to Reverend Dr. John Caleb Morris, III. God used John to save my life and my sanity, for which I am forever grateful.

Contents

Introduction xi

Part I
The Pathway to Spiritual Rest and Healing

1. When They Don't Love You the Way You Want 1
2. SHOCK #1: Give Thanks 9
3. SHOCK #2: How To Make It When the Most Important
   People Don't Love You 17
4. Shock #3: Why Is All This Happening to Me? 23
5. I Will Bring the Blind By a Way That They Knew Not 32
6. A Touch of Grace.. 40
7. Everywhere I Go, There I Am 46
8. War with Amalek.. 52
9. Dealing with Negative Messages..................................... 60
10. A Lesson In God's Pursuit Of A Relationship With Us............... 66
11. A Checkup on Motivations 75
12. A Discussion with Paul about Holiness 83
13. The Pathway into Spiritual Intimacy with God..................... 90
14. Our Identification with Christ................................... 99
15. Entering In – From Crisis and Captivity to Freedom 106

Part II
The Pathway to Emotional Rest and Healing

16. Down for the Count 119
17. My "Picker" Is Broken 127

18. Who's Responsible For Your Happiness? 134

19. God's Assertiveness Training
    Part I – Identifying the Source of the Drama............................ 140

20. God's Assertiveness Training
    Part II – Going Back to School 147

21. Taking a Break...162

22. Feasting on Crumbs...171

23. Why We Are So Attracted to Certain People 181

24. The Blessing..189

25. Rejoicing in Heaven..196

26. What Is Your Name?.. 201

27. The Two-Fold Dream...210

28. Know When to Hold 'Em, Know When to Fold 'Em 217

29. How's That Working out for You? 224

30. There Is No Plan B..231

31. No Greater Compliment – Zechariah 8:23 239

32. Remember Whence Thou Came 245

Afterword.. 249

Notes 251

Introduction

This book may not be the typical Christian book you are expecting. I did not attend church on a regular basis until the age of twenty-four. I have no professional theological training nor did I attend seminary. Neither of my parents were church-goers. The subject of church was simply not discussed during my upbringing. The only place I heard about God was in school from a teacher. This led to a very short period of only a few months when I attended church as a child with my sister, Julia, and one of her friends before our lives were ripped apart through our parent's divorce and our dad's death. Although I had accepted Christ as my Savior at age twelve, it seemed nothing more than "fire insurance," and I had no idea there could be more to gain from this relationship.

This book explores the search which I began at age twenty-four to find answers in life and, in doing so, how I reconnected with my Savior and developed an intimate relationship with Jesus Christ. I asked God to be my Teacher and for Him to take up my training. While I engaged in intensive Bible study, I also read hundreds of books by many of the finest writers and theologians of their time, including Theodore H. Epp, founder of the Back to the Bible Broadcast, Miles J. Stanford, Dr. Alan Redpath, Watchman Nee, Major W. Ian Thomas, C.S. Lewis, and many more. While the extent of my knowledge probably would not enable me to answer a challenge from someone trained in Systematic Theology, I would be able to answer a question from a person desperately seeking hope and healing from years of mental or emotional turmoil or those carrying the scars of physical or sexual abuse. Although I don't claim to have the ultimate answer for everyone, the answer for me is Christ. As a Christian I have witnessed lives going up in smoke, and the only equipment most Christians are equipped with are proverbial garden hoses. It's time for discipleship-equipped believers to deal more effectively with life issues.

The road to healing was long and difficult, and in some instances, there are simply no shortcuts. However, the amount of *time* it takes is different for each person, and my prayer is that you will identify with the path and journey the Lord brought me through and will apply the principles and truths the Lord showed me as well. In doing so, I hope you will experience a greatly reduced duration in time on your own journey as you encounter these truths.

Each one of us can benefit from doing our "homework," which involves both the spiritual search and principles found and the application of those principles, as well as the emotional and psychological work of dealing with childhood wounds and negative messages. It involves the discovery of what binds us or keeps us captive, both spiritually and emotionally, and the subsequent release through healing. You know you've done your homework when the drama and roller coaster ride of the past transforms into a restful and peaceful relationship with the Lover of your soul, our Lord, and your personal relationships will reflect this change as well. Thus, as you follow along, you will discover answers given both in a spiritual form through counseling and intense study of the Scriptures as well as psychological training. It is not my intent to have theological expositions or debates. I simply questioned God through both His Word and through my life circumstances, and these are the personal answers that came to me. The theological portions may take a little time to digest. My prayer is that your understanding will come in *days* and not *years*, like it did for me. The search of how I discovered these truths is included for a two-fold purpose: first, to show the steps of one moving from complete lack of knowledge of Scripture to a deeper, more meaningful heart knowledge for all to understand. Secondly, this search not only profoundly changed my life, but the heartfelt acceptance of what I learned literally *saved* my life.

The overriding truth that came out again and again is that God has a process for each of us as believers to bring us to a peaceful, restful, intimate, and abundantly full relationship with Him. That process begins when we find ourselves in a dry and thirsty land and ends in a place He wants all His children to discover – The Promised Land. Walk with me as we enter in. The invitation extends to all believers. Come on in. Bring them in. Come with me into the Promised Land.

Part I

The Pathway to Spiritual Rest and Healing

When They Don't Love You the Way You Want

How in the world could I make it? Why was everything in my life so constantly topsy-turvy? Why couldn't I have a decent, lasting relationship with anyone?

I had married at age twenty-four in December 1980. By twenty-six, I was separated and would be for another two years. With eighteen divorces within my family—parents, grandparents, and siblings—I didn't know what a successful marriage even looked like.

I searched the world over for answers but found none. Finally, I decided to start going back to church to see if I could find any answers, as I had just started reading the Bible again. I had quit going to church when I was twelve after only attending for a few months with my next older sister, Julia. During that same year, one of the very few kind men in my life, my seventh-grade choir teacher, had shared his faith in Christ with us all year in school, and I accepted Christ as my Savior the following fall. However, we were then yanked away from church when, during a short twenty-four-month period, our family suffered the three Big Ds: our parents divorced, our dad died, and we moved to Dallas, Texas, where my mother could get better-paying work. (I wondered as a kid if that's why people call Dallas the Big D. That's sure why I do.)

After failing in multiple marriages, our mother later told my younger sister, Penny, and me that she had given up ever figuring out how to have a successful relationship with a man and that she was passing the quest down to us two girls. Both my two older sisters and half brother had already been through or would later go through divorce themselves, and now here I was, facing the likely prospect of marriage failure myself.

We didn't grow up in church. My father was a self-proclaimed atheist, and my mother never attended church as an adult. My father grew up in Sabinov, Poland, and later immigrated to the United States, and my mother was raised by her Swedish grandmother in Seattle, Washington.

For six years, I was the youngest of three girls. Monica was the oldest, and then Julia, and then me. I also had an older half brother, Cary, and then another sister came along behind me named Penny. I would be twelve before I learned there was another half brother, Tom, who had lived with my grandparents since he was a baby.

There was so much strife and fighting in our home between our parents that Julia and I ran away when I was five, hoping to find a farm with animals, because animals were the only creatures who loved unconditionally and didn't fight with one another. We only got a few blocks when we decided that, wherever we went, we would probably meet other people just like our family. That certainly appeared to be the case on the block where we lived, for the other kids and their families we knew were dysfunctional as well. Two other kids my age lived on the same block. One's mother had committed suicide, and the other's parents allowed their children to be sexually abused. This occurred in what would be considered an upper-middle-class neighborhood in Waco, Texas, during 1961 and 1962.

I couldn't trust anyone. When I was five, I faced three incidents of abuse, two from adults and one from a six-year-old boy who lived across the street from us.

One day, neighbors came to rescue me from the six-year-old after hearing my screams from our backyard. It would be thirty years before I realized that he was merely acting out what was being done to him behind closed doors in his own home, with no one to rescue him.

Later, a close friend of the family took a liking to me and would often ask my father if he could take me to go get a Coke. The first couple of times it was great fun, and he bought me coloring books. But the third time, he took me to his house and started acting very inappropriately. I begged him to take me home, which, thankfully, he did. I was very lucky to not have been killed or raped. Still, I was ashamed to tell my parents what had happened and just looked down to the floor and went to my room. Then Julia asked me what had happened and then told our parents. No one ever talked with me about it; we simply never saw this individual ever again.

The third incident that same year was when I was, once again, playing by myself in the backyard while my siblings were at school. I kept seeing a car slowly circling our block, and I hid in the bushes, looking out. Something told me not to move. The third time the car circled the block, it turned down our alley, and the guy kept looking into our backyard. I was too scared to run, afraid he would catch me before I could get to the back door, so I stayed still. He stopped at the house next door and got out of the car, looking around, especially in our backyard. I don't know how he didn't see me in the bushes. Finally, he got in the car and drove off.

When I was finally able to get up and, with great trembling, get to the house to tell my mother, she didn't believe me, and completely dismissed my claims. A few hours later, when we were watching television, the newscaster stated that a man had been arrested while trying to abduct a six-year-old from the local schoolyard. When I saw the picture of him, I told my parents that that was the man I had told my mother about that morning. I think they finally believed me. Child predators and pedophiles would constantly torment me every year until the age of twelve, when I was finally saved. Although we moved numerous times, predators seemed to keep finding me. The question was not who *was* a pedophile but rather who *wasn't*. Thank God they never won.

The worst day of my life was the day our dad died. I was thirteen, and he was only forty-four. He had married a younger woman, a nurse, and they fought all the time, too. They were living in an apartment complex, and one Sunday, according to the neighbors, there was a big fight and then silence for about an hour. After that, an ambulance showed up and took my father to the hospital after he appeared to have had a heart attack. He was an insurance agent, and his boss came to the hospital to see him. When his boss arrived, my dad was stable but had a second heart attack and died a few minutes later. We found out about his death when his boss called our mother.

My father had been a compulsive gambler for much of his adult life. He was very intelligent and spoke seven languages, but he was unable to keep a regular job very long or maintain a relationship. I'm convinced that, after much studying about it, he had been a victim of Munchausen Syndrome by proxy. In these cases, one parent is often a doctor, as my dad's father was, and the other parent repeatedly takes the child to the doctor, claiming that the child is sick. In my dad's case, his mother got the attention from his father (the physician) by using the "sick" child (my dad). Unfortunately, the children in these relationships usually struggle when they grow into adulthood with maintaining commitments, jobs, and relationships. When my dad died, he had not paid his life insurance policy, which had a thirty-day grace period that ended at 12:00 p.m. He died fifteen minutes before the end of that thirty-day grace period—a compulsive gambler to the end.

I was the one who answered the phone when our grandparents called the house and asked why we were not at the funeral. They had forbidden our mother from coming, so she forbade us from attending as well. On the phone, my grandmother cursed me out and then hung up on me. We had some friends who lived at the end of the block who were like grandparents to me, and they advised me to write my grandparents and explain what had happened. I knew that if our mother found out, she would kill me, but I went ahead and did it. Grandmother did receive the letter and wrote me back to say that I was forgiven. We never saw them again, as they both died a couple of years later. Any inheritance went to second and third cousins who lived near where they had lived.

I don't ever recall a single incidence of either of my parents hugging us kids; perhaps it was because their parents never hugged them either. The first time I even saw people hugging was when I was twenty-four and was attending church for the first time. It was also the first time I saw happily married people. One of those couples was a younger couple close to my age. Another couple I would later meet at a different church who were happily married were also a younger couple close to my age. Their names are Johnny and Frances Coffman, and they were a great model of what I hoped to attain someday. They later moved to a different church, and I used Johnny as my mechanic for over thirty years. We have remained friends all these years later, although I don't see them very often.

The church I attended was what I would later consider to be extremely legalistic. I truly believe that the Lord wanted me there, and as I look back, I'm convinced that the purpose of my attendance there was to break me forever of legalism as well as to teach me to *not* put my trust in the messenger, but in the One who sends and *is* the Message. I already thought that God was more of a policeman than a loving Father. I knew nothing about His love, mercy, and grace. I also knew that there was no way I could go *back* and learn what I needed to learn about relationships, either with Him or in a marriage, so I just had to start where I was. I had read in the Bible that "when my father and my mother forsake me, then the Lord will take me up." (Psalms 27:10, KJV) I wouldn't know for years that this meant that he would sweep me up into His arms, so I simply asked for years, "Lord, since my father and my mother forsook the spiritual training that I needed because they were unable to, please take up my training and teach me Yourself, Lord!"

When I first started at the church there, it was led by a very kindly, older pastor for just a few months, but he soon retired and a new pastor replaced him. As I sat in church and heard mostly fire and brimstone, I studied more and more, and from time to time, the Lord's Spirit would give me understanding to help me. For example, on one occasion the pastor was preaching that if a branch doesn't bear any fruit, it should be cut down and thrown in the fire. (John 15:1-6, KJV) I went home shaking in fear, as I knew I didn't have any fruit to show, yet His Spirit gently led me to turn a few pages further in the Bible and read about when the Master came to see the Husbandman of the vineyard and requested why there was no fruit after three years. The Husbandman requested that they place fertilizer around it and allow it another year to bear fruit. (Luke 13:7-9, KJV)

I was continually fearful and terrified of God, yet His Spirit consistently comforted my wounded spirit.

"Lord, I feel so captive and I'm trying so hard and seeking so hard," I would say.

Then His Spirit would gently show me, "And you shall seek me and find me, when ye shall search for me with all your heart. And I *will* be found of you, saith the Lord: and I *will* turn away your captivity." (Jeremiah 29:13-14, KJV)

"Lord, I am simply blind to Your Ways, and I'm so afraid You will throw me away if I don't do just right," I would reply.

"I will bring the blind by a way that they knew not, I will lead them in paths that they have not known, I will make darkness light before them and crooked things straight. These things will I do and *not* forsake them," His Spirit would soothingly then show me. (Isaiah 42:16, KJV)

"I will *never* leave you nor forsake thee," His Spirit whispered to my heart. (Hebrews 13:5, KJV)

5

"For God hath not given us the spirit of fear; but of power, and of love, and of a *sound mind.*" (2 Timothy, 1:7, KJV)

"Lord, I sure would like to have a sound mind." I began to view His Word as a cleansing agent, like pouring clean water through a filthy clogged filter, slowing clearing away simply by the action of pouring, slowly cleansing the filth, mire, and muddiness of my thoughts toward God, myself, and those around me.

My father and his parents had escaped Hitler in 1939, and his view had always been one of questioning, "How could there be a God who allowed such suffering to happen to His people?" I felt just the opposite – "There has to be a God in spite of all the suffering that happens to His people."

In the few months that I attended church as a child, I learned just enough to understand that I was a sinner and needed forgiveness and grace. Yet, here I was, all these years later, wondering if my decision to accept Christ even "took." There certainly wasn't anything in my life to demonstrate that it did, and there certainly wasn't any grace at the tiny church where I attended and where the people knew I was separated. I might as well have worn a scarlet letter on my forehead. It seemed that you could be a murderer and be forgiven, but not if you were separated or going through a divorce! When I had tried to get help from the pastor, he sent me to his wife, who simply told me, "You can't question God, and don't go outside of this church for anything."

"That's strange," I replied. "I know I don't know much about the Bible, but wasn't there some guy named Hezekiah that questioned God and he got to live longer?" I wasn't asking out of rebellion, I was simply desperate for answers. Yet somehow, I knew I couldn't give up. Somehow I knew that if my life didn't change, I wouldn't live to see the age of thirty.

When I found this little church two years before, I had re-dedicated my life to the Lord and asked Him to teach me and help me to answer the questions that poured from my broken, wounded heart. After working for four years at the Dallas Police Department as a civilian, working the late night tour in the Records Division, and seeing only the lowest, darkest side of humanity, I figured that if there were no answers from God, there would be nowhere else to look. I had met my future husband there and had left the police department for better paying work, ultimately transferring to Tyler, Texas, where we would later marry. He was several years older than me, and before marriage he had promised a home together as well as the prospect of children. After marriage, he wanted me to quit my good job and live in a travel trailer, traveling around the country working part time as a waitress while living in South Texas as a "winter Texan" and somewhere else during the summers. The differences between us continued to magnify, but he did agree to attend church for a short time. This didn't last long, however, and he left the church, and then he left me. Even though he saw how serious I was about getting my life turned around and he later would tell me that he liked what church attendance did for me, he simply couldn't accept that kind of lifestyle for himself.

While waiting during our separation for any kind of speck of hope for our relationship to work, I volunteered to work with the fourth and fifth grade class so I could also begin to learn where I had left off so many years before when I attended church in Waco, Texas. During the second year, I volunteered to work with the high school kids, and by the third year I started teaching adults. Every Sunday I would think to myself, *maybe today will be the day that I hear something that will help.*

I decided to try to find a counselor of some kind, but in 1982, there weren't many to be found. There was a local public health agency that offered counseling, so I thought I would start there.

After pouring out my heart for forty-five minutes, the lady simply said, "Well, you just need to stop feeling the way that you do," to which I responded, "Lady, if I knew how, I wouldn't be here!!"

I walked out the door and cried out to God in tears and frustration, "Please, dear God. Is there anyone out there who can help me? If there is, please send him or her to me. I can't take it anymore. Please help me!"

Within twenty-four hours, I received a phone call. It was one of my girlfriends.

She said, "You've been on my heart. I've been meaning to tell you about the pastor/counselor I have been seeing. He was one of the founding fathers of the church I attend, and he is so helpful. I was wondering if you might consider coming to see him. I'd be willing to go with you if you are afraid or anything."

"Absolutely," I replied. "No, I'm not afraid, I'll answer any question he has for me." That day, the appointment was set. I tell people to this day that the Lord used this man, John Morris, to save my life. He gave me a jump start to life and to the Christian faith that I so desperately needed while telling me the three most shocking truths I had ever heard in my life.

HOMEWORK:

- What are the circumstances that have brought you to your knees? _____

- What is the heartache from which you need healing? _____
_____

- How have you tried in the past to deal with it? _____
_____

- What is your relationship with Jesus Christ? Do you know Him? _____

- Has your experience with church been different than what you expected? _____

- Have you ever considered meeting with a Christian counselor? _____

SHOCK #1: Give Thanks

The first shock came at the end of the very first appointment with John Morris.

"Before you come back for your second appointment, I want you to write down forty reasons why you're thankful for going through this separation and potential divorce," John told me.

"Do what?!" I said as I looked at him in absolute shock.

"Don't come back without it," he repeated his request.

"That's like saying that I'm thankful for having two flat tires!" I replied. "Where in the world do you come up with such a bizarre request?"

"I Thessalonians 5:18," he replied, "In ALL things give thanks, for this is the will of God in Christ Jesus concerning you."

"I have never heard of such a thing," I replied.

"Nonetheless, I will expect to see this when you return," he replied.

"I can't even think of one," I retorted, but I was desperate to come back. He was so kind, and he wasn't shocked by anything I said or that had happened to me. He didn't treat me like I was crazy, and he had given me a crumb of hope that things could, and *I* could, get better. I couldn't argue with his logic either; he had reminded me that it was not my husband who had come requesting help, but me, so let's work on me and not be so concerned with trying to change him.

I didn't come up with forty, but I did come up with more than twenty. To this day, I still use this truth and will always start in the same way:

- I give thanks for what I'm currently going through in obedience to Your Word.
- I give thanks for what I'm currently going through, because it will bring a time of self-examination.

- I give thanks for what I'm currently going through, because You, Lord, are going to teach me something I could learn in no other way than this.
- I give thanks because this is another opportunity to respond to God's grace rather than to circumstances.

I would later add:

- I give thanks because this is an opportunity to get to know God in a clearer way – to understand His ways with His children, rather than His works. Moses knew God's *Ways* while the children of Israel only knew His *Works...* (Psalms 103:7, KJV)
- I give thanks because this is another opportunity to learn or demonstrate contentment. Is my happiness and contentment based on another person or circumstances or on my relationship with Christ?
- I give thanks because this is an opportunity to learn or demonstrate completeness. "Ye are complete in Him." (Col. 2:10, KJV) I am a whole, complete person who does not have to look to a human being for completion – they are to complement and enhance me, not complete me, for I am complete in Him.
- I give thanks because this is an opportunity to learn to love or to demonstrate love. This is His greatest commandment – to love Him with all my heart, mind, and soul, and then my neighbor as myself. What would love do?

Once I began the list, thoughts began to come to me about what I needed to learn, and it would take some time before I realized this was the Holy Spirit, our Heavenly Counselor, performing His work in my life. Ephesians 5:20 (KJV) also says, "Giving thanks always for all things." This certainly doesn't mean that we thank God for the evil happening to us, but it changes our mindset to one of victor instead of victim. When I saw the verse in Psalms 50:23 (NIV), "He who *sacrifices* thank offerings honors me, and he prepares the way so that I may show him the salvation of God," I readily realized that sometimes offering thanks *is* a real sacrifice. When we realize that "all things work together for good to them that love God,"

(Romans 8:28 KJV), and that "He that hath begun a good work in you will perform it until the day of Jesus Christ," (Philippians 1:6, KJV) then we can realize and relax in our relationship with Him that whatever has happened *to* us can be transformed *in* us to be a message of grace and hope to others. For example, when I realized that the little boy who tortured me in the back yard that day was himself being tortured in his own home, I was able to forgive and pray for him, wherever he was in life.

Am I thankful that my dad died? Not in a direct sense, but I am thankful for the thirteen years that I did have with him and that I knew him, and I'm thankful that I would later find a Heavenly Father who tells me to call him, "Abba, Father," which means: "Daddy, Daddy!" (Romans 8:15, NIV)

Am I thankful that I'm divorced? I'm not happy that I wasn't able to maintain God's standard for marriage, "until death do you part," but I've discovered that, although God loves the institution of marriage, as He's the one who invented it, He even more loves the two people who make it up. He sent His Son to die and ransom *us*, not the institution of marriage. I have kept the newspaper insert written by Paul Powell, former pastor of Green Acres Church for over 30 years, called, "God Loves Divorcees." In it he clearly explains that sometimes choices in life are not black and white, that sometimes we have to choose the lesser evil. It is better to divorce than be killed or beaten, etc. God has called us to peace. That message spoke to my heart in a profound way as I struggled in that small church I was attending. While I was being told there that God couldn't even speak to me because I was so rebellious, I saw grace – God loves divorcees! It was also during this time when I faced divorce that I heard the words that I'd longed for all my life from my mother: "I love you." Now that's something to give thanks for!

Am I thankful that I spent four and a half years in a legalistic church? It sure wasn't fun, but I am so thankful because the rejection I felt in the church was used by God to force me to look only to God for relief. When they would tell me *not* to go outside the church for answers and *not* to question God, I searched day and night and studied day and night, bringing all my questions to God for which He led me and taught me so I could understand His ways with His children. Being there was like looking at the Law, which is, as His Word describes, a taskmaster who leads us to

Christ. I hung on for dear life to His Word, which gave me hope when no hope could be found and drew me to others in His Word who felt as I did: "I had fainted unless I had believed to see the goodness of the Lord in the land of the *living....*" (Psalms 27:13, KJV) This illustrated the possibility that I could do more than just wait for heaven where there is no pain and sorrow, but see that there is something here in this life as well. "And I will restore unto you the years the locusts hath eaten...." (Joel 2:25, KJV) I knew life was full of devouring sorrow, suffering, and rejection, but somehow God would make up for it in *this* life if I would not give up.

Am I thankful that I was pursued by a pedophile? Absolutely not, but I am thankful I *survived*, and that showed me that many of us are simply survivors, doing what we have to do in order to make it to adulthood.

Now if you told me that I was going to be forced to travel in time back to when I was child, I would almost rather die, yet in looking back years later, I am thankful for the family I grew up with, as I truly do not believe I would have the relationship with God that He pursued in me had I lived in a wonderful, loving, Christian home. I simply would not have searched and would have more likely been satisfied with mediocrity. I was simply a natural-born quitter. You see, as a child, if an adult told me that I couldn't do something, I believed them and didn't even try. Yet, the biggest fight I had with my mother was just over that. I've told her to this day that she is the one who started the pattern in my life for sticking with something.

My family moved a dozen or more times during my childhood, and I started my freshman year and the first six weeks of my junior year at David W. Carter High School in South Oak Cliff, Dallas, Texas. During the second six weeks, we had moved closer to the White Rock Lake/Casa Linda area on the east side of Dallas, and I attended Bryan Adams High School. The very first day I showed up, I discovered I was thirty lessons behind in typing and fifteen behind in shorthand, and the science class was using an entirely different chemistry book, so it was essentially starting over. All three teachers told me it would be impossible for me to catch up and that I should drop these three classes and take them during my senior year. When I told this to my mother, she became angry and insisted that I would not be dropping those classes. We had a huge fight over it, and even though we didn't have a typewriter, she instructed me to do what I could while the others were typing or studying during these classes. When

I told the teachers that she had insisted that I not drop the classes, they all allowed me to try. I became the fastest first-year typist in the school as well as the fastest shorthand taker. When I had gone into the chemistry class, I asked who the smartest kids were. All of the students pointed to two boys and one girl. I walked over and sat next to the girl, told her what had happened, and begged her to allow me to watch and learn as much as I could from her. It was the most difficult class I had ever taken, and the teacher was very difficult to be around. Despite trying my best, I was only able to earn a C, but I felt very grateful to get it.

After attending my twenty-fifth high school reunion, and having not kept up with any of the few friends I had met in high school, I noticed that my science class friend had not attended. We were given a booklet with names and email addresses and bios on many of our old classmates, and there she was in the booklet. I decided to email her to thank her for tutoring me and helping me all those years ago, and at first she didn't remember me. When I explained to her all that had happened, she asked me if I remembered what had happened to her. I told her I had no idea. She had dropped the class toward the end of the year because even her father who had tried to tutor her and who was himself a chemical engineer couldn't help her, and she felt like she would fail and she absolutely hated the teacher. I told her I didn't know she had dropped the course. She said she had become a teacher herself just to prove to herself that she could overcome that awful teacher. This account made me even more grateful for that "C" I had received.

Once I asked my mother (during a time when I happened *not* to be in trouble) what my greatest strength and my greatest weakness were.

"That's easy," she said, "Your greatest strength is gentleness, and your greatest weakness is stubbornness." I've thought to myself all these years since that stubbornness is just the negative demonstration of the positive attribute of perseverance, tenacity, and endurance. Yet it took great tribulation to bring those qualities out.

You see, it took a great trial just to get me to come back to church. While others freely came and while it had been easy to get to go when I was a kid, it became an impossible task that I couldn't achieve just to go these past two years, from age twenty-four, when I rededicated my life to the Lord, to my current age of twenty-six, when I needed God the most.

When I had left the Dallas Police Department in 1978, I had become the youngest civilian supervisor in the history of the department at age twenty. I had hired a girl who had previously worked in the Post Office. She had been making what a twenty-year veteran at the Dallas Police Department with a college degree made in comparison to my salary, but she had been injured early in her career and had to leave. I went and took the test for the Postal Service several months, later, got hired, and then left the Police Department for the Post Office.

While working at the Police Department and again at the Post Office, I had to work late nights and sleep during the daytime. After working for one year in Dallas, I transferred to Tyler, Texas, where I was put on the evening shift. It was during this time in late 1979 and into 1980, when I left Dallas and started my career in Tyler, that my heart became heavy with the realization that I had to get back into church, but my shift wouldn't allow it. My evening shifts started anywhere from 3:00-4:00PM and went until 11:00P.M-12:00 midnight. Unfortunately, on Sunday, I was scheduled to come back and work during the morning and afternoon, usually from 11:00A.M.-7:00P.M., as there was no evening or late night shift for that one day. This prevented me from attending Wednesday evening or Sunday services.

I told my supervisors what I wanted to do and asked what I could do to change shifts so I could start attending church. The only alternative was the late-night tour, since I didn't have any seniority to work the day shift. I had no problem volunteering for the night shift, but before I could start I had to learn two city schemes, which included every street in Tyler, Texas, a population at that time of about 75,000. This included all breaks in block numbers and which carrier delivered to each street and be able to do this in one second, at 4:00A.M., while working on a machine. There were approximately two thousand of these blocks and breaks, and the scheme was broken up into two parts – I had to pass one before I could start on the next. I requested both of them at the same time, because the desperation in my heart was growing by the day. Employees were given approximately six months to learn each scheme, but I passed them both in four months – barely. The supervisors allowed me to move to the late night shift, at which point I immediately started attending church.

After only working a few months and attending church faithfully, the lead supervisor called me into his office one afternoon.

He said, "I have good news and bad news for you. The good news is that, although you have been working forty hours a week, you have been considered a part-time flexible employee. A late-night opening is coming up for you to apply to where you will be full time and not be moved around. Unfortunately, you have no seniority, and if even one person bids on the same job, you will not get the job, and the union will force me to put you back on the evening shift."

I was terrified, because going back to the evening shift meant I couldn't attend church. Although the late-night opening was a terrible job as far as hours go, with split days off and late nights, I would discover that the night before the bidding closed, three other people also bid on the job.

I went into the break room by myself with tears streaming down my cheeks, and I cried out to God. "I've tried to be faithful to come to Your house. I've done everything humanly possible to be able to be there. Lord, do You not want me in Your house anymore?? There is nothing else that I can do!" I went home deeply depressed, knowing that that evening I would get the results and I would have to make plans to go back to the evening shift and stop attending church. I got in bed at 7AM and the phone rang about 11AM. It was a personnel representative in Dallas, Texas:

"We are so sorry to wake you, we realize that you have just gone to bed, but we had to call you and tell you what has happened. There were four bids on this particular position – yours and three other people. It really is a rather low seniority position, so we don't understand why there is such a fuss going on about it, but for some reason, all three of the other people have called back their bids on that job, so it is yours!"

I know for a fact that no one but God Himself heard me in that break room that night, since the machines were too loud for anyone to hear me. I would later approach each of the three people who called their bids back in, none of whom were aware of why I had bid on the job or what would have happened if I hadn't gotten it. I believe God wanted me to see His power that night.

As I came before the Lord about it that next day, it was as though He were asking me, *Will you leave Me too when the going gets rough? Will you quit Me? You have much to learn, and you need to be able to withstand. I have tested you to see if you will stay when you do get to come. You wouldn't*

15

come when the door was wide open all those years ago. Will you come and stay when the door opens again? Will you leave Me?

"Lord, You are all I have right now," I replied. "I'm so low that I have to reach up to touch bottom! There is nowhere else to go and no one else to turn to but You." Little did I know that I would enter a wilderness of three and a half years of wandering from the time I rededicated my life to the Lord until there would be any kind of true peace in my life. All I knew was that my life depended on these actions, and later I would discover that this was literally true.

HOMEWORK:

Perhaps this is a tremendous surprise to you as well to think of "giving thanks in all things." I encourage you to begin your list as well. Try it for yourself. Some people say, "Don't test God," but I believe He is pretty clear on some things like this, and as long as you're are not testing God out of anger and rebellion, I think He can handle it. He says,

"Try Me, Prove Me..." (Malachi 3:10, KJV).

"Taste and see that the Lord is good." (Psalms 34:8, KJV)

GIVING THANKS:

- Lord, I give thanks for _____
  in obedience to Your Word.

- I give thanks because this brings a time of self examination. I ask for You to search my heart, cleanse me, and lead me in the ways everlasting. Teach me Your ways, not mine.

- I give thanks because You are going to teach me something I could learn in no other way than going through _____
  _____.

- I give thanks because _____
  _____.

SHOCK #2: How To Make It When the Most Important People Don't Love You

The second shock came after the first few visits with John Morris. After pouring out my whole family history and what was currently happening within my marriage and now separation, I threw out *THE BIG QUESTION:*

"How do you make it in life when the most important people in your life don't love you?"

"You can not only make it, but you can thrive," John quietly answered.

"How is that possible?" I implored. John answered me with a question of his own.

"Do you know what the greatest commandment is?" I had not been reading the Bible very long, but had been spending time in the Gospels and Psalms quite a bit, so I told him,

"I don't know why the Gospels tell the same story four times, but isn't it something like 'love God with all your heart, mind, and soul?'"

"Correct," he replied, "and what is the second greatest commandment?"

"Love your neighbor as yourself," I responded.

"Correct again," he replied. "You see, in those two commandments, four relationships are discussed. Two are vertical and two are horizontal. First, God loves you ↓. Secondly, you love God ↑. Third, you love yourself ←. Fourth, you love your neighbor as yourself →. Nowhere in there does it say that your neighbor loves you back."

"What!!" I said in shock.

"Nor your husband, nor your mother, nor your father," John replied.

"How can that be?! Don't you have to be loved?" I responded.

"Yes," he replied, but here is love, God loves you first ↓, you love Him back ↑, you love yourself ←, and with the overflow of the love God has given you, that is what you love your neighbor with, whether or not they ever love you back, whether it be your neighbor, your husband, your mother, or your father."

"Are you telling me that a person can make it without the most important people in life ever loving them?" I implored.

"Once again, YES, and not only make it, but thrive," John replied.

I thought about this for a few minutes and then said, "You know, I've been mad at my mother for too many years, and I guess the thing that made me so angry was that she couldn't seem to show unconditional love. Yet, *her* mother hated her, and *her* dad wasn't around either. How can I be mad at someone for not giving me something they themselves never received either?!" In that moment, I was able to forgive my mother. Now in the more than thirty years that have followed, she has never apologized for any of the ways she raised us or any of the ways she dealt with us, but I'm not responsible for her actions. I'm certain that, if she were asked, she would reveal that life was completely different from her perspective as an adult than it was for us as kids.

I was allowing my mother to control me through my swallowed anger at her (called depression), resentment, bitterness, and sadness. It was taking a physical toll on me as well. I had long-term stomach problems, and there was a lot of history of cancer in the family as well. Both my mother and her mother suffered from cancer, and I could see how all that hurt, resentment, and bitterness were just going from one generation to the next. All of my siblings were doing the same thing I was doing – trying, trying, and trying. We were great achievers, all calling our mother to tell her what we had achieved, but it became so clear that we were all trying to gain her approval, to get her to say, "I love you," and "I'm proud of you," which she most likely truly felt but had simply not been able to express.

Several of my siblings are still struggling with physical ailments to this day, and I believe it is because we all need to forgive our mother. Does she deserve it? Do any of us deserve forgiveness? Regardless of whether we deserve it, it has been offered to us. "Forgive one another even as God for Christ's sake has forgiven you." (Ephesians 4:32, KJV)

"If God loves us first, how does He show us that He loves us?" I asked John.

"Why don't you ask Him to show you?" John replied.

"Oh no," I responded. "I'd be too afraid to ask. My mother told me I had given up ever getting my own father's attention by the time I was three. I don't remember any of that, but I do know that I always longed to just one time sit in his lap and for him to say he loved me, but I knew not to ask because I knew what the answer would be. My sister, Julia, was his favorite and I never saw her in his lap, so what chance did I have? No, I won't ask, because I'm just too afraid of rejection."

"I want you to think about asking Him, and we'll talk again later."

A few weeks later, during a Sunday sermon, the pastor stopped preaching and suddenly hollered out, "How many of you love Jesus – raise your hands?!" Everyone was waving their hands high, but I was just barely raising my hand to wave. When I got home that day, I got down on the floor and just cried out to God.

"Lord, I love You the best I know how, but I'm not sure if I even know how to love. If it is possible, is there a way that you could show me in a personal way that You love me? I know You spread Your arms wide and died for all of us. In those Gospels – and I still don't know why you told the same story four times, but wasn't there a guy who referred to himself as the disciple whom You loved. Somehow he knew in a personal way that You loved him. Is there any way that could be possible for me?"

I got up off the floor and then thought, *You fool, who do you think you are, asking God for something like that?*

I went to work that night at the Post Office and forgot about my request, but God didn't forget. At about 4:00AM, I went into the break room to take my "lunch" break and was reading in Psalms. When I came out, I walked up to the machines to take my turn to run the mail using the schemes I had previously learned. I started to sit down, but these words starting flowing through my mind, and they were so vivid that I had to shut the machine down to take dictation. It took less than ten minutes, and I skipped my last break to make up for it, but I tell people that I had to temporarily delay their mail so I could take down a letter from God. He had remembered the desire I had in my heart concerning my own dad, and his answer came in the form of a poem called, "Daddy's Little Girl." It would be years before I comprehended that "Abba, Father" truly means "Daddy, Daddy!" I have shared this poem as often as I could through the years, and it seems to be just as much a blessing today as it was then.

This poem provided what I would call a mountaintop experience. I would keep it as a daily reminder of His love and tell people that the memory of this poem was my hug from God that I so desperately needed and that He miraculously supplied. Most of the questions I asked God weren't quite as miraculously and quickly answered like this request, but I find that He meets us where we are with what we need at that time, and if we seek Him with all our heart, He will answer our questions, especially when it pertains to understanding who He is and how He deals with us, His children.

DADDY'S LITTLE GIRL

I came before my Father's throne
One eve when I was down.
And this my observation was...
Lord, You're nowhere to be found.

I finally tired of fretting so
My head I did then nod,
For I heard a voice so softly say
Be still, and know I'm God.

I cried, Dear Lord, from up above
Oh please, look down on me,
Sin and strife have made me but
A black sheep in the Family.

For just one day if in Your arms
That You would let me curl,
If just this *once* that I could know
I'm "Daddy's" little girl.

And suddenly there was an urge
And a Voice that spoke to me,
Open up the Book, my child
To Psalm of David, 103.

You see, My child, I have not dealt
The penalty that's due,
As the heaven is high above the earth
So is My love for you.

As far as the East is from the West
That's where My mercy lies,
Thy sin and strife have been removed
The blood of My Son applies.

I pity you, My little one
And yes, I know your frame,
That dust you are and dust you'll be
And yet you love My name.

Your life is like a vapor mist
A trail that tags along,
But when the wind blows down on it
It disappears, it's gone.

But listen to me, little one
My child, I say to you,
My love and mercy know no bounds
They're everlasting true.

Unto this world be not conformed
My child, you must believe,
But through renewing of your mind
Be transformed unto me.

Oh, I may not don the eldest spot
Nor was I born the youngest tot,
But when my soul on high was bought
Just look what I got.

Oh, the peace of knowing there's a home
Of knowing I won't go it alone,
Of knowing "Dad" is always there
His Son for whom my sins to bear.

Of knowing that my prayers He'll hear
And knowing that He'll always care...
That irritations bear a pearl
I'm "Daddy's" little girl!

"I will *never* leave you nor forsake you."
Hebrews 13:5

HOMEWORK:

- Do you have someone in your life who doesn't or didn't love you the way you want or need?

- Do you need to forgive that person?

- Are you willing to ask God to help you to forgive?

- Is it possible that this person could not give you something he or she never received themselves?

- Have you experienced the love of God?

- If not, are you willing to ask Him to show you His love?

- If you already know the love of God in your own life, can you consider allowing the overflow of that love to flow towards this person who could not love you?

Shock #3: Why Is All This Happening to Me?

During those four and a half years in which I attended the small church, I carried two other books besides my Bible with me on a daily basis that greatly influenced my walk with Christ. One was called <u>The Ins and Out of Rejection</u>, by Charles R. Solomon.[1] The first time I read it, I cried and cried, because it was so apparent that someone knew and understood how a person feels who has experienced repeated rejection and how the Holy Spirit can bring us out of that mindset. It took three years of reading the second half of the book to move from complete lack of understanding to mental assent and finally to a spiritual grasp of what he wrote concerning what he called "The Way Out or The Cross."

You see, I am told that there are three kinds of people: those who *make* it happen, those who *watch* it happen, and my kind, those who wonder *what happened!* This book is written for those of us in the third group. When I came to see John Morris, I had zero comprehension of the second half of the book and thus I would ask him about it. I still quote from time to time the first four lines of a poem called "Acceptance" from C.R. Solomon's book that I loved (later I got to meet him in person at one of his seminars in Dallas, Texas!):

> Oh, to know acceptance
> In a feeling sort of way:
> To be known for who I am –
> Not what I do or say.

> C.R. Solomon, Ed. D (from <u>The Ins and Out of Rejection</u>) [2]

The second book that I carried daily was from a question that I had for God and His answer. It would take three and a half years before I could get a spiritual grasp on and comprehension of what God was really doing. I underlined and wrote notes in all of the books that I studied during that period, including these two, with questions, feelings, and thoughts that the Lord would bring to mind. I had sought for years to discover what horrible sin I had committed to have to have grown up the way I did and for things to be going as they had, but I couldn't find it.

I recall coming home from that small church one day and sitting all alone on the edge of the bed in my apartment and feeling rather sorry for myself.

I finally looked up and blurted out, "God, why are You trying to hurt me?!" In an instant, I could sense as though Heaven opened up and I could hear the unmistakable sounds of a Man crying, and I *instantly* knew I had blamed the wrong Person!

I cried out, "Lord, please forgive me, I have grieved You and blamed the wrong person, I know I am the one with sin, but if there isn't some great sin that I have committed, then how could and why would You allow your children to suffer so much, especially if we didn't do anything wrong?! Is there anyone in Your Word that had to suffer that didn't do anything wrong?" As I perused through His Word, I found the beginning of an answer....

"Have you considered my servant Job....?" (Job 1:8, KJV) The book I would quickly be led to find and study was called, "Job, A Man Tried As Gold" by Theodore H. Epp.[3] I carried this book and not only did I read it on a daily basis for those four years but also read it yearly thereafter. Every book I found by Theodore H. Epp was profound in its depth and help in understanding God's Word, but this was the first and by far the most influential for me.

I wrote in the front cover of this book my question concerning why we have to suffer as well as each year that I would read and reread this book. Underneath that question I inserted "Look at page 19 for answer" which says:

> "It is well to note that in the Book of Job, which deals with
> the purpose of the suffering of the godly, such suffering is

not imposed by a judge for wrongdoing on the part of the individual. Nevertheless, it is suffering allowed to remedy something in the believer's life. It is not punishment, and yet it is designed to correct wrong. It is not retribution for wrong done, but discipline to refine the life to where the likeness of Christ becomes clear." (Job, A Man Tried As Gold, Theodore H. Epp, pp. 19).[4]

Both The Ins and Out of Rejection and Job, a Man Tried as Gold began to draw a picture and present a plan that God applies with *all* His children for bringing us out of the bondage of sin into a land of abundant living. God called this place of abundance The Promised Land. This plan is laid out in the New Testament, particularly in Romans chapters 6-8, Galatians 2:20, all of Galatians Chapter 5, as well as Ephesians and Colossians. It is seen in word pictures through the Old Testament counterparts in the stories of the Israelites with Moses as their leader, being brought through the Red Sea and their wilderness, wandering before being brought into the Promised Land by Joshua and their conquests. Something is done *for* them, something done *in* them, and finally, something is done *through* them.

Through the story of Job, I began to get an inkling that there is something within us all that God has to deal with. Even though Job loved and served God and was an upright man, God used his sufferings to reveal to him and to us all down through the ages that he, and we, possess a fallen, incurably evil nature that cannot be tamed, shamed, or changed into something better. We inherited this from Adam. I discovered that the New Testament calls this nature the "old man" or the "flesh" and that it was primarily addressed when Christ died on the cross. I didn't have a clue what this really meant, but I remembered some words when I was baptized and could understand that they were in reference to this concept. We are buried with Christ in baptism and rise up to walk in the newness of life. As I was still walking around, I knew something had been buried but wasn't sure what, and it felt like I was being held captive.

The end of the book of Job presents that he, too, had been held captive, but God released him. "And the Lord turned the *captivity* of Job, when he prayed for his friends; also the Lord gave Job twice as much as he had before." (Job 42:10, KJV) There was a hint of hope again that things would someday get better, and there would be a *double portion* of joy to come. In those beginning moments and months though, I simply understood that I had to get even lower before I could be brought up and to experience greater humility.

When I brought the question before John, I asked it in a different way: "I truly don't have the assurance of my salvation yet, but if it did "take", then did something happen afterward, perhaps during those twelve years I *didn't* attend church to lead me to where I am today?" His answer and subsequent "homework" shocked me to my core.

"I want you to go home and study Romans 1:21-32," John told me. "I am going to draw you some stair steps, both going down and going up, and I want you to allow the Holy Spirit to help you fill out the rest of the steps down and up and show me what you learned at our next appointment." Romans 1:21-32 reads as follows:

"Although they know who God is, they do not glorify him as God or thank him. On the contrary, they have become futile in their thinking; and their undiscerning hearts have become darkened. Claiming to be wise, they have become fools! In fact, they have exchanged the glory of the immortal God for mere images, like a mortal human being, or like birds, animals, or reptiles!"

"This is why God has given them up to the vileness of their hearts' lusts, to the shameful misuse of each other's bodies. They have exchanged the truth of God for falsehood, by worshipping and serving created things, rather than the Creator – praised be he forever. This is why God has given them up to degrading passions; so that their women exchange natural sexual relations for unnatural; and likewise the men, giving up natural relations with the opposite sex, burn with passion for one another, men committing shameful acts with other men and receiving in their own persons the penalty appropriate to their perversion. In other words, since they have not considered God worth knowing, God has given them up to worthless ways of thinking; so that they do improper things. They are filled with every kind of wickedness, evil, greed and vice; stuffed with jealousy, murder, quarrelling, dishonesty and ill-will; they are gossips, slanderers, haters of God; they are insolent, arrogant and boastful; they plan evil schemes; they disobey their parents; they are brainless, faithless, heartless and ruthless. They know well enough God's righteous decree that people who do such things deserve to die; yet not only do they keep doing them, but they applaud others who do the same." (Complete Jewish Bible)

What John started for me looked like this:

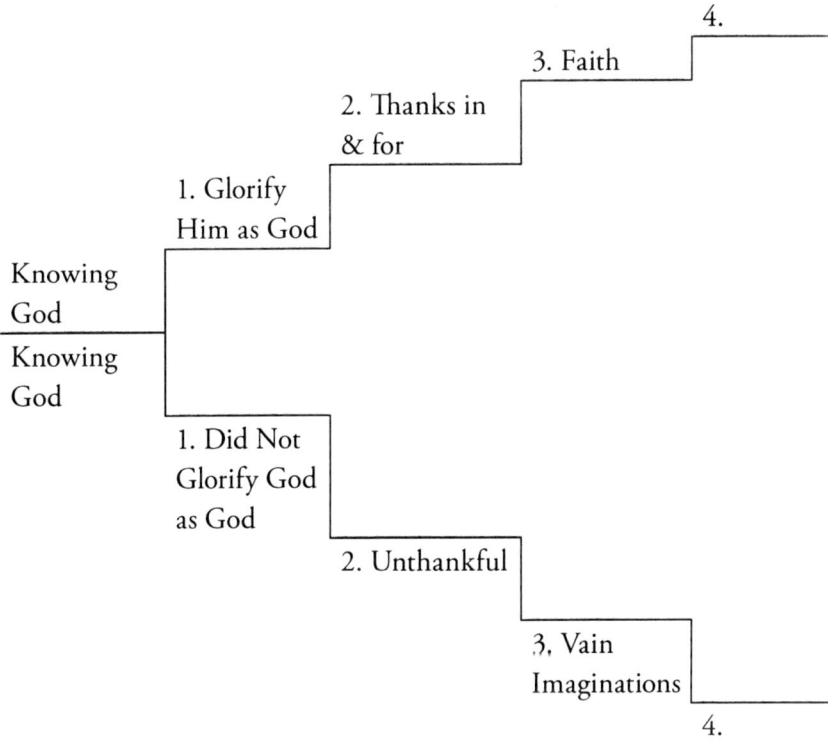

```
                                                      4.
                                       3. Faith    |_____
                          2. Thanks in          |
                          & for                 |
            1. Glorify                 |_____|
            Him as God                 |
Knowing              |_____|
God                  |
Knowing              |
God                  |
            1. Did Not                 |
            Glorify God                |
            as God          |_____|
                          2. Unthankful         |
                                      |_____|
                                      3, Vain            |
                                      Imaginations    |_____
                                                      4.
```

When I went home and looked at the verses, I could see myself there and what had happened after I had been saved but did not continue in church, pursuing to know Him more. I didn't know I was even supposed to do that. In fact, I had felt sorry for the other kids who continued to go because they were only hearing the same thing week after week as far as I could tell: "get saved and go serve God and receive heaven by and by." At age 24, the message of the church was: get saved, go serve God, put on the full armor of God, and go out and war with the Devil, bring forth fruit so you can be pleasing to God by winning others to Christ; if you mess up, go to the Christian "bar of soap," 1 John 1:9, and it's heaven by and by.

(Oh, and by the way, don't get divorced or God will never speak to you or ever use you again.)

My dad sold life insurance for a living, and it would take a long time for me to understand this truth as applied to scripture; I have a problem with someone trying to sell term insurance with decreasing value, when the whole life has already been paid for. "I am come that they might have life, and that they might have it more abundantly," meaning to super abound, beyond measure! (John 10:10, KJV)

What the Holy Spirit began to show me, and what broke my heart, is shown below and while some apply it in regard to homosexuality, I believe this applies to *each of us*, individually, or as a nation that turns away from God from when we first knew Him:

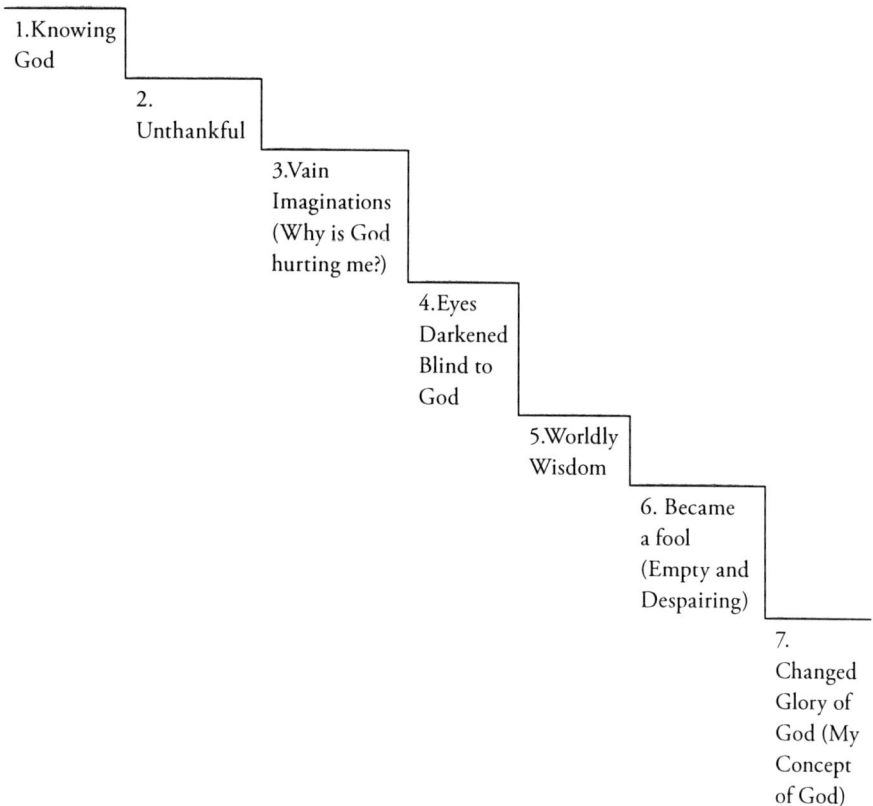

1. Knowing God

2. Unthankful

3. Vain Imaginations (Why is God hurting me?)

4. Eyes Darkened Blind to God

5. Worldly Wisdom

6. Became a fool (Empty and Despairing)

7. Changed Glory of God (My Concept of God)

FRUITS OR CONSEQUENCES:

1. Uncleanness – Sought contentment in the physical – sex, marriage, children, job, etc.
2. Vile Affections – Perverted God's ideal of all these things, especially sex.
3. Reprobate Mind – Wanted to break covenant, unmerciful toward others and judgmental, unable to see God's mercy; no sense of a sound mind.

At first I simply wept in grief and sorrow as I saw how far I had fallen, so full of worldly wisdom from working with the police department, but only seeing the "mud" in life; all growth had been stagnated because I had become spiritually and emotionally dead; I had the worldly wisdom of an adult but the emotions of a child. I wondered how to get out of this pit. Should I try to climb back up all those stairs?? Then the Holy Spirit showed me grace; I felt compelled to simply go back to the beginning where I started – Knowing God:

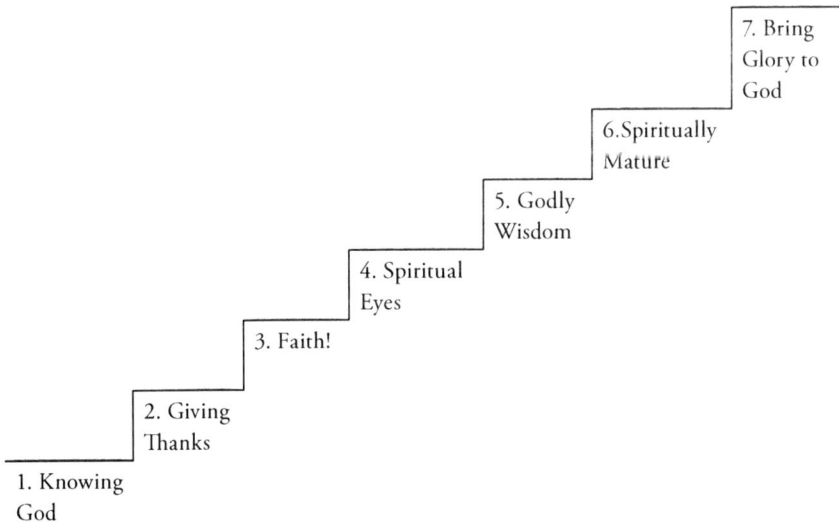

```
                                                         7. Bring
                                                         Glory to
                                                         God
                                              6. Spiritually
                                              Mature
                                    5. Godly
                                    Wisdom
                          4. Spiritual
                          Eyes
                3. Faith!
      2. Giving
      Thanks
1. Knowing
God
```

FRUITS OR CONSEQUENCES:

1. Cleansing – Casting down imaginations and false reasoning. 2 Cor. 10:5
2. Getting to Know God – Where your treasure is, there will your heart be also. Matt. 6:21
3. Goal: To have pleasure with God and *rest* in God and share with others the way out. Spiritually and emotionally *alive!!*

These tasks were what John had started me with – while knowing God, give thanks! This focus gave me a goal and more to study about! I could see in His Word that He spoke about the peace of God that surpasses understanding, abundant living, and rest for God's people. I had no clue what these meant, but I sure wanted to know more!

John would later invite me to be a part of the ministry of his church called Evangelism Explosion[5] (which was outside my church!). I had asked him about sharing the gospel with something other than the Roman Road to Salvation, and it would be in this ministry that the assurance of salvation would finally be cemented in place for me, through such soul-searching questions like, *If you were to die tonight and were to stand before God and He asked you, "Why should I let you into My Heaven?" what would you say?* Anything except putting our faith in what His Son had already done for us through His sacrificial death would indicate that we were trusting in ourselves rather than in the Heavenly provision of the blood of Christ. Along with that came word pictures of faith, such as, *"If you had a chair here in front of you, and you believed it would hold you up, how would you prove it?* The quite obvious answer is to go and sit in it. The chair was a picture of what Christ had done for us, and our sitting in that chair was the act of putting our trust in Him and completely resting on that provision, not any good works or deeds we could ever do.

HOMEWORK:

- Have you thought to yourself, "Why is God hurting me?" or "Why are you allowing this to happen to me, God?"

- Are you beginning to get a different perspective about that?

- What is your understanding at this point of why God allows suffering? _____

- Have you ever searched for some great sin which you think is the cause of all your suffering?

- Have you ever heard of these biblical terms before: "old man" or "the flesh"?

- Do you too feel as though you have been taken captive?

- What is your concept of God?

- If you know God, is it your pattern to glorify Him as God? Have you demonstrated thankfulness?

- What has been the message of the church for you?

- Where are you on the stair steps – going up or down?

- Can you see now how to take steps up in your faith to a closer relationship with God?

- What would you say if you were to die tonight and you were to stand before God and He asked you, "Why should I let you into My Heaven?" _____

I Will Bring the Blind By a Way That They Knew Not

As I continued in the quest for answers from God, several things became rather apparent:

1. I was an outsider and a misfit.
2. Church attendance is not enough to feed or satisfy you.
3. Pain is the greatest motivator to change, thus personal tribulation/ suffering is the chief motivator of spiritual growth.
4. *Spiritual* answers and healing would most likely come before *emotional* healing and any change in circumstances.

As I did not grow up in church and came in as an adult, I struggled to feel a sense of belonging, and when you include the experience of separation and divorce, I was very much a misfit. It appeared to me (and later it became very clear) that being the only single adult there and also being in my twenties made most of the other women in church very uncomfortable to have me around them. I just hung on more tightly to God and studied even more. I didn't have any children of my own, and I didn't cook much at all, so swapping recipes and exchanging baby and toddler stories was certainly not in my range of experience. In fact, when I later remarried, a couple brought their two-week-old baby over to our house and the baby boy was drinking out of a bottle. The mother complained that the doctor had told her not to give him anything but milk for the first six months, but when he was born he weighed eleven pounds. Now, I knew *that* was a *big* baby! She told me that she got tired of hearing him cry all the time, so she started giving him rice cereal in his bottle, but said he would still cry out of frustration. I looked at her and then at the baby, and then asked, "Is he trying right now to eat cereal?"

She replied that he was, and I looked at her and said, "Well, it's no wonder that he's frustrated. How's he supposed to suck Rice Krispies through that bottle?" She busted out laughing and said, "You really don't know anything about babies, do you?"

"No," I replied. She explained there was a difference between baby rice cereal and Rice Krispies cereal. There was another lady there who had come to visit, and she had not had any children either. She not only thought the same thing I had, but asked what was the difference between "real" diapers and "fake" diapers (the first being cloth and the latter being disposable). The mother got a good laugh at us both.

At the time, I had also just started teaching an adult class after finishing one year with the high school kids and the previous year with the fourth and fifth graders. I called the little Sunday School booklets that we handed out, "teaching out of a box," and there wasn't very much to it in those days, but I had to start somewhere, and that seemed to be the logical place. On the side, I was studying day and night with whatever books I could find along with my Bible as I asked God questions. It became very apparent that just waiting each Sunday to hear something from God at church that would help me would take too long, and it simply wasn't enough for me at that point in my spiritual journey. The Lord began to show me that church attendance alone wasn't intended to satisfy us, that He wants us to approach Him every day and that His Spirit will lead us, teach us, and feed our hungry soul as we continue to seek Him. The personal, emotional pain was what goaded me onward with the desire for relief and the tidbit of hope that, as I studied, somehow, the tide would turn, and somehow I would feel better and finally *normal* – whatever that meant.

What came across the pulpit and from some of the church members was the idea that, if you simply had enough faith, you could make your marriage work or fix whatever other problem ailed you. To be perfectly honest, I don't think that faith has as much to do with a successful marriage as having one modeled before you will. Think about it. If you were invited to a scrumptious meal and you didn't know how to cook, and you were told that if you just had enough faith you could make a meal just like that, you would laugh. No – you must be *shown* how to cook successfully!

How much do you need of each ingredient, what temperature to bake, etc? Is it not the same for relationships and marriage? When all you've ever seen modeled before you, *your normal,* is misery and failure, how *do* you overcome? Who is there to teach us?? My only hope was that God, Himself, would be my instructor.

As I began the Adult Sunday School class, I was given permission to teach from my own materials, so I simply shared what the Lord was teaching me by performing character studies of different people in the Bible. I discovered that, in preparing to teach, God's Word became more cemented in my heart, and I understood more and more as I taught each week.

After I asked God to show me one person (besides Christ) who had to suffer who didn't do anything wrong and He showed me Job, I asked could there be another. God then showed me Joseph. I was led to do character studies on each of the people that God would have me study as they would pertain to a question. I found the book Joseph, God Planned It for Good [6] by Theodore Epp and thoroughly enjoyed it.

The emphasis from Joseph seemed to be that so many times we find ourselves in trying circumstances that just seem to imprison us. Our first response is to do everything possible to escape, including prayer, but this is not necessarily God's way. It was within God's will for Joseph to be brought to Egypt as a slave so that he could later be used to provide a way for his family to live in safety in Egypt. God's Word doesn't always imply that we will be delivered *out* of all our problems; many times we are told that we will be comforted and strengthened as we go *through* the fires and *through* the waters and that God will always be with us to encourage us. For faith to be built within us, we must go through trials and adversity. Could it be possible that God is the One who allows our present circumstances to help us rather than to hurt? Maybe instead of trying to get God to change our *circumstances,* we should ask Him to change *us.* "Change me, Oh God – Search my heart – lead me in the ways everlasting...."(Psalms 139:23-24, KJV)

Through Joseph, I could see that, as a child and teenager, he wasn't ruined by his home environment because God became his priority. Joseph was influenced by God to overcome the death of his mother, the bitterness and jealousy of his brothers and their wives and children, and (worst of all) the murderous intents of his own brothers toward him that led to him to be sold into slavery. Joseph would later be able to look back and say, "you thought evil against me; but God meant it for good." (Genesis 50:20, KJV) I saw in studying Joseph a term that I would see again and again – *death of self.* I wasn't clear on entirely what it meant, but it was clear that Joseph was put in a place of death, and God brought him out. Joseph knew that there was nothing physically he could do, and he had to rely on God alone. I would see the pattern repeated with each person I studied.

After studying Joseph, I went to God once more.

"Well, Lord, could you show me someone who really messed up and had to suffer and yet You showed them how much you still loved them?" The person the Lord showed me became my favorite Bible character. I even did a Paul Harvey-type introduction when I shared his story with the Sunday School class:

"His name meant 'well-beloved.' He occupied a special place in the eyes of the Lord unequaled by anyone to follow except Christ, Himself. Yet he was a liar, a sneak, and a murderer. His hot temper almost led him to murder another time except for the Lord's intervention.

"He was a tremendous actor, convincing others he was a lunatic and feigning madness in order to preserve his life.

"His closest friends were a motley group of depression-ridden, irresponsible misfits whom he later led to some of the greatest victories his people ever witnessed.

"He had an uncontrolled eye for the ladies, having numerous wives and whose sins of passion were surpassed only by those of his own household.

"Although promised a position of leadership among his people, it was fifteen years before he gained their allegiance, only to be ousted for a time and then to return. Yet it was this man who, in type, portrayed Christ possibly more closely than any other Bible hero, having a city named in his honor, and whose name is most closely tied into the ancestry of Christ.

"Who was he? Well, as a young man, he was known for his great strength – he killed a lion and a bear with his hands and his staff as he grabbed the lion's beard and smote it. But it was his simple trust in his great Jehovah that brought him to the world's attention when he aimed for the mark and killed the man who dared to defy the armies of the living God for whom cheering crowds later sang that the king had killed thousands, but *David* had killed ten thousands. And now you know the end of that story!"

The Holy Spirit then led me to study the book <u>David – A Man After the Heart of God</u>[7] by Theodore Epp. Just as I had experienced a personal set of three "Ds" (death, divorce, Dallas), I would discover in the Bible another misfit who became a leader of a group of misfits like myself who surrounded him who had their own three "Ds": "…and everyone that was in *Distress*, and everyone that was in *Debt*, and everyone that was *Discontented,* gathered themselves unto him; and he became a captain over them: and there were with him about four hundred men." (I Samuel 22:2, KJV) David had also cried out to God and said, "I had fainted unless I had believed to see the goodness of the Lord in the *land of the living.*" (Psalms 27:13, KJV) These stories fortified me, and for the first time, I did not feel alone.

I began to see through David a similar pattern that had been followed by Job and Joseph: a time of preparation – God's servant may be *called or even anointed,* but usually there is a *time of preparation* before he/she is *sent.* David was tested deeply for eight years before becoming king of Judah, and it was during these years that he wrote many of the Psalms. He had to hide and was constantly in danger, as King Saul wanted to kill him, and yet he did not fight for his rights as the anointed king but waited until God enthroned him rather than trying to take the throne himself. It seemed that David, Joseph, and Job all had the same experience of finding themselves in a place where there was no human form of deliverance available, and they each had to turn to God for mercy and grace. It was so comforting to see Bible characters feeling and doing as I had felt and done. Each time each man arrived at this place, they called it "coming to the end of self." It was helpful to see that, even though Job and Joseph hadn't truly committed great sins, they had to be brought to this very same place as David did, even though he committed heinous sins such as murder and adultery. I was in awe that the worst sinner I could find was the one that God would say was a man after His own heart! I wondered what made David so special in God's eyes, and I could see that, in sin and without sin, David would repeatedly cast himself on God's mercy and had learned to trust God implicitly. Even when his loyal men would try to encourage him to take action against Saul, David waited for God to deal with Saul and to bring David to the throne. This was so different than what was being presented in my church – "get saved and go, go, go, do, do, do!!"

During the four and a half years that I stayed at this small church, I read probably a couple hundred Christian books along with my study of the Bible. I could also see other Christians also going through these same patterns of working very hard in their ministries and lives, burning out, and going down in flames. Somehow this concept of "getting saved and going to serve God" is just a myth, one that leads to burnout. Something must occur between the two tasks. Although I knew I could leave the church and try to find another one, I felt as though I was five again, and running away was not a viable answer for me. Other churches were probably like this one. I didn't know for sure, but I did know that God wanted me to learn something by staying here for the time being, and when He had opened that door for me to attend, it didn't matter to me what was behind or beyond that door, as long as He was there with me. I would stay until He put it on my heart that it was time to go.

I know one of the many lessons to be learned was to listen and discern God's Voice or Message. I needed to learn to discern as a baby Christian when God was correcting me or when I was just beating myself up through His Word or the words from other people or if Satan was twisting God's Word. For example, I remember seeing God's Word, "Walk in the Spirit and you shall not fulfill the lusts of the flesh." (Galatians 5:16, KJV) What I *heard* was, "*Try* not to fulfill the lust of the flesh *in order that you may* walk in the spirit." There was a continual pouring of God's Word into my heart, like the pouring of a pitcher of clean, pure water to wash away the mud and mire of wrong thinking. I wanted that *sound mind* that His Word spoke of!

Staying at this church also meant that I needed to learn when His Spirit was directing me or if I should stay in submission to what was being told to me at church; sometimes they were two different things. I never could understand that, if I was so bad for being separated (which was completely out of my control), then why would they let me teach, and teach not only them, but also teach their precious children? They couldn't find anything wrong with what I taught, and they couldn't get rid of me either – I was there Sunday morning, Sunday night, and Wednesday evenings for prayer service.

During Vacation Bible School one summer, I had the privilege and opportunity to lead eight fourth and fifth graders to Christ. I kept telling them all week to make sure to attend that Thursday evening, as it might be the most important day of their lives. All of them attended that day, and I got to share with them that scientists had discovered that our ability to learn is at one of its greatest levels during the fourth and fifth grades; that was why school seemed more difficult with less time for play and more schooling after the third grade. Our ability to memorize and remember things is also at one of its highest at this point in childhood, and I shared with them two songs that I remembered from my own childhood. We chose to sing one of those songs to the parents on Friday evening at the close of Vacation Bible School, so they all worked on it all week and eventually had it memorized. On the night of the performance, the kids sang loud, and everyone laughed and laughed! The song was called, "Be Kind to Your Parents," by Pete Seeger.[8] The first few lines started:

> Be kind to your parents
> Though they don't deserve it,
> Remember they're grownups
> A difficult stage of life.

When the parents heard that, they busted out laughing. The rest of the song spoke of the daily dilemma which parents are faced with, reminding all kids that not only were parents once kids, but most kids will grow up to be parents themselves. Thus, we are all reminded to deal with one another with patience and understanding. This message was delivered in such a hilarious way that everyone had a wonderful time singing it and hearing it together.

I also told the children how I was saved at age twelve, and thus, physically, emotionally, and for some, spiritually, life could change for them during this very time. I told them we were all sinners, that Christ had come and given His life to pay for all our sins, and that He wanted to come into their hearts and lives if we would just invite Him. We prayed a prayer of salvation, and I asked how many had already prayed a prayer like that in their lives; five or six children raised their hands. When I asked how many wanted to pray that prayer to accept Christ for the very first time and did so, wanting Christ to be their Savior, the remainder of the class raised their hands in unison. I started crying and sent one of the kids to go find the pastor, who thought perhaps there was some trouble happening in the class. I repeated everything that we said and did, and then he started crying, and there were a lot of tears of joy that day and in the days to come as the baptisms and the families came together to celebrate.

However, although it was okay for me to teach adults and the children at Vacation Bible School, somehow, because I wouldn't "repent" of the separation and impending divorce, I was told that God couldn't talk to me and that He wouldn't hear my personal prayers until I would repent. The leadership of that church also made it plain that, even though my husband had left me, if the divorce went through, I could never ever remarry for any reason and would have to remain single for the rest of my life. I couldn't argue with them, because I simply didn't know God's Word the way they did. I just hung my head and kept digging. I would constantly turn to the lyrics to a song I wrote down in the back of The Ins and Out of Rejection called "More of You" by Bill Gaither.[9] I changed a couple of lines where he wrote, "nothing's changed, I'm not new" to "something's changed, I want You," thus better matching the stage I was in – a baby Christian seeking nourishment and care. During my praise time, I would sing these words to the Lord:

"More of you... more of you. I've had it all, but what I need, just more of you. Of things I've had my fill, and yet I hunger still, empty and bare – Lord, hear my prayer, for more of You!"

HOMEWORK:

- Do you feel like an Outsider or a Misfit?

- Are you learning to feed yourself on God's Word or are you just waiting for a tiny morsel of His Word on Sunday mornings?

- Have you used prayer to try to escape your prison?

- Are you burnt out in your Christian walk – do you merely go, go, go, do, do, do?

A Touch of Grace

One of the grace areas in my life from the Lord at that time was a friendship with a much older Christian man who joined the church after I did. He was thirty years older than me, and he worked with the pastor at their regular full-time job in insurance sales. His name was Walt Blanch, and his ten-year-old daughter, Jackie, was in my fourth and fifth grade class. She and another girl named Lori became my adopted kids at church. He and many members of his family from California had been involved with Campus Crusade for Christ, Navigators, etc., and he was (and is to this day) the most positive person I have ever met. He became my mentor while attending this small church. He came with his daughter to the church to work and assist the pastor. Not long after he started attending, his wife divorced him, due to her lack of interest in any of the ministries he was involved in and she didn't like the neighborhood they lived in and wanted something nicer. They had lived in a simple frame home and had two or three other frame homes in the same block to provide rental income to supplement his insurance sales income. When his wife left and moved to the Ft. Worth area, his daughter stayed with him for a while before rejoining her mother. Then, there we were, two "rebellious sinners" and we have remained friends until this day, which for him is age 87. He is still involved in ministry and drives every week to one of the local prisons to teach and minister, and he has run a halfway house for prison inmates for almost thirty years out of his home, which he started a few years after his wife left.

Walt showed me and taught me the love and grace of God, while the church showed me the hell, fire, and brimstone side of religion. He spent a lot of time sharing with me how the Lord leads us, how to discern the Lord's timing, and how to discern the leading of the Holy Spirit. When my husband left me, he talked Walt into coming and staying with him rather than going back to Dallas, and Walt wanted to see if he could minister to my ex and to work with is to see if there was any chance for reconciliation. My husband stayed with Walt for *two years*, so through Walt, I kept up with how my husband was doing. I never dated during that two-year separation or even entertained the idea of doing so, with the hope that something would change and things might work out. Walt would later give me away when I did remarry and he shared Christmas at our home and attempted to minister to my second husband as well. He never remarried during the more than thirty years I've known him.

During the separation, I shared a house with my younger sister for about a year after leaving the apartment my husband and I had shared. After she met a guy that she really liked who was spending a lot of time with her, I decided that we both needed some privacy and I needed some time to be alone and to rest emotionally. Walt told me to ask God to show me a place to rent and not to be afraid to ask for little things. We prayed together for God's leading, and I started looking in the paper for a place to stay. Walt and I would meet at the donut shop sometimes as he was heading into work and I was just getting off work at the Post Office. I told Walt that I was looking for a place that would be peaceful and restful, so he told me to ask God. I did just that.

The next morning I got a paper out and looked at available rentals, and one caught my eye – a small two-bedroom frame house that said it was close to a pond. That sounded nice to me, a house with a pond and maybe ducks in it, but was it available, and could I afford it? When I called the number, the man who answered the phone said the place was available and the cost was $250 per month. I couldn't believe it; everything else was at least $600 per month, so I told him I would be right out to look. I was there before 10:00AM.

As I drove up to the place, there was a sign at the entrance that the owner had made and he had named the area Restful Valley. I thought to myself, "Now Lord, You really have a good sense of humor!" The house was very simple and the pond was beautiful, and it was the only house that was close to the pond. I loved it, but I wanted to be sure it was right for me.

I took a deep breath and then blurted out to the owner, "Sir, I really like the place, but I'll have to pray to be sure this is the house for me."

The owner took a step back, looked at me hard and said, "My wife goes to church." He paused. Then he said, "I'll have to tell you, ma'am, the last time I had this house up for rent we had several hundred calls for it, so I wouldn't wait very long."

I took another deep breath and then said, "Well, if this is the house the Lord has for me, it will be here when I get back." (I thought to myself, *Gee thanks, Walt – now look what you've influenced me to do!*) We both looked at one another kind of strangely, and I left. I decided to pray about it for the rest of the day.

That evening, I finally felt peace about the house and called the owner. The man I had spoken to earlier answered the phone. I told him who I was and asked if the house was still available.

"Yes ma'am, it is, and I don't understand it. We haven't had even a single call on this house – not before you called or after. It's the strangest thing I've ever seen."

"I'll take it," I replied.

The story didn't end there. I had planned to move in the following weekend, and Walt and several kids in the neighborhood were going to help. The pastor had agreed to let me use his pickup, and everything was set – or so I thought. On Saturday morning I called the pastor's house to get the pickup. His wife answered the phone and said that the pickup had broken down and wasn't available; I didn't know what I was going to do. About that time, I heard a knock at the door; it was the little girl from across the street, Missy. She was nine – in her "late nines," she would say – and I would bring her and her older brother, John, who was eleven, to Vacation Bible School. I was a tomboy when I was growing up, so I used that expertise to show John how to throw a spiral with a football.

Both Missy and John were planning to help me move. I told Missy what had happened with the pickup. I had my little car all packed up and was just putting the last box in when she came by. I told her she could ride with me over to the house and we would have to pray on the way, praying for specifics, like Walt had suggested.

We prayed with our eyes open as we drove: "Lord, You know I needed a house and You were the One who led me to this house. You know I wanted a restful place, and You provided me with Restful Valley. Now You know I need a pickup to move, and I've lost the one I was supposed to use, so please provide us with a pickup for today. Oh, and while You're at it, would you please be sure it's an automatic, as I'm not comfortable at all shifting gears with a manual transmission?"

"Yeah!" Missy replied.

We drove up to my new place, and while I was bringing in the last box, I saw a pickup driving up the driveway towards us. I had no idea who it belonged to.

I turned to Missy and said, "Maybe this is the pickup the Lord is going to give us."

"Yeah!" Missy responded again.

The pickup stopped and the owner of the house got out and started walking towards us. He had come to check on us as I started the move-in. I thanked him for his inquiry.

I then asked, "Sir, I have a really big favor to ask of you."

"What is it?" he very gruffly responded. I then told him all that had happened and that I was in desperate need of a pickup. He looked at me for a minute and then a slight smile came to his face.

"Is that all you need? Here, take the keys." Missy and I looked at one another in surprise.

"Is it standard or automatic?" I stuttered in response.

"It's automatic," he replied. Missy and I looked at one another again in disbelief.

"Yeah!" Missy shouted in delight.

We got in the pickup and headed back toward the house. I then remembered that we were now a little *early*, and I wondered if Walt would be at the donut shop. We drove by, and there was his car in the parking lot. We walked in the door, and he looked at us and asked us what we were doing there.

"God gave us a pickup!" Missy shouted. "God gave us a pickup!" I told him the whole story.

"See what I've been telling you?" he said.

"Yeah!" I replied.

The memory of the funniest thing I ever saw Walt do still brings a smile to my face. We all have down times in our Christian walk, and Walt was no different. A group of Cowboys for Christ had been invited to the church to give their testimonies. Walt had a sister who had a ranch in California, so he knew all about the cowboy lifestyle. We both sat towards the back as the men got up and began giving their testimonies, and Walt began to cross his arms and you could hear him huffing under his breath. I asked him what was wrong.

"I know cowboys," he told me, "and I can't believe that God would have anything to do with these guys, let alone for them to claim they have been saved." I crossed my arms and leaned over and whispered in his ear,

"I know what you mean. I used to think the same thing about insurance salesmen!" He busted out laughing, uncrossing his arms.

"You got me!" he said.

Not long after that, was when I was perusing the newspaper one Sunday morning, I just happened to glance at the religious section where the churches would post their worship times and the occasional article written by some of the pastors. On that particular Sunday morning, I pounced on an article that caught my eye and brought a copy for Walt as well. I've saved this article for over thirty years, and as I read it the first time, I remember thinking, "I sure would like to go to that man's church one day." Later the Lord would lead me there.

God Loves Divorcees
By Dr. Paul Powell

The other day while shopping, a clerk asked me if she could speak with me privately. She is a divorcee and is having a hard time dealing with her feelings. Her life consists of working all day in the store and then going home to a lonely apartment at night. She doesn't enjoy going to bars, and she feels out of place in her church. She feels that she just doesn't fit anywhere and wanted to know what she should do.

I told her that my church understood her problem and that we have a large Single Adult Ministry, whose attendance averages over 250 people every Sunday. In fact, these divorcees, widows, and widowers are so important to us that we have provided a full-time staff member to work with them, and we have developed a full program for them. We have also provided the best facilities in our church for them to meet in. I assured her that God loves her and that we love her also. Not all churches feel this way. Some mistakenly think that, because God hates divorce, He also hates divorcees. These churches look upon these formerly married people as second-class citizens and either ignore them or treat them as outcasts.

Divorce is wrong. There can be no doubt that God's ideal for marriage is one man and one woman living together for life. But while God does hate divorce, He loves the divorcee. This doesn't mean that He condones sin. But it does mean that He still loves and accepts people who have failed to reach His ideal.

Sometimes divorce is the lesser of two evils. Choices in life are not always between good and evil, right and wrong, black and white. Sometimes our choices are between the bad and the worse. While divorce is wrong, so are alcoholism, child abuse, homosexuality, perversion, and wife beating. It's better to divorce in such instances and live in peace. Marriages are not to be held together at all costs.

The Christian faith calls for unconditional love and forgiveness for anyone who comes to God with an attitude of repentance. It is imperative that we adopt the same spirit and attitude as Jesus toward all people – including divorcees.

The entire thrust of the Christian message is good news. It is good news about a second chance. Divorce is a sin, but it is not the unpardonable sin. If you are a divorcee, take heart. God loves the divorced, and so do we.

God bless you, Paul Powell, wherever you are!

HOMEWORK:

- Are you willing to seek out a mentor? Do you know anyone who would be spiritually mature and available? Are you willing to be accountable to this mentor?

- Have you experienced the love and grace of God while still understanding that there is a just and righteous God?

- Are you willing to ask God for specifics in your prayers and allow Him to show you His glory?

- Are you divorced? If so, have you found a church home that provides spiritual comfort and healing? Do you know God loves the divorced?

Everywhere I Go, There I Am

The uneasiness in my heart during the separation in 1982-1983 drove me ever onward in the quest for answers and relief. I continued with my character studies, but the Lord also led me to study the Book of Romans and Galatians. In church I would hear that we needed to "present our bodies, a living sacrifice, holy, acceptable unto God, which is your reasonable service," from Romans 12:1. For most, this meant we presented ourselves for service, and the amount of time we gave might be a sacrifice. I struggled with this idea as it also said that *what* we presented was to be *holy*, and I knew I wasn't very holy. In fact, it was a constant problem just struggling with my thoughts, let alone the constant struggle of *trying* to be obedient, and there seemed to be quite a list of things to do or not do.

"Can a Christian go twenty-four hours without sinning, Lord? Is there no choice?" I brought these thoughts before Him, tired of just going to "The Christian Bar of Soap," 1 John, 1:9, and asking again and again for forgiveness. Does God just leave us like this? Surely he doesn't! There had to be more. I almost felt like I was living back home again – I couldn't win, no matter what I did; I knew I would end up in trouble and I couldn't get away. Everywhere I went, there I was!

So the Lord led me to start from the beginning of Romans and really focus on chapters 6, 7, and 8. I began to see Paul discussing some of the same issues I was facing and he put names to his discourse: "dead to sin," "the law," "old man," "the Adamic nature," etc. The only Bibles that were available that I was aware of at that time were the King James Version along with The Living Bible, but I was able to find a Scofield Reference Bible in the KJV, and the notes there were very helpful as well. Scofield's notes stated that each believer has two natures, "the flesh" and "the Spirit," and the law causes the two natures within us to be in continual strife to see which one will be in charge. He also stated that the believer is not made holy by the law, so I also wondered what *does* make us holy?

At the same time, I found a book by Watchman Nee called <u>The Normal Christian Life</u>.[10] It should have been called "The *Abnormal* Christian Life," since I couldn't see any aspect of his description in the ordinary lives of any Christians I knew (and it certainly wasn't in mine!). He insisted, however, that the principles of freedom and walking in the Spirit should be the norm for every Christian. I could also see where Charles Solomon's second half of his book, <u>The Ins and Out of Rejection</u>, was in complete harmony with Watchman Nee's book, as both began with The Blood and The Cross, where Christ's blood deals with what *we have done*, hence our sins, but the Cross deals with *what we are or what we have*, which is a sin nature.

In Romans 6:4 (KJV), I found the verse that is used by many pastors in baptism: "Therefore we are buried with him by baptism into death: that like as Christ was raised up from the dead by the glory of the Father, even so we also should walk in newness of life." Our pastor would always say, "Buried with Him in baptism, raised to walk in newness of life" as he was baptizing. Here, it was clear that something died at salvation, portrayed in baptism, and I finally saw what "it" was in verse six: "Knowing this, that our *old man is crucified with him*, that the body of sin might be destroyed, that henceforth we should not serve sin." Also in Galatians 2: 20 (KJV), it reads, "I am crucified with Christ, nevertheless I live, yet not I, but Christ lives In me, and the life which I now live in the flesh I live by the faith of the Son of God, who loved me, and gave himself for me." I didn't know exactly how to apply this, but Romans 6 seemed to suggest that you have to know first, then, reckon it to be true, and then yield to God and not to sin.

When I took this idea to the adult Sunday School class, I started with two questions, hoping to gain more insight: "How many of you can view in your mind's eye Christ dying on the Cross for you, raise your hand?" All of them raised their hands.

So then I asked, "How many of you can view in your mind's eye *yourself on that cross with Christ*, raise your hand?" Not one person raised their hand.

"Before you think I'm a heretic," I replied, "would someone please read Romans 6:6 and Galatians 2:20." So the next question that I brought up was this:

"Can a Christian go twenty-four hours without sinning?" Although the discussion was lively, it didn't take long, as it appeared that everyone was in the same boat as I was, and they all simply defaulted to 1 John 1:9 as the answer for sin. Just confess and repent again and again and again. I knew there was more. Why would God deliver us from the *penalty* of sin by sending His Son to die on the Cross for us, and one day, when we get to Heaven, deliver us from the very *presence* of sin, but do absolutely nothing about the *power* of sin in our daily lives?! What I could understand was that *before* a person is saved, they have *no choice* but to sin, but *after* a person is saved, they do have a choice. The word picture I formed was a butterfly and its metamorphosis.

A caterpillar has no choice but to crawl, but once it enters into the cocoon, which is like a place of death, a transformation occurs, and it comes out a butterfly. As a butterfly, it now faces a choice. Does it want to crawl on the ground like it did before or fly as it was intended to do? I don't know about you, but I would want to fly! For us as Christians, we have gone through a transformation as well. 2 Corinthians 5:17 (KJV) tells us, "If any man be in Christ, he is a *new creation,* old things are passed away; behold *all things are become new!*"

Another word picture I formed involved cars. If you decided that the world would be better if there were no cars, how would you go about getting rid of them? Would you try to destroy every car you see? Would that do any good? The answer is most likely not, as the automobile manufacturers would keep making more. Thus, it is the same with us; we can try to do away with every sin we commit through repentance and confession as in 1 John 1:9, but it won't do any good until we do something about the sin-producing manufacturer within us all, "the flesh," or "the old man," or sinful nature. Paul discovered in Romans 7 a tremendous battle. It seems that understanding God's law and trying to obey and keep it reveals this monster within us all, and it seeks to destroy us and keep us in failure. Paul's answer seemed to be that *something happens in order that we may* "walk after the Spirit" and not "after the flesh," Romans 8:1, but that took me back to "*try* not to fulfill the lusts of the flesh in order to walk in the Spirit." I wasn't sure how one walks after the Spirit. The KJV of Romans 8 did make clear a couple of things about two words: "in" and "after," which reminded me of that butterfly life cycle.

A lost person is "in the "flesh" and has no choice but to walk "after the flesh." A saved person is "in the spirit" and needs *to choose* – will he or she walk "after the Spirit" or "after the flesh"? What became very apparent to me at this point was that God does NOT want us to go to Romans 12:1 and present "the flesh" to Him, because *that* is not holy, no matter how we try to present it.

The Lord began to show me that practically every New Testament truth could be seen in a word picture through an event in the Old Testament. The Old Testament became for me a Picture Book of New Testament truths. Although the character studies I was doing suggested that many of the people of the Old Testament, such as Joseph, and David, and Moses, etc., showed what writers referred to as "types" of Christ or different aspects of Christ, such as Joseph portraying Christ as the Savior of the people, etc.; this was different. These were *principles* that were taught in the New Testament and *revealed* in the Old Testament. There might be a historical event that occurred to support these principles, but it might indicate a revelation of a future event or the fulfillment of a past prophecy or sometimes even a double fulfillment such as in Daniel where an antichrist is spoken of and history shows there was a certain leader who fit that bill in biblical times named Antiochus Epiphanes, and yet there will be one in future times. Or, as I saw repeatedly with Job, Joseph, David, etc., a person could be brought to this so-called "end of self" or "death of self," which apparently was referenced in Romans 6 and 7 and in Galatians. In other words, there was one interpretation but many applications.

An example of a literal or historical event in Old Testament scripture that was used or applied with a different application or principle in the New Testament can be seen when reading in Galatians Chapter 4, verses 22-24 (KJV):

"For it is written, that Abraham had two sons, the one by a bondmaid, the other by a free-woman. But he who was of the bondwoman was born after the *flesh*; but he of the free-woman was *by promise. Which things are an allegory....*"

Webster's dictionary defines an allegory as "a figurative treatment of one subject under the guise of another." The rest of the verse shows what was being figuratively spoken about: "for these are two covenants," one is bondage and other is freedom, according to verses 25-26. There was an actual historical event of two women having children, but God used them to portray, through Paul, a New Testament truth about Law and freedom in Christ.

Another example is what I call a "progressive revelation," in which God, over hundreds of years, shows His people in the Old Testament and us, as believers in the New Testament, what His true plan really is. With Adam and Eve and again with Cain and Abel, we saw a blood sacrifice offered that was accepted by God. In fact, God uses an *innocent substitute* of an animal to clothe Adam and Eve. God seals that idea again in the case of Cain and Abel, in which only *the blood of an innocent substitute* is accepted; thus we get the picture of One Innocent Substitute for One Man. Hundreds of years later, while the Hebrews are in Egypt, they are told that they will be delivered from the death angel if they put the blood of an innocent lamb or substitute over the door posts of their homes. If they do this, their entire family will be saved, as the death angel will pass over their homes, thus we get the picture of One Lamb for One Family. Later, once again after hundreds of years, we see the High Priest going once a year to the Holy of Holies, the inner sanctuary of the Tabernacle to offer the blood of an innocent substitute for all the Israelites, thus we get the picture of One Lamb for One Nation. Finally, what are the first words out of John the Baptist's mouth when he sees Jesus?

"Look, the Lamb of God who takes away the sin of one man – NO! the sin of one family? NO! the sin of one nation? NO! the sin of the *world!"*(John 1:29, NIV)

Where in the Old Testament was a picture of what *not* to offer God? Is there a Romans 12:1 example in the O.T. depicting an offer *wrongly* presented for sacrifice or preparing to sacrifice, in which a person God had chosen and anointed was attempting to present the best of this so-called "flesh" to God as holy, and it was rejected? I remembered the story of Cain and Abel of where one offered an animal sacrifice and the other offered a grain sacrifice, which was rejected because it was a picture of God wanting man to see that there had to be a blood payment for redemption of mankind, but I was remembering an incident that more closely matched the issue of holiness or lack of holiness in a sacrifice demanded in Romans 12:1. In fact, this incident actually led to that person being removed from their position of leadership! I learned this during my study about King David – It was King Saul!

In 1 Samuel 15, the prophet Samuel tells Saul that God sent Samuel to anoint Saul to be king over Israel and that God expected Saul to do one thing as king: to utterly destroy Amalek and all his belongings, such as sheep and oxen. This was a king who tried to defeat the Israelites in the wilderness. Although Saul did kill some of the Amalekites, he purposely saved their king and the best of his sheep and oxen to offer *as a sacrifice* to God. Samuel offers up his famous words, "What meaneth then this bleating of the sheep in mine ears, and the lowing of the oxen which I hear," (I Samuel 15:14, KJV) which will not be forgotten, as Saul is then told that, because he tried to offer the best of what God hated, "I will war with Amalek from generation to generation," (Exodus 17:16, KJV), he would be removed as king and someone else would take his place – David. Of course, this leads us to wonder, who in the world is this guy Amalek, and why is God so mad at him that He wants him killed, all his family, and even his sheep and goats? What does this have to do with us?"

HOMEWORK:

- Is it your norm to walk in the Spirit and be free?

- Are you discovering "rules and regulations" in the Christian life and finding them to be taskmasters over you?

- Are you tired of trying (and failing) to live the Christian life?

- Are you guilty of offering the best of your self-effort to God as a sacrifice?

War with Amalek

As my quest for answers progressed, three more truths became evident:

1. God's ways are typically not our ways.
2. God makes it plain that He wants us to learn His ways.
3. Most of the Christian life is spent discovering what God has *already* given us, in and through the person of Jesus Christ.

The search for Amalek led me to study about the Israelites wandering in the wilderness after Moses led them out of Egypt. God wanted this entire group brought to what was called The Promised Land, whose boundaries were described in Genesis 12, and which was a place filled with milk and honey, according to Exodus 3:8. Yet God did not have Moses lead them directly to this place, but instead brought them through a way where they would not see warfare, as this would overwhelm them (Exodus 13:17-18, KJV), as they had been *slaves* in Egypt for four hundred years and thus had a *slave mentality*.

"But God led the people about, through the *way of the wilderness* of the Red sea..." When Pharaoh pursued them, and they were *in a place of impossibility – a place of certain death*, God miraculously delivered them by having the waters rolled back, allowing the people to pass through, then causing those same waters to return to their former place, drowning Pharaoh's army instead. Moses instructs the people to "stand still and see the salvation of the Lord." (Exodus 14:13, KJV)

I wondered whether there could be any reference to slavery in the New Testament principles that I was studying by this group of people. And there it was in Romans 6:20 (KJV): "*When you were slaves of sin* you were free from righteousness..." New Testament believers begin with a slave mentality as well! "But now that you have been set free from sin and *have become slaves of God...*" (Romans 6:22, NIV), thus *ownership* changed as well. John 8:34-36 (NIV) states, "Jesus replied, Very truly I tell you, *everyone who sins is a slave to sin.* Now a slave has no permanent place in the family, but a son belongs to it forever. So if the Son sets you free, you will be free indeed." I certainly felt like I was being held captive! I wanted to shout like Patrick Henry did, but for different reasons – "Give me liberty or give me death!" Boy, was I in for a surprise with God's answer!!

When the Israelites were brought into the Promised Land after forty years of wandering, I noticed that they crossed over in a very similar manner as they had at the Red Sea – the waters were at flood stage, and yet they rolled back for them to cross on dry ground, and it was also a place of impossibility, although no one was chasing them. I knew this had to be significant, but I didn't understand yet what this meant. However, I could see that *once they were in the Promised Land,* they did a lot of fighting, thus, somehow *they no more carried a slave mentality but a warrior mentality.* Did the New Testament reference a warrior mentality? Once again, I saw it in several places, and we would even sing songs about it, as in the hymn "Onward, Christian Soldiers." The book of Ephesians had lots of notes and verses about warfare, what armor we are to wear and shields to hold, and all the fighting we are to do in Ephesians 6. It even tells who we are fighting against: "For we wrestle not against flesh and blood, but against principalities, against powers, against the rulers of the darkness of this world, against spiritual wickedness in high places." (Ephesians 6:12, KJV) To me, though, it didn't seem that "spiritual wickedness in high places" could be the same as what Paul said he was warring about, because his warring was different. His warfare appeared to be internal, although spiritual:

"But I see another law *in my members, warring* against the law of my mind, and bringing me into *captivity* to the law of sin which *is in my members.*"(Romans 7:23, KJV)

I then wondered, *Lord, how did the Israelites change from having a slave mentality to having a warrior mentality and where in the story of the Israelites would there be a picture of what Paul was warring with? What is the power struggle about?*

In looking at the forty years during which the Israelites wandered in the wilderness, it first became apparent that God intended for them to come through this way for a reason, but didn't intend for them to stay there as long as they did. In fact, it became a punishment for them to have such a lengthy stay. This particular generation would not be warriors in the Promised Land; only Joshua and his family and Caleb and his family would go across. God got mad at all of the other Israelites because they didn't believe, and so they didn't get to have all that God had intended for them through His promise to Abraham. However, the next generation did go across and began to take the land. I wondered if there was a New Testament application of this, and when I found Hebrews chapters 3 and 4, it shook me to the core.

Hebrews 3 and the first part of chapter 4 depict the story of the Israelites, who wandered in the wilderness. In Hebrews 3:19, Paul says they couldn't go into the Promised Land "because of unbelief." Yet Paul compares this "entering into the Promised Land" as something different in verse 18, (KJV): "And to whom sware he that they should not enter into *His rest*, but to them that *believed not*." Now *there* was the word I wanted to see – rest, and God likened it to coming into the Promised Land *as a warrior* in the Old Testament! Now *that* was very interesting! How can you "rest" and be engaged in warfare at the same time?! Chapter 3 also indicated *why* there was such unbelief in verses 10-11: (KJV) "Wherefore I was grieved with that generation, and said, they do always err in their heart; and *they have not known **my ways.*** So I sware in my wrath, they shall not enter into *my rest.*"

Well, of course, that led me to ask the Lord, "Was there anyone who *did* know Your Ways?" That led me to a character study about Moses.[11] In Exodus 33:13, (Complete Jewish Bible), Moses *directly asks God* to show him *His ways!*

"Now please, if it really is the case that I have found favor in your sight, *show me your ways so that I will understand you* and continue finding favor in your sight." Would God answer that request? Absolutely! We see that answer in Psalms 103:7 (NIV): "He made *His ways known to Moses*, his mighty *deeds* to the children of Israel."

I also noted that Moses had an extended stay in a wilderness for a forty-year period *before* he led the children of Israel into theirs. I *thought*

I noticed a pattern here. Were there others in the Old Testament and especially in the New Testament that also had a "wilderness experience"? It appeared so! David was in a wilderness; Moses was in a wilderness, the children of Israel were in a wilderness, and in the New Testament, John the Baptist lived in the wilderness and said he was "the voice of one crying in the wilderness." (John 1:23) Paul went to a desert wilderness for three years before preaching, and even Christ Himself went to the wilderness to be tested!

Yet even more disconcerting was Hebrews 4:1 (KJV), which shouts out a warning to all believers: "Let us therefore fear (and in the Complete Jewish Bible it states "be *terrified*"), lest a promise being left us of entering into *His rest,* any of you should seem to come short of it." I found several verses that told us NOT to fear, but here we are told we DO need to fear! To my knowledge, there are only two places in the Bible in which we are told to fear. One is to have a reverential fear or respect of God Himself. This is called "the fear of the Lord." It is referenced in numerous places in the Bible. For example, in Psalms 34:11, (KJV) we are invited to learn this fear: "Come, ye children, hearken unto me; I will teach you the fear of the Lord." The only other time I've ever seen where we are instructed to be fearful is here, in Hebrews Chapter 4:1, "Let us therefore *fear....*" "Let us *strive* therefore to enter that rest." (Hebrews 4:11, KJV)

After I read that passage, I got on my knees right then and pleaded with God, "Lord, please teach me and show me Your Ways! Your Word says that "My thoughts are not your thoughts, neither are your ways My ways, saith the Lord." (Isaiah 55:8, KJV) While You're at it, Lord, please show me what's going on in the *wilderness*"!

I began to see that the wilderness is *where* we learn God's Ways! It's also the same place that Amalek showed up. In fact, Amalek seeks to attack the Israelites at their very weakest point: "Remember what Amalek did unto thee by the way, when ye were come forth out of Egypt. How he met thee by the way, and smote the hindmost of thee, even all that were feeble behind thee, when thou wast faint and weary; and he feared not God." (Deuteronomy 25:17-18, KJV)

Amalek was the grandson of Essau. Although there is a blood kinship here with the Israelites, as Essau was the twin brother of Jacob, Amalek, Essau's grandson, comes out of Canaan specifically looking for a fight with the Israelites and attacks them at their weakest. We know that Essau gave up his birthright for food (Genesis 25:27-34), and this was driven by more than simple hunger – he *despised* the birthright (verse 34), and according to the Scofield notes, it was because it was a spiritual thing. The Scofield notes state:

The birthright had three elements:

1. Until the establishment of the Aaronic priesthood, the head of the family exercised priestly rights.
2. The Abrahamic family held the Edenic promise of the Satan-Bruiser (Gen. 3:15), thus Abel, Seth, Shem, Abraham, Isaac, and Essau.
3. Esau, as the firstborn, was in the direct line of the Abrahamic promise of the Earth-Blesser.

Someone once said, "What one generation allows in moderation, the next generation excuses in excess." Thus, if Esau *despised* his spiritual birthright, it stands to reason that his grandson will also despise God. Then, what was God's response to both these men? God despised them! Romans 9:13 (KJV) states, "As it is written, Jacob have I loved, but Esau have I hated." Exodus 17:16, (KJV) states, "I will war with Amalek from generation to generation."

When we think about entire groups of peoples in the Old Testament that are wiped out by God or per God's instructions, it seems most likely due to the fact that they will NEVER bow down before God and despise anyone who does and often will try to destroy them! Galatians 4:29 (KJV) seems to suggest this as well: "But just as then he that was born *after the flesh* persecuted him that was born *after the spirit*, even so it is now." With some of these people, God waited for hundreds of years in mercy, but they never changed.

Romans 9:22-24 (Complete Jewish Bible) suggests why: "Now what if God, even though he was quite willing to demonstrate his anger and make know his power, patiently put up with people who deserved his punishment and were ripe for destruction? What if he did this in order to make known the riches of his glory to those who are the objects of his mercy, whom he prepared in advance for glory – that is, to us, whom he called not only from among the Jews, but also from among the Gentiles."

Esau took his wives and concubines from the people of the land of Canaan and thus Amalek is the offspring from one of the children (Eliphaz) and of these concubines and is raised in the ways of the Canaanites who worship Baal and detest God, thus becoming everything God hates!

Now, in looking to see how Amalek was defeated, it seems that there is again a *progressive revelation,* through which God shows us one thing in the Old Testament and explains His true intention in the New Testament. The Israelites defeated Amalek when Moses stood on top of the hill with the rod of God in his hands; thus, the picture is that of *fighting and praying.* According to the Scofield notes, the Old Testament victory is a man under the Law, but the New Testament victory is under Grace, where the Holy Spirit gains the victory over the flesh on the believer's behalf as the believer walks *in the Spirit.*

So this also matches what is seen in the New Testament, in which Paul's experience told in Romans 7 depicts the *warfare* of the Spirit and the flesh, *not* the Ephesians' warfare against "spiritual wickedness in high places." The wilderness warfare and the Romans 7 warfare depict warfare conducted *within,* while the Joshua and The Promised Land warfare and the warfare in Ephesians depict warfare conducted *without.* Apparently, this warfare conducted in the wilderness and all that they were supposed to learn in the wilderness is what should have transformed them from having a slave mentality to that of a warrior mentality, and they didn't get it! Yet we know that Moses did get it! So what did Moses learn in his wilderness? To answer this, once again I returned to Theodore Epp and his book, Moses Vol. 1, God Prepares His Man.

In Acts 7, much is written about Moses, and verse 22 (KJV) reads, "Moses was learned in all wisdom of the Egyptians, and was mighty in words and deeds." His training occurred during a time when a new Pharaoh ruled that was not kindly towards the Israelites, as those had previously been with Joseph. Moses' training included military training, and he received the best in the world at that time. Thus his deeds included military deeds as well. Epp presents the following from Moses, Vol. 1 (p. 30):

"At that time, the queen was the rightful heir to the throne; thus, the king held power only by right of marriage to her. The king then on the throne had no son, but he had a daughter of outstanding ability, and she was in line for the throne. However, she would not be allowed to reign, because, according to Egyptian custom and law, the reigning monarch was to be a man. But because of her connection to the throne, she could determine who the next king would be." Page 31 reads:

"Although Pharaoh's daughter could not rule on the throne herself, she could adopt a son who could rule on the throne."[12]

Hebrews 11:24 (KJV) states that Moses "refused to be called the son of Pharaoh's daughter"; Moses denied his rights to the throne. He then went and tried to identify with his people by devoting his own effort to deliver them, and he failed miserably and completely, killing an Egyptian in the process. He had hoped his people would see that he was there to deliver them, but they didn't understand him. So he then fled to the desert – *his wilderness.* Here he became a shepherd, which was something the Egyptians despised.

What did Moses learn?

1. Human sympathy or pity would not carry him when the Israelites would later constantly provoke him. Sympathy or pity led to impulsive actions, which God does not use. Sympathy and pity would not be enough to lead a man to be the intercessor for his people, like Moses became.
2. Self-will and self-reliance led Moses to take matters into his own hands. Moses had zeal without knowledge of what God wanted and when. His actions were thus premature and not led by God.
3. Human strength would not be enough to deliver God's people. This battle would be God's and not man's. Due to his military training, it is not inconceivable that Moses would plan deliverance by force, but this was not what God had planned. Zechariah 4:6 (KJV) says, "Not by might, nor by power, but by my spirit, saith the Lord of hosts."

4. Dependence on God and not independence is what Moses needed. Moses may have surrendered to a task as well as to a people, but he needed to surrender to God.

5. "By faith" are the key words identified when Moses comes out of his desert experience.

6. Intimacy with God is learned in the desert, as Moses is then known for speaking with God face to face.

7. New name for God – Moses knew God as Elohim, the Strong One, Creator and Judge of the Universe, but in the desert, he learns a different name – I Am (Exodus 3:14). This "I Am" had always been in existence and always would be, including among His people in terms of whatever their needs would require.

8. Death of self – There was that term again. It seemed that every person chosen by God was going through this experience!

9. Meekness – After his desert experience, Moses is known for his meekness, only to be surpassed by Christ Himself.

Again and again I faced this concept of "death to self." I wondered how one brings this about in life and how one enters into the "rest" that God refers to. I could see all of the rules and regulations and the need to obey, but was overwhelmed by it all. Yet it seemed that the Lord was showing me that if I wanted to try to do something, there were two things to strive for:

1. Strive to know Him.
2. Strive to enter His rest.

HOMEWORK:

- As a believer, do you feel enslaved by sin? Does there seem to be one particular sin you can't overcome?

- Have you considered the possibility that you, too, can know God's Ways, and more so, you can incorporate them into your life?

- As a believer, are you striving to know Him? Are you, too, desirous of the rest God's Word speaks of?

Dealing with Negative Messages

In early 1984, I approached the adult Sunday School class about the admonition in Hebrews 4:1 of entering God's rest. No one had ever heard of it. I asked the pastor and his wife, but they didn't know what I was talking about either. I told them there were three things in the Bible that I really wanted to understand better: the peace of God that surpasses understanding, the abundant life, and this rest of God. The pastor's wife told me she didn't believe any Christian could have the peace of God in their heart as long as there was un-confessed sin in their lives, so if I wanted peace and rest, I had to have a clean heart. She told me that it would be difficult for me to have this peace due to the roller-coaster ride of emotions I was experiencing and my separation, since it appeared to all that I was not working toward reconciliation with my husband, as we had been separated for quite some time. She emphasized that I needed to focus on being obedient to the Lord. I told her I was trying so hard to be as obedient as I could and that, somehow, I was going to find the answer to this quest. She just shook her head and said, "We're praying for you."

I really didn't believe that the pastor's wife was trying to be cruel or to mistreat me intentionally. I truly believe she was speaking from her understanding, and alas, for many during that time period, with the church's view and lack of understanding towards the divorced or separated. My emotions *were* in an upheaval, and although much of this was due to the divorce, in looking back, I also believe that much of it was due to being a "baby Christian" as well. Even without having children of my own, I could understand that babies cry, whine, and are bottle fed with milk. Even though I was twenty-seven years of age physically, I was spiritually more like a toddler in the Lord, as I had been attending church and studying for about three years at that point. Paul talked about "milk babies" in 1

Corinthians 3:1-3, and it appeared to me in studying Moses that *for forty years* Moses led around about two to three million "milk babies"!

Almost every time I talked with the pastor or his wife during this separation, I felt ashamed of myself for not doing better and was afraid that God might be mad at me as well. Yet His Word constantly reminded me that He "*hath not given us the spirit of fear,* but of power, and of love, and of a sound mind." (1 Timothy 1:7, KJV) Something they would say would "push my buttons," and I felt the same fear and anxiety as when I was at home as a little kid with no way out.

It seemed to me now that the answer again would be the same, except spiritually I needed to "grow up" and eat the "meat" of God's Word, like Paul said. Paul also said something else about immature and mature Christians in 1 Corinthians 13:11 (KJV):

"When I was a child, I spake as a child, I understood as a child, I thought as a child: but when I became a man, I put away childish things." I knew it was time to do something about those negative messages that they instilled in me each time we spoke. Previously, I had responded the same way as in childhood by becoming hurt, depressed, and afraid of the one in authority over me, as well as of God and His authority. Then I engaged in a wrestling within and with God about what His Word really says. I needed to be free from what other people thought – and even more, my own thoughts – and rely *only* on what God thinks of me. So I wrote down those negative messages from childhood, the exact words I heard or felt and then what I thought I heard, either in church or from my own heart, and finally, what God had to say about it all. Was God really a policeman, or was He my Heavenly Dad?!

Negative Messages from Childhood: What I Heard and What God Has to Say

1. **"Nothing in life is fair."** Rather than say, "I'm sorry," or "I was wrong," tell the person that you're just trying to teach him or her that nothing in life is fair.

   In Church or My Heart: God owes you nothing – you owe Him. If you got what you really deserved, you'd be in Hell. God does not owe you happiness, contentment, peace, satisfaction, etc., so don't expect it.

In Christ: He will work all the "unfairness" for my good. Although He owes me nothing, He freely gives of Himself to me without demanding in return. Instead, He issues an invitation: "Come unto me all ye who are weary and heavy laden and I will give you rest." (Matthew 11:28, KJV)

2. **"You are a burden – don't ask for anything."** You have what you need – just don't ask.

In Church or My Heart: Don't look to humans to meet any of your needs – see how Christ meets all your needs. Give expecting nothing in return – not even from God. You have what you need. We all deserve Hell, and you shouldn't complain if you're getting a mere taste of that which you deserve. Do for God because He's done so much for you.

In Christ: I'm a child of the King!! *Before* I even speak or call out – He answers. While I am yet speaking, He will hear! (Isaiah 65:24) To Him, I am a blessing and not a burden. He knows my needs and wants to supply them with Himself, for He is my greatest need.

3. **"Things are more important than me."** Things are an asset – I'm a liability.

In Church or My Heart: Giving is more important than receiving. Serve God, Serve God, SERVE GOD – do, do, DO!! Always think of others. Always deny self and all needs, wants, and desires. Give them up to God and without expectation of return.

In Christ: I am so important that He gave His life for me! He wants me to "be" in order to "do." I am loved; I am accepted, not based on what I do, but because of whose I am! (Ephesians 1:6).

The Holy Spirit does not reason from what man is or does for God, but from what God is to man.

Theodore H. Epp

Fear produces the obedience of a slave;
Love produces the obedience of a son.

C. I. Scofield

4. **"Who would want to hear *your* opinion?"** You do not have permission to share feelings; keep them to yourself.

In Church or My Heart: Your gender and your marriage failures disqualify any testimony. If you couldn't make your marriage work and trust God for its success, you have no faith. You have absolutely nothing to offer God's people.

In Christ: He looks at my heart- at my longing to seek Him, to be with Him to hear Him, and speak on His behalf to those who are hurting. He desires intimacy with me. He is my Heavenly Husband! He is investing His love in me to develop a life message through me. Our greatest messages come out of our greatest failures and weaknesses, as His love shines through us.

5. **"Children are neither to be seen nor heard."**

In Church or My Heart: You have no rights. You are to suffer as a good soldier and not complain. Turn the other cheek. Deny yourself.

In Christ: He rejoices over me and has seated me in Heavenly places, far above for all to see, and He has placed all things under my feet because I am in Him. He is my inheritance, therefore I cannot help but sing His praises. (Ephesians 1).

6. **"If you want me to spend time with you – you will have to pay me."**

In Church or My Heart: WORK for God so He will be pleased with you. DO all the right things so He can draw close to you. If you mess up – even if it's just in your thought life – you'll still belong to Him, but you won't have any fellowship. He won't have a thing to do with you.

In Christ: There was no higher price than that which He paid to not only have a relationship with me, but fellowship and intimacy <u>in spite</u> of what I do. His <u>goodness</u> draws me to desire Him and His ways, and there's no payment I can make to attain His acceptance, for I already and forever will be accepted in the Beloved!! When I'm at my worst, His love shines the brightest. This draws me to Him and builds within me the desire to follow Him. His love (not His rules) draw me to *want* to be with Him, to *want* His ways, to *want* to follow Him.

7. <u>"Do not allow yourself to be subject to any man, and certainly don't depend on one."</u>

In Church or My Heart: You must subject yourself to God, even if He has to beat you into subjection. The beatings just demonstrate the "stripes" of His *love* for you and mark that you are His child.

In Christ: He *loved* me into subjection, insisting that I know His love for me before submitting, knowing I could not truly submit out of fear and terror but only out of love. I can depend on His love and care for me no matter what happens. He has carved me upon the palms of His hands! (Isaiah 49:16)

8. <u>"No one is satisfied – no one gets along."</u> No role model for intimacy, conflict resolution, love.

In Church or My Heart: Set off on a life-and-death search for more – for a role model, for Freedom, for answers in Christ to a troubled world. We are amid a forest of lives going up in smoke, and most Christians are only equipped with garden hoses. Do not accept mediocrity in the Christian experience. Have a vertical relationship with God, healed in order that my horizontal relationships with others might also be healed.

In Christ: He is my El Shadai – the Breasted One, the God who satisfies. He is my satisfaction. Just as a babe is satisfied at the breast of its mother, so too does He satisfy me. I am complete in Him and have communion and intimacy with Him.

HOMEWORK:

- One of the negative messages of my childhood was:
  _____

- What has your heart convicted you about this message all these years? _____

- What does Christ really say about that message? _____
  _____

A Lesson In God's Pursuit Of A Relationship With Us

The relationship we enter into with God is first started by God, as He seeks to *restore* that which was lost in Adam through sin – our relationship with Him. Even though we may think we are the ones who thought up the idea of seeking God, He reminds us that it is He who seeks us. He tells us in Luke 19:10 that He came "to seek and to save that which was lost." In Romans 3:11-12, we are also reminded that, when it comes to sin, "there is none that seeks after God." I thought about this as I pondered about the groups of people in the Old Testament that were given hundreds of years as God waited for any change before they were destroyed as they would come against God's people. It was during the long wait of all those years that God prepared His own people, the Hebrews to become a great people in number. Even so, the grace of God was present and available for both the Hebrew and the Gentile nations. I was never more keenly reminded of this truth and of the overwhelming love of God that pursues each one of us then during my experience with my friend Bob, which continues even to the present.

While trying to learn from my friend Walt about the Lord's leading, one Sunday evening as church was letting out, I sensed this overwhelming need to stop at Sambo's, the local coffee shop that I frequented on a regular basis and had just been to right before church that evening. My sister, Penny, worked there as well. I really didn't want any coffee, but there seemed a great heaviness in my heart that I needed to go.

Maybe Penny needs to see me about something, I thought at first. I drove by the restaurant and didn't see her car, and I started to drive out of the parking lot to go home. As I tried to drive away, the heaviness and the thought that I needed to go inside became greater.

Maybe there's someone there I know that maybe I need to run into, I mused, as I knew I didn't want any coffee. So I drove around the parking lot to see if there were any cars I recognized, and there were none, so I started again to exit the parking lot.

You need to go inside Sambo's. This became such an overwhelming thought which was so heavy, I finally spoke out loud:

"Lord, if this is You, and I don't know for sure, I sure don't want any coffee, and I don't see any cars I know, but if this is You, I'll go inside for ten minutes and if whoever or whatever it is You want has not occurred, I'm going to leave after ten minutes, because I'm not sure if this is You or not."

I parked the car and headed inside. I no more than walked through the door when two guys hollered out my name.

"Susan, can you come over here?!" I looked over at them in surprise, because I had no idea who they were and wondered how they knew my name.

"Do I know you?" I asked as I walked towards them.

"No, you don't know us, but we know you. Would you sit with us for a minute?" There were several people there, so I didn't feel afraid, and I went and sat in the booth with them.

I asked, "How do you know me?"

"Well, we see you in here all the time, and every time we see you here, you're studying that Bible like your life depends on it."

"My life *does* depend on it," I responded. I then began to share with them about the life and death search I was on for answers from God and the premonition that, if things didn't change, I didn't think I would live to see the age of thirty. One of the guys was a Catholic believer who simply hadn't been to church in awhile, but it was very apparent immediately as to why I was there. It was for the other guy. His name was Bob. He was a great skeptic and a non-believer, and it became very clear that, even though I didn't know a lot about the Bible, the passionate search I was on was the key that opened the door that perhaps a pastor or other more scholarly person would not be allowed to go through to reach him. Bob was simply very curious as to what I could find so intriguing with "that Bible."

I talked with Bob and his friend for *three hours* and shared what was going on in my life, including the separation and the struggles of understanding God's purpose in all of it. There was never even a hint from either man to hit on me, they asked just questions about what I had been studying. I asked Bob if he was a believer, and he said no, and I asked if he was interested in becoming a believer. He said not at this time, but he was just interested in what I had learned and had to say. After three hours, we said our goodbyes and went our separate ways, and I didn't think any more about it. I never expected to see either one of them again.

Two years later, I decided to walk through the booths and vendors set up at the Azalea Trails celebration at Bergfield Park in Tyler. As I was approaching the booths, I saw Bob walking towards me about fifty yards away, and he glanced at me and immediately looked away. I knew he recognized me, but it was obvious he didn't want to talk, so I kept walking.

Five years later, after I had remarried and visited the Henderson Syrup Festival with my new husband, I ran right into Bob! Because I knew the Lord had instigated the original meeting in the first place, I was (and always have been since then) very bold with Bob. When I saw him there, I approached him as though he was a long-lost friend.

"Bob!! It's so good to see you! How are ya?!" He smiled and seemed genuinely glad to see me.

"Fine," he replied, "and you?" I gave him a big hug and introduced him to my husband.

"Bob, have you become a Christian yet?" I asked.

"Naw," he replied, "I'm just not into that."

"Ok," I replied, but continued, "You do know God loves you, don't you Bob?" I asked.

"I'm just not into all that right now. I see you got that divorce after all, right?" he replied.

"Yes, Bob, I regret to say, that it did happen. After two years of separation, my ex-husband decided he didn't want church or God to be any part of his life." Bob quickly changed the subject and we exchanged a few pleasantries before saying goodbye to go our separate ways to enjoy the festival.

"It was good to see ya, Bob," I said.

"Good to see you, too," he replied.

"I want you to think about what I said," I replied. He nodded and kept walking.

Ten years later, I happened to walk into a different diner for lunch one day, and as I sat down, I saw Bob leaving the restaurant. He seemed so bubbly with joy, and there was a bounce to his step, but I couldn't get to him before he left. I had forgotten his last name by that time and asked the waitress if she knew him,

She replied, "Oh yes, he's in here all the time." So that evening, I got bold again and looked his name up in the phone book and dialed his number. He answered the phone.

I said, "Is this Bob?"

"Yes, it is," he replied. I told him who I was and reminded him of when I met him at Sambo's, of seeing him at Bergfield Park for the Azalea Trails, and then seeing him at the Syrup Festival.

"I remember you," he replied.

I told him that I noticed that he seemed very happy at lunch today and just wondered if he had become a Christian yet.

"Naw, I have a new girlfriend!"

"That's great, Bob," I responded, "but that's not gonna last!"

Bob just laughed, and we visited for a couple of minutes before ending the conversation.

Five years ago, I was teaching a lady's Bible study based on the book by John Ortberg, called If You Want to Walk on Water, You've Got to Get out of the Boat. The book includes a testimony of a friend of the author's named Doug Coe from Washington D.C., who led a man named Bob to faith in Christ and the outlandish yet marvelously bold behavior Bob exhibited as a new believer in Christ while learning the power of prayer. Bob was an insurance salesman (see, Walt, I told ya!!), and Bob stayed connected with his mentor, Doug (who sounded a whole lot like my mentor, Walt) in order to learn more about his newfound faith. Ortberg relates the following:

> One day, Bob came in all excited about a statement in
> the Bible where Jesus says, "Ask whatever you will in my
> name, and you shall receive it."
>
> "Is that really true?" Bob demanded. Doug explained,

"Well, it's not a blank check. You have to take it in context of the teachings of the whole Scripture on prayer. But yes – it really is true. Jesus really does answer prayer."

"Great!" Bob said. "Then I gotta start praying for something. I think I'll pray for Africa."

"That's kind of a broad target. Why don't you narrow it down to one country?" Doug advised.

"All right. I'll pray for Kenya."

"Do you know anyone in Kenya?" Doug asked.

"No."

"Ever been to Kenya?"

"No." Bob just wanted to pray for Kenya.

So Doug made an unusual arrangement. He challenged Bob to pray every day for six months for Kenya. If Bob would do that and nothing extraordinary happened, Doug would pay him five hundred dollars. But if something remarkable did happen, Bob would pay Doug five hundred dollars. And if Bob did not pray every day, the whole deal was off. It was a pretty unusual prayer program, but then Doug is a creative guy.

Bob began to pray, and for a long while, nothing happened. Then one night he was at a dinner in Washington. The people around the table explained what they did for a living. One woman said she helped run an orphanage in Kenya – the largest of its kind.

Bob saw five hundred dollars suddenly sprout wings and begin to fly away. But he could not keep quiet. Bob roared to life. He had not said much up to this point, and now he pounded her relentlessly with question after question.

"You're obviously very interested in my country," the woman said to Bob, overwhelmed by his sudden barrage of questions. "You've been to Kenya before?"

"No."

"Then how do you happen to be so curious?"

"Well, someone is kind of paying me five hundred dollars to pray..."

She asked Bob if he would like to come visit Kenya and tour the orphanage. Bob was so eager to go, he would have left that very night if he could.

When Bob arrived in Kenya, he was appalled by the poverty and the lack of basic health care. Upon returning to Washington, he couldn't get this place out of his mind. He began to write to large pharmaceutical companies, describing to them the vast need he had seen. He reminded them that every year they would throw away large amounts of medical supplies that went unsold. "Why not send them to this place in Kenya?" he asked.

And some of them did. This orphanage received more than a million dollars' worth of medical supplies.

The woman called Bob up and said, "Bob, this is amazing! We've had the most phenomenal gifts because of the letters you wrote. We would like to fly you back over and have a big party. Will you come?"

So Bob flew back to Kenya. While he was there, the president of Kenya came to the celebration, because it was the largest orphanage in the country, and offered to take Bob on a tour of Nairobi, the capital city. In the course of the tour they saw a prison. Bob asked about a group of prisoners there.

"They're political prisoners," he was told.

"That's a bad idea," Bob said brightly. "You should let them out."

Bob finished the tour and flew back home. Sometime later, Bob received a phone call from the State Department of the United States government:

"Is this Bob?"

"Yes."

"Were you recently in Kenya?"

"Yes."

"Did you make any statements to the president about political prisoners?"

"Yes."

"What did you say?"

"I told him he should let them out."

The State Department official explained that the department had been working for years to get the release of these prisoners, to no avail. Normal diplomatic channels and political maneuvers had led to a dead end. But now the prisoners had been released, and the State Department was told it had been largely because of Bob. So the government was calling to say thanks.

Several months later, the president of Kenya made a phone call to Bob. He was going to rearrange his government and select a new cabinet. Would Bob be willing to fly over and pray for him for three days while he worked on this very important task?

So Bob – who was not politically connected at all – boarded a plane once more and flew back to Kenya, where he prayed and asked God to give wisdom to the leader of the nation as he selected his government. All this happened because one man got out of the boat.

How about you? What are you praying for? Give it six months. I'll make you a deal – I'll give you the Bob Challenge...

John Ortberg, Author

<u>If You Want to Walk on Water, You've Got to Get out of the Boat</u>

(Printed with permission.) [13]

Immediately upon reading this story aloud from Ortberg's book, I shared with the ladies in the Bible study about my own friend Bob and our escapades over a twenty-five year period. Then the Lord laid a thought upon my heart, and I shared with the ladies that I would be running into *my* Bob again, and very soon. We all agreed to pray for Bob as a class. *Five days later,* the Post Office sent me to pick up some vehicle parts from the Goodyear Tire facility. As I walked in the door and approached the counter, there was a man ahead of me just finishing up paying his bill. He looked familiar from the back, and when he turned around, I saw that it was Bob!

"Bob! It's you!" I gleefully shouted. "How are you, Bob? Have you become a Christian yet?" (I can assure you that I've never been led to be this bold to any other person in my life!)

"Naw. I was just talking the other day to a priest about...." Bob then began to relay about a religion I had never heard of that he had been reading about. I thought, *At least he was asking something, anything, about God.* I reminded Bob of our last visit and asked if the girlfriend he had started seeing at that time was still with him.

"Naw, she left." Bob retorted. I told Bob there was One who would never leave him or forsake him.

We visited a couple more minutes and parted ways again. I shared with the ladies from Bible study class what had happened, and we prayed again for Bob and for salvation.

As I ponder these past *thirty-two years* that I've known Bob, it is overwhelming to think that God's love would pursue one man so long. Who knows how many other people the Lord has stirred to speak to Bob and pray for Bob as well. Can any of us comprehend the love of a God who would do that for him and did that for each one of us? I think not! I am assured that I will run into Bob at least one more time. In the very brief moments that we have talked since that first night, I never got to share with him how and why we even met the very first time. I also need to share with him how God's love has pursued Him all these years. I can't help but imagine that maybe God has a marvelous adventure similar to the Bob from Ortberg's book. I can only pray that will be the case....

HOMEWORK:

- Child of God, are you overwhelmed with the love of God that pursues you?

- Are you allowing the Lord to direct your thoughts and lead you into divine appointments?

- Do you have a tendency to limit God as to what kind of people you are willing to talk to?

- Are you waiting until you have a "perfect" testimony before sharing with others about your relationship with Christ, or are you willing to share right where you are in that relationship?

A Checkup on Motivations

While my search for answers was ongoing in the spring of 1984, a door opened at work that I wasn't expecting – an offer came up for a supervisory position. When working at the Dallas Police Department, I had moved up quickly from a Clerk 3 to a Clerk 6, and finally to a Supervisor 8, all within two and a half years, making me the youngest civilian supervisor in the history of the department. It seemed that this would be the natural step to take, yet within my heart a dilemma arose. Somehow I knew that, within thirty days of taking the new position, I would be looking for something different to do, which usually meant to keep trying to move up. I wondered why there would be no satisfaction with the position. It was certainly something I could do and had done well, but the idea left a gnawing in my soul for something more.

At that time, I was working the late night shift and was the only female working with fifty men. The only other lady who had been there had recently retired. I enjoyed working around the guys but realized that a handful of these men, for some reason, had an issue with me. For some, it had been quite some time, and there was one who hadn't even spoken to me since right after I had arrived, three years previously. The thing was, to be perfectly honest, I really hadn't cared before. I figured it was *their problem*. I was pretty easy to get along with, and at least most of the guys seemed to indicate this to be true.

It had taken about six months after learning those two city schemes to really get a handle on running the machines with speed and accuracy, which we were tested on regularly, but within a year, I could run the mail through at a letter per second, and there were only two other employees who could consistently do the same. If I didn't compete against them, I would compete against myself to see if I could run it faster each time. But

75

now with the offer of becoming a supervisor over these guys, I wondered if it would be worth it, in light of the gnawing within and especially having to supervise that handful of guys who, for whatever reason, had an issue with me. I talked to Walt about it and, of course, he encouraged me to pray with him about it, which we did, asking for truth and God's leading.

While continuing counseling with the pastor/counselor at the time, I found out through his church about a seminar for all denominations to be held in Dallas, Texas, called the Bill Gothard Institute of Basic Youth Conflicts, which Gothard started at Wheaton College, where he attended college. These seminars were wildly popular during the 1970s and '80s, and there were approximately five thousand who attended the particular week-long seminar I went to, which covered seven basic subjects:

1. Accepting God's design in the way He made us.
2. Getting under the protection of God-ordained authorities.
3. Responsibility – Clearing our consciences of past offenses.
4. Suffering – Forgiving those who offend us.
5. Ownership – Yielding our personal rights.
6. Freedom – Having physical drives under the control of the Holy Spirit.
7. Success – Engrafting Scripture into our souls.

After attending the seminar, I shared with the pastor and his wife where I attended church about the seminar and finally found one thing that they really approved of. They had five daughters, and the pastor's wife, Joan, and two of their daughters went with me to the next one that was held in Austin. These seminars were life-changing. The first thing I did after returning home was contact my mother and ask her forgiveness for when I had wronged her during the incident when I left home. Although I truly believed she carried the heavier burden of wrongdoing, I wasn't responsible for her actions, only mine, and it brought great relief to follow through with getting rid of the "beam" that was in my eye (Matthew 7:5) and leaving the "mote," or small dust particle, to God.

Although I did not agree with everything that was presented through the seminars, especially concerning divorce and remarriage, the vast majority of the material was phenomenal for me to hear. One of the subjects discussed in great detail during the week which really caught my attention was what motivates each of us while discovering our "spiritual gifts" spoken about in Romans 12 and 1 Corinthians 12.[14] Gothard broke down the gifts Paul speaks about into seven basic *motivational* gifts (Prophecy, Serving, Giving, Teaching, Mercy, Exhortation, Administration), from Romans 12:3-9; *ministry gifts* from 1 Corinthians 12:27-31 and Ephesians 4, and *manifestation gifts* from 1 Corinthians 12:7-11. Each Christian has at least one gift. We were offered the opportunity to take a spiritual gift "test" to help determine what our motivational gift was. I jumped at the opportunity and thought for sure that administration would be my top gift. This would be a great help in understanding God's leading in terms of the promotional opportunity waiting back home.

I was utterly stunned to learn what motivated me. Instead of administration being the area of highest score for me, it was my *lowest* score. No wonder there was such a gnawing in my soul about that position – it would *never* satisfy me. It was something I could be good at, but I would be at my best while exercising what really motivated me – mercy! This really began to make sense! The gift of mercy is much more concerned with the mental/emotional well-being of others. In an instant, I understood that I would be more successful and more fulfilled in future promotions as a servant leader helping others to be successful in their positions by encouraging them and removing barriers that kept them from being successful. Coworkers would need to *feel good about themselves and their work,* rather than be led by a taskmaster, rewarding only achievement and disciplining based only on results, with no concern as to what may be happening in their homes or families. I then received what some call their *life verse or verses.* The mercy verse that so grabbed my heart was 1 Peter 4:8 (KJV): "Above all things have a fervent love amongst yourselves, for love shall cover a multitude of sins." The second verse, Galatians 6:10, addressed ministry: "As we have therefore opportunity, let us do good unto all men, especially unto them who are of the household of faith." I absolutely loved teaching the kids at church and also the adult Sunday School class, but now it was easy to see that it wasn't the facts that were satisfying, it was the seeking for each of them to discover or share the same thing I was seeking – our minds, wills, and *emotions* at peace and at rest in God.

So why was I so concerned about achieving? What was the payoff that my entire family of high achievers was attempting to get while at the same time failing miserably in achieving satisfying marriages? The Lord would show me more. I thought about the rest of my family; we were all doing the same thing – seeking to achieve something. Then it dawned on me! We would all call Mom to tell her what we had achieved, *in hopes of gaining her approval, love, and acceptance!!* No wonder I was always looking for something else to achieve or do!! We couldn't win! We couldn't seem to gain approval when we lived at home (even though it may have been there and we couldn't see it), so why in the world did we think as adults we could do any differently?! That took me right back to John Morris and Shock #2, which reminds me that *my neighbor* is not responsible to provide me with love, acceptance, or approval; only God is! We are *accepted* in the Beloved, and He *loves* us first! I was still working on the approval, but somehow God would help make that clear. Do we obey in order to gain His approval, or does He already approve of us, therefore motivating us to obey? Is it what we do or who we are?

When I remembered other high achievers in life besides our family, there seemed to be a prevalent motivation for their accomplishments as well, at least in my mind:

1. They either had a Jewish mother who told them they were the smartest and greatest kid on earth (1%), or,
2. They came from a loving, encouraging, family atmosphere, with parents who helped them "see" their hidden talents or potential (5-15%), or
3. They came from a dysfunctional family where love and acceptance were never truly attainable, *no matter how hard they tried.*

There were other interesting observations from the above three groups:

Group I – Average to above average intelligence.
Group II – Average intelligence.
Group III – Above average to exceptional intelligence!

(My father spoke seven languages and my mother was a member of Mensa, purely for the purpose of showing herself and *her mother* that she wasn't dumb!)

Groups I and II – Demonstration of more harmonious and longer-lasting marriages.
Group III – Innumerable divorces but exceptional achievements.

This leads to a rather logical conclusion or question: *How could people that were so intelligent be so stupid, (at least in their relationships)?* This was easier to understand when I thought back to my history and then looked at the *emotional maturity* of those in Group III. Their need for *love and acceptance* were never met as a child, therefore all of their adult relationships show the marks or consequences of an adult person walking around with the emotional maturity of a child in some ways!

Another observation (and none of this is true for every person, but it seems to appear for most), is the astronomical amount of physical and/or emotional illnesses present among those in Group III. These are seen especially in the area of depression (I struggled with low-grade depression until age 35!), shame, anger, and physical ailments from one extreme to the other, such as stomach problems to cancers (I had stomach problems for years and cancer abounds in our family!). Research does show a direct correlation between unresolved bitterness and some types of cancers.

In Group III, you will find a person very likely to be highly intelligent, yet emotionally immature, who consistently enters into relationships that won't work, resulting in physical, emotional, and/or mental down time.

What *is* the greatest achievement? According to surveys, it is the ability to have an intimate and loving relationship! Well, that goes back to the first and second Greatest Commandments – love God and love your neighbor!

Right then, a new goal would be born that would last the rest of my life: "Lord, I want to love You, number one, and number two, I want the opportunity to love one man and have that man love me back." What were we made for? To be successful in relationships! First with Him, and then with one another!

I decided it might be good to write down, like I had regarding the negative childhood messages, why I thought we do "church work or service" and perhaps what could be learned about godly motivations. That's when the Lord showed me 1 Thessalonians 1:3, which speaks of *works, labor or ministry, and endurance.* Okay, so what was my understanding of what motivates our works, ministry, and endurance? When I looked at the research available in the 1980s, obviously, I wasn't the only one thinking like this:

Fleshly or Dysfunctional motivations:

Sacrificial works of obedience – produced by fear of reprisal from God. When I picked up a Christian magazine, there was a survey at that time of Southern Baptists showing that *80% attended church out of fear of reprisal from God.*
Our labor or ministry – prompted by a desire for acceptance and approval.
Our endurance – inspired by desperation and survival skills

Godly motivations: 1 Thessalonians 1:3

Our works – inspired by *faith*!
Our labor or ministry – prompted by *love*!
Our endurance – inspired by *hope* in our Lord Jesus Christ!

Hebrews 12:18-24 also showed another of those so-called *progressive revelations*:

"You have *not* come to a mountain that can be touched and that is ' burning with fire: to *darkness, gloom, and storm;* to a trumpet blast or to such a voice speaking words that those who heard it begged that no further word be spoken to them, because they could not bear what was commanded: If even an animal touches the mountain, it must be stoned to death. The sight was so terrifying that Moses said, *I am trembling with fear.* But you have come to Mount Zion, to the city of the living God, the heavenly Jerusalem. You have come to thousands upon thousands of angels *in festive, joyful assembly,* to the church of the firstborn, whose names are written in heaven. You have come to God, the Judge of all, to the spirits of righteous people who have been brought to the goal; to Jesus the mediator of a new covenant, and to the sprinkled blood that speaks a better word than the blood of Abel."

Well, so long, Hell, fire, and brimstone!! God has not given us the spirit of *fear*, but of power, and of *love*, and of a sound mind! When I thought back to that job promotion opportunity, I did some research and discovered that 80% of job success comes from not job knowledge, but the ability to work *harmoniously* with others. When I thought about the handful of guys who were avoiding me, the Lord laid on my heart that I had a spirit of *competition*, and what was needed was a spirit of *cooperation*. The next day I went to our immediate supervisor and told him I would be turning down the promotional opportunity, as there was a handful of guys that I would have supervised that the Lord had convicted me of having a competitive spirit with, and I needed to spend more time on the work floor working to demonstrate a cooperative spirit. The immediate supervisor was also a Christian, but he warned me that this had never been done before and there was a strong possibility that I might be "blacklisted" for turning down the job. I told him it didn't matter – I had to do this.

Within twenty-four hours of informing the supervisor, every one of the guys that had an issue with me, except for one, *came to me and asked forgiveness for the way they had been acting!* I asked for forgiveness as well, and one of those guys became a very supportive friend for the next thirty years until I retired (the one who hadn't spoken to me in three years!). There was one guy left who was no longer working late nights and had already been promoted and had moved to a different station, so I determined to seek him out to ask his forgiveness as well.

One month later, a job position was posted for a day job at the very station where this man had gone. Typically, it takes ten to fifteen years to have enough seniority with the postal service to move to a day job as a clerk. I had the lowest seniority of all fifty guys and one of the lowest in the entire city. But I went ahead and put in for the job and waited. The job required a typing test, and there were numerous people who applied for the job who had much greater seniority than I did. However, *no one* showed up for the typing test but me. Guess who got the job! When I arrived at the new station, within a couple of days, I was able to find that last guy and apologize for my competitive spirit. He forgave me, and within a few weeks, he moved on to another station with a different assignment. There had been just a small window of opportunity to be able to seek forgiveness. With regard to the supposed "blacklisting," when the lead manager heard that I had turned down the promotion, he asked me why. After I explained, he paused and told me he had taken a position for 364 days that would have locked him into it after one more day but had turned it down and went back to his previous position. He then told me, "I have no problem with what you've done." Our God is an awesome God!

HOMEWORK:

- Have you discovered what your spiritual gift is? If not, your local church will likely have the resources available for you to discover your gift.

- Have you discovered a "life verse" that motivates you in your service in God's kingdom? If not, why not ask God to show you?

- What are your motives when seeking achievement? Are you seeking approval or acceptance from others, not realizing that both approval and acceptance are with God?

- What are your motives for serving God?

- Do you have a spirit of competition or cooperation?

A Discussion with Paul
about Holiness

While attempting to gain a better understanding concerning holiness and *how a person becomes holy*, I decided to have an imaginary conversation with the Apostle Paul. I needed to know if we are considered holy because we are doing our best in trying to keep God's laws and being as obedient as possible, and this seemed to be the message I was getting at church as well. Although many books had been studied thus far, it was still unclear to me what our role is in the matter, if any at all. We seem to be instructed or commanded to do this according to 1 Peter 1:16 (KJV): "...be ye holy; for I am holy..." and we are instructed to "present our bodies, a living sacrifice, *holy* and acceptable...." (Romans 12:1, KJV)

I had previously purchased a Strong's Concordance that worked with the King James Version and had found it to be beneficial when struggling with certain verses or words in verses. For example, Psalm 66:18 (KJV) states, "If I *regard* iniquity in my heart, the Lord will not hear me." To me, the word *regard* suggested thinking about or considering something, thus, if I even thought about a sin, then God couldn't hear me. It seemed to be this way as the pastor's wife, Joan, had talked with me about the separation, suggesting that God couldn't hear me as I was even *thinking about and considering* the possibility of a divorce occurring. When I looked up the word *regard* and saw the original Hebrew meaning, I was very surprised. It meant "to cherish or enjoy." Wow! *That* gave me a completely different meaning than before! If I *cherish* or enjoy sin in my heart, the Lord will not hear me. Now that made much more sense than the idea that if we are struggling with a sin in our life and don't know what to do, but go to the Christian bar of soap, 1 John 1:9, then the Lord would not hear me. That sold me on getting the Strong's Concordance so I could see the Hebrew meaning for the Old Testament and the Greek meaning for the New Testament. Of course, today, there are so many different versions of the Bible available with more updated verbal usage, one doesn't often see the dilemma I was in.

The Strong's Concordance stated that the term *holy* indicated to be set apart for God, sacred, or consecrated. The Scofield notes stated that, at salvation, in *position* we are called "saints" and "holy" from the moment of believing, but in *experience,* it is a *process* brought about through the work of the Holy Spirit and that some day it will be *consummated* when Christ appears. This reminded me of the different applications of salvation – as Christians, we *have been saved* from the *penalty* of sin, we *are being saved* from the *power* of sin, and one day, we *shall be saved* from even the *presence* of sin.

The Lord had been leading me to study in Romans and now into the Book of Galatians. I became fixated on Galatians 5:1, (KJV): "Stand fast therefore in the *liberty* wherewith Christ hath made us *free,* and be not entangled again with the yoke of bondage." I sure wanted to be free, but I wondered what this *yoke of bondage* was all about. What was binding us?

Typically, I didn't use The Living Bible, as it was written by a father to help his daughter understand Scripture better and was not good in word studies or the like. But this time, as I thought about what was being taught in church and the questions from my own heart, this version seemed to be very clear on this struggle about obeying all these rules and regulations called "the Law." It seemed that the believers in the Galatian church may have been struggling with the same problem as well. According to Paul, ***holiness does not come from obedience, holiness comes from death!***

"I am crucified with Christ (I died to my own self-effort), and I myself no longer live, but Christ lives in me. And the real life I now have within this body is a result of my trusting in the Son of God (and His faithfulness to me), who loved me and gave himself for me." (Galatians 2:20, Living Bible).

In the Ryrie Study Bible, the question is asked concerning this verse, "If God wanted obedience through law, why would He send His Son to suffer and die on a cross?

The KJV affirms the answer:

"I do not frustrate the grace of God: for if righteousness comes by (obeying) the law, then Christ is dead in vain." (Galatians 2:21, KJV)

"For it was through reading the Scripture that I came to realize that I could never find God's favor by *trying* – and failing – to obey the laws. I came to realize that acceptance with God comes by believing in Christ." (Galatians 2:19, Living Bible)

"Wherefore my brethren, ye also are become *dead to the law* by the body of Christ; that ye should be *married to another*, even to him who is raised from the dead, that we should bring forth fruit unto God." (Romans 7:4, KJV) From this I realized that I need to "die" to the husband I was married to previously – the Law – in order to be free to be married to another, because my husband, the Law, will not die, thus I must "die."

But one might say that this is fine for salvation, but what about my everyday walk? Don't I have to *try* to be obedient? Isn't that right?

Paul addresses this question: "Oh foolish Galatians! What magician has hypnotized you and cast an evil spell upon you? For you used to see the meaning of Jesus Christ's death as clearly as though I had waved a placard before you with a picture on it of Christ dying on the cross. Let me ask you this one question: Did you receive the Holy Spirit by *trying to keep the laws?* Of course not, for the Holy Spirit came upon you only after you heard about Christ and trusted him to save you. Then have you gone completely crazy? For if trying to obey the laws never gave you spiritual life in the first place, *why do you think that trying to obey them now will make you stronger Christians?* You have suffered so much for the Gospel. Now are you going to just throw it all overboard? I can hardly believe it! (Galatians 3:1-5, Living Bible).

But Paul, doesn't God tell us that we must *be holy and obedient!* How is a person holy and obedient unless we are *doing* something?

Paul's answer: "Yes, and those who depend on (obeying) the laws to save them are under God's curse, for the Scriptures point out very clearly, Cursed is everyone who at any time breaks a single one of these laws that are written in God's Book of the Law. *Consequently, it is clear that no one can ever win God's favor by trying to keep the laws,* because God has said that the only way we can be right in His sight is *by faith.* As the prophet Habakkuk says, The man who finds life will find it through trusting God. How different from this way of faith is the way of law which says that a man is saved by obeying every law of God, without one slip. But Christ has bought us out from under the doom of that impossible system by taking the curse for our wrongdoing upon himself. For it is written in the Scripture, Anyone who is hanged on a tree is cursed – as Jesus was hung upon a wooden cross." (Galatians 3:10-13, Living Bible)

Well, that sounds to me, Paul, like you are doing away with or negating God's law – what was it given for, then?

Paul's response: "Well then, are God's laws and God's promises against each other? Of course not! If we could be saved by his laws, then God would not have had to give us a different way to get out of the grip of sin – for the Scriptures insist we are all its prisoners. The only way out is through faith in Jesus Christ; the way of escape is open to all who believe him.

"Let me put it another way. The laws were our teacher and guide until Christ came to give us right standing with God through faith. But now that Christ has come, we don't need those laws any longer to guard us and lead us to him. For now we are children of God through faith in Christ Jesus, and we who have been baptized into union with Christ are enveloped by him. We are no longer Jews or Greeks or slaves or free men or even merely men or women, but we are all the same – we are Christians; we are one in Christ Jesus. And now that we are Christ's we are the true descendants of Abraham, and all of God's promises to him belong to us." (Galatians 3:21-29, Living Bible)

Well Paul, I can sure understand now why you were criticized about preaching grace – it sounds to me like I can just do anything I want; after all, it's all covered by the Blood – right?

Paul's response: "Well then, shall we keep on sinning so that God can keep on showing us more and more grace, kindness, and forgiveness? Of course not! Should we keep on sinning *when we don't have to?* **For sin's power over us was broken when we became Christians** and were baptized to become a part of Jesus Christ (baptized into His crucifixion – I am crucified with Christ...); through his death the power of your sinful nature was shattered. Your old sin-loving nature was buried with him by baptism when he died, and when God the Father, with glorious power, brought him back to life again, you were given his wonderful new life to enjoy. For you have become a part of him, and so *you died with him,* so to speak, when he died, and now you share his new life, and shall rise as he did. Your old evil desires were nailed to the cross with him; that part of you that loves to sin was crushed and fatally wounded, so that your sin-loving body is no longer under sin's control, no longer needs to be a slave to sin; for when you are deadened to sin you are freed from all its allure and its power over you. And since your old sin-loving nature died with Christ, we know that you will share his new life." (Romans 6: 1-8, Living Bible)

So Paul, we know that sin often feels good at the time. So what's to keep me from just doing what I want?

Paul's answer: "Sin need never again be your master, for now you are no longer tied to the law where sin enslaves you, but you are free under God's favor and mercy. Does this mean that we can go ahead and sin and not worry about it – for our salvation does not depend on keeping the law, but on receiving God's grace! Of course not! (Romans 6:14-15, Living Bible).

So what is the purpose of all of this? Why go through it? What is the end result?

Paul's response: "Your husband, your master, used to be the law, but you "died" as it were, with Christ on the cross, and since you are "dead," you are no longer "married to the law," and it has no more control over you. Then you came back to life again when Christ did, and are a new person. And now you are "married," so to speak, to the one who rose from

the dead, *so that you can produce good fruit,* that is, good deeds for God."
(Romans 7:4, Living Bible)

But Paul, how does one know how to get this liberty? How do I get
free? I see the Church as being so disobedient and without power, I see my
loved ones, and finally I see myself as powerless.

Paul's answer: "I know I am rotten through and through so far as my
old sinful nature is concerned. No matter which way I turn I can't make
myself do right. I want to but I can't. When I want to do good, I don't, and
when I try not to do wrong, I do it anyway. Now if I am doing what I don't
want to, it is plain where the trouble is: sin still has me in its evil grasp. It
seems to be a fact of life that when I want to do right, I inevitably do what
is wrong. I love to do God's will so far as my new nature is concerned; but
there is something else deep within me, *in my lower nature, that is at war*
with my mind and wins the fight and makes me a slave to the sin that is
still within me. In my mind I want to be God's willing servant but instead
I find myself still enslaved to sin. So you see how it is: my new life tells
me to do right, but the old nature that is still inside me loves to sin. Oh,
what a terrible predicament I'm in! Who will free me from my slavery to
this deadly lower nature? Thank God! IT HAS BEEN DONE by Jesus
Christ our Lord. He has set me free. We aren't saved from sin's grasp by
knowing the commandments of God, because we can't and don't keep them,
but God put into effect a different plan to save us. He sent his own Son
in a human body like ours – except ours are sinful – and destroyed sin's
control over us by giving himself as a sacrifice for our sins." (Romans 7:18-
25; 8:3, Living Bible)

Paul, I understand now, you are saying we are *not* have our eyes on
the rules and regulations, but to realize God's law is fulfilled when Christ
lives His life through us. Yet, it is so easy to put our eyes back on what we
are *supposed to be doing in order to be pleasing to God* – how do we keep
from doing that?

Paul's response: "Now make sure that you stay free and don't get all
tied up again in the chains of slavery to laws and regulations. Christ is

useless to you if you are counting on clearing your debt to God by keeping those laws; you are lost from God's grace. But we by the help of the Holy Spirit are counting on Christ's death to clear away our sins and make us right with God. And we to whom Christ has given eternal life *don't need to worry about* whether we have been circumcised or not, or *whether we are obeying the laws or not;* for all we need is faith working through love. You were getting along so well. Who has interfered with you to hold you back from following the truth? It certainly isn't God who has done it, for he is the one who has called you to freedom in Christ. For dear brothers, you have been given freedom: *not freedom to do wrong,* but freedom to love and serve each other. For the whole Law is summed up in this one command: "Love your neighbor as you love yourself." But if instead of showing love among yourselves you are always critical and catty, watch out! Beware of ruining each other. *When you are guided by the Holy Spirit you need no longer force yourself to obey laws.* But when the Holy Spirit controls our lives he will produce *this kind of fruit in us: love, joy, peace, patience, kindness, goodness, faithfulness, gentleness, and self-control;* and here there is no conflict with laws. If we are living now by the Holy Spirit's power, let us follow the Holy Spirit's leading in every part of our lives." (Galatians 5:1, 4-8, 13-15, 18, 22, 25, Living Bible)

Now you would think that it finally clicked for me, but, alas, what I was gaining was a mental assent and understanding, but the experiential aspect was "yet for an appointed time...." (Habakkuk 2:3, KJV)

HOMEWORK:

- Where is your focus? Do you focus on rules and regulations and the struggle to keep them, or is your focus on getting to know Him?

- Are we holy – physically pure, morally blameless, set apart for God – based on what we do or by living in the truth of what has already been done for us?

- Do you seek to obey Him in order to gain acceptance or approval or simply because you love Him?

The Pathway into Spiritual Intimacy with God

The pieces were beginning to all fit together for me as God was teaching and showing me His Ways:

1. There is a journey that begins at salvation – our conversion, with the purpose of getting us *out* of something (sin), and *into* something (victory).
2. God had to go back to work and restore something (our relationship with Him), and we were redeemed by the blood of His Son.
3. There are four relationships of utmost importance: God's love for me; my love for God, my love for myself, and my love for my neighbor.
4. The Old Testament is a picture book of New Testament truths.
5. The deliverance of the Israelites from the hands of the Egyptian taskmasters is a picture of our salvation – a work done FOR US where they were told to "*stand still* and see the salvation of the Lord." (Exodus 14:13, KJV, emphasis added)
6. The Israelites came out of Egypt with a slave mentality, and between the place of slavery and the place of victory lays our wilderness experience, where we learn the ways of God *before* we can become warriors.
7. The wilderness experience is also a picture of Romans 7, the warfare of the spirit and the flesh, a work done in us.
8. In the wilderness experience, through the law, we become aware of our sin producing natures and we are faced with a power struggle between the flesh and the spirit – represented by Amalek.

9. In the wilderness experience, there was no fruit, only manna – wafers that had the taste of honey and oil, which was never intended to satisfy; thus, God does not want us stay here indefinitely – He has a Promised Land full of milk and honey and fruit for us to enter into.

10. During our Romans 7 experience, we typically will not produce much fruit either, such as the fruits of the spirit – love, joy, peace, patience, gentleness, goodness, faith, humility, and self-control –until after the warfare is complete. Attempting to produce fruit from our own self effort will lead to burnout and failure.

11. The victory comes through our surrender and entering into the experiential aspect of Galatians 2:20 (KJV) - "I am crucified with Christ, nevertheless I live..." in other words, we have to die to our own effort to live the Christian life or keep the Law.

12. This is done by grace and is not a second work, but the realization of what was provided in our salvation experience.

13. The law does not disappear, but is now fulfilled as we live day by day through grace, and every time we see the law and attempt to try to live it through our own efforts, it is a school master that brings us to Christ so that we may "die daily" to our own effort to fulfill its requirements. We are to continue to realize that we are "dead to sin" and have a choice now to live after the Spirit rather than after the flesh. When we do this, we have fruit – love, joy, and peace, "against such there is no law." (Galatians 5:22-23, KJV)

14. The Promised Land is a picture book of the New Testament Book of Ephesians, where the Israelites are no longer slaves but warriors, and it demonstrates a work done through us.

15. Through the conflict of the wilderness experience, God's purpose was for each one that went through it to enter into a greater intimacy with God.

16. Between the wilderness experience and entering the Promised Land is the Jordan River, a picture of Galatians 2:20, also crossed through *by faith*. Those who "get it" and learn God's ways enter into the experiential aspect of God's Rest.

So my question was this: What is God's Rest and how does one enter into it? It seemed pretty apparent that there might be another Old Testament progressive revelation and a New Testament application as was seen in previous studies. I knew it would include the Israelites in the wilderness, because I'd already looked at Hebrews, Chapter 3, and I knew it would also include Jesus Himself, as it appeared that He purposely performed some miracles on what is called the *Sabbath.*

From the very beginning, I could see there were differences in the Old and New Testament concerning this Sabbath or Day of Rest, as it was issued as a *command* in the Old Testament:

"Remember the Sabbath day, to keep it holy. Six days you shall labor, and do all your work; but the seventh day is a Sabbath to the Lord your God: in it you shall not do any work, you, or your son, or your daughter, or your manservant, or your maidservant, or your cattle, or the sojourner who is within your gates; for in six days the Lord made heaven and earth, the sea, and all that is in them, and rested the seventh day; therefore the Lord blessed the Sabbath day and hallowed it." (Exodus 20:8-11, KJV)

I couldn't find anywhere in the New Testament a commandment regarding this issue. In fact, there were verses that specifically stated that it *didn't apply as a command or part of the Law* for Gentiles *or Christians:* "When Gentiles, *who have not the law...*" *(*Romans 2:14, KJV); and in Colossians 2:16, (KJV): "Therefore let no one pass judgment on you (believers or Christians) in questions of food and drink or with regard to a festival or a new moon *or a Sabbath."* I knew from Hebrews 4:1 that somehow, we as Christians are supposed to understand, because we are to fear if we *don't* and enter into His rest, so I continued to study.

The command was given specifically to the Israelites, and I knew the Israelites are a picture of the New Testament believer, so I wondered what I was missing. Why was this Sabbath related to the Creation account: "in six days the Lord made heaven and earth and *rested* the seventh day" (Genesis 2:2, KJV), and why would God want His people to not work and "rest" on the seventh day?

I decided to pull out the trusted Strong's Concordance, as this could be like that word "regard" I had so much trouble with previously. I was thinking that the Sabbath surely meant the seventh day, but was surprised to see it meant an intermission, to repose, desist from exertion, *to rest*! So why did God give this commandment *specifically* to the Israelites? I found the answer in Exodus – it was a *sign* given to them after they had been redeemed from slavery in Egypt to remind them that God had set them aside for Himself: "Say to the people of Israel, You shall keep my Sabbaths, for this is a *sign* between me and you throughout your generations, that you may know that I the Lord sanctify you...." (Exodus 31:13, NIV)

So, whatever this *rest* was, God wanted His people to reflect back on the same *rest* God had when He blessed the seventh day. "So God blessed the seventh day... because on it God *rested* from all His work which He had done in creation." (Genesis 2:3, KJV) I could see why many might think as I had that *Sabbath* meant "seventh" instead of "rest," but this led to an even bigger dilemma: Did God wear Himself out from the act of Creation and need to rest up and be restored? Was God *tired?* Isaiah 40:28 (NIV) shouted out the answer to that question for eternity: "Don't you know? Haven't you heard that the everlasting God, the Creator of the ends of the earth, *does not grow tired or weary?*"

This really confused me. If God's rest does not mean seventh and it doesn't happen because we or God are tired, then what *is God's rest?!* So I went back to the beginning... again. When God finished with the Creation, He stood back and repeatedly stated, "It was good." In Genesis 1:31, it states that, when God saw everything He had made, it was *very good.* Perhaps when God was standing back and looking at all that He created, He was simply relaxing and enjoying what He had made. So if God was resting and enjoying what He had made, which included Adam and Eve, and they were enjoying Him, what made Him *stop* resting and enjoying? Well – as we say in East Texas, "duh" – *sin entered the picture!* So this is the great Gospel story – God had to go back to work to restore the rest that was lost for both God and man! God couldn't rest *in* man because of man's sin, and because He loves us, He couldn't rest *apart* from man, so God had to redeem man and make man a new creation that could rest in Him!

In Isaiah, I found that God is asking for a resting place: "Heaven is my throne and the earth is my footstool; what is the house you would build for me, and *what is the place of my rest?" (*Isaiah 66:1, KJV, emphasis added) Heaven and earth appear more like furniture to God, in asking this question, but He answers His own question in the very next verse:

"this is the man to whom I will look, he that is humble, and contrite, and trembles at my word." (Isaiah 66:2, KJV) The phrase *trembles at my word* would indicate to me that reverential respect, or "fear of the Lord," and *humble* or lowly reminded me of how Moses was when he came out of his wilderness experience – he was the meekest or most humble man alive, except for Jesus Himself. When I looked in the Strong's Concordance for that word "contrite," I was amazed to learn that it meant "smitten, maimed, and dejected"! *Smitten* means to strike or hit extremely hard; to kill by striking hard; to afflict or affect seriously. These are the same words spoken of by God concerning His Son in Isaiah: "yet we did esteem him stricken, smitten of God, and afflicted." (Isaiah 53:4, KJV)

So where does God find rest? In the heart of a person who is not prideful, but humble, who trembles at God's Word, and who demonstrates contrition of spirit. This is a person whose focus is on God and is not resisting Him like the Israelites did while they were in the wilderness. This is why God said they didn't understand and thus would never enter His rest. God intended for the Israelites to learn this while they were in the wilderness and when the next generation passed through the Jordan River and entered into the Promised Land, their leader was Joshua, whose name means "the Lord saves." Our New Testament leader is Christ, and His name, Jesus, is the English equivalent of the name Joshua. God wants us to learn this as well while we are in our wilderness experience, and this is why we are told, "let us therefore *strive* to enter that rest." (Hebrews 4:11, KJV)

The reason I couldn't find a New Testament parallel of a *command* to keep the Sabbath is because of that progressive revelation aspect that God uses. What is issued as a command in the Old Testament is offered as an invitation in the New Testament, by Christ: "Come unto Me, all ye who are weary and heavy-laden, and I will give you *rest*. Take my yoke upon you, and learn from me, for I am gentle and humble in heart and you will find *rest* for your souls." (Matthew 11:28-29, KJV) The soul is made up of our mind, will, and emotions, and Christ is offering emotional *peace,* a mind at *rest,* and a will that is secured to Christ if we come to Him. That peace offered is the peace that surpasses understanding that I was so longing for.

The act of associating rest with the usage of a yoke suggests to me that rest is something to be tied into work, as a yoke was what was used on oxen during that time. It seems that God wants us to be *resting while working!* So it's not a seventh-day issue, it's a twenty-four-hour-a-day, seven-day-a-week resting *in* God while He rests *in us!* This is why Jesus did not break any laws by doing good on the Sabbath. He was not the one who instituted legalism; the Jews did at that time, and we do today!

I was finally beginning to get a grasp on what the Lord wanted to bring about in each of our lives. I was understanding in my head but not yet with my heart. I could see the way, His Way, but just didn't know how to bring it all about. For some, it is simply hearing it as in our conversion experience itself, and for others it is brought on by perhaps a crisis in which we find ourselves completely helpless. For me, it was the latter.

The Lord would give me a song, one of two concerning this period in my life. I didn't have a clue how to write a song and could only read music somewhat from having taken eighteen months of piano lessons. I had a wild notion that perhaps after a year of piano lessons I could, if needed, be the backup piano player at a little church in case no one was there. I figured a beginner piano player was better than none – right? (Wrong!)

I had bought a piano with this thought in mind right before moving from Dallas to Tyler. It was odd the way I even found the piano, since at that time, I wasn't yet attending church. I could picture the one I wanted, a beautiful walnut or burl wood antique upright with beautifully carved legs. I set aside $800.00 for the piano and drove down an older commercial street in Dallas, Texas, that I hadn't driven by before on a Friday evening. When I turned a corner, I noticed a piano store with an antique white piano in the store window; all the rest were new. I drove on, instantly knowing that the piano I was looking for would be there waiting for me in the morning. On Saturday morning I got up and got $800.00 in cash and enough for tax and drove back to the store as soon as it opened. I walked in the door and told them I was there to buy a walnut or burl wood antique piano they had. The lady told me there wasn't one like that there, only the white one in the window. I told her, "No, no, it's here, I'm just not seeing it yet," as I walked all over the store. She followed me, bewildered, and I described it to her. "It's an antique upright with shiny wood, either walnut or burl, and it has beautifully carved legs, *and I'm not leaving without it because it's here. I've got cash for the purchase as well.*" Of course, she looked at me as though I were nuts, but I started opening closet doors at that point. She followed me as we looked behind doors, and when we got to the last door, she told me this one was locked. I asked her to get the key, and then the owner walked in, wanting to know what was going on. I told him I was there to buy the antique piano with the carved legs and he told me the only one for sale was the one in the window. When I explained the one I was wanting, he looked at me in shock.

"It's not for sale yet, it just came in last night off an estate sale, and we haven't even gone through it to inspect it. How did you know it was here?" I told him I really didn't know, but while driving by the evening before, something told me it would be there. I asked where it was and he said it was behind the locked door. He opened the door, and *there was my piano!* It was more beautiful than I had imagined. Sure enough, it was a shiny burl wood with *three* carved legs on each side! It was a 1901 Lester piano made in Philadelphia. The sales lady was absolutely shocked. I asked the owner how much he planned to ask for it, and he said at first he hadn't even thought about it yet. I told him I had brought cash, and he said it was $795.00 plus tax.

"I'll take it, and I'll pay for it right now, just let me know as soon as you get it ready," I replied.

As soon as I moved to Tyler and got settled in, I began to look for a piano teacher while also looking for a church. But after eighteen months of piano playing, when I tried to keep up with the crowd singing, I kept making too many errors and found it very difficult to keep up. No one bothered to tell me that it usually takes five to ten years before you are truly proficient! When that happened, along with my separation, I quit taking piano lessons but kept the piano for twenty years before selling it.

So when the Lord gave me these two songs, the only thing I could do was sing them a cappella on a cassette tape and take them to a song director at a different church and ask him to listen to them and write down the notes I was singing.

The first song relates to this time period during which I sought rest. In 2 Chronicles 20, I read of Jehoshaphat, king of Judah, who was besieged by enemies and was helpless. He called for a fast and prayed, and the Spirit of the Lord came upon Jahaziel and he spoke out, "Thus saith the Lord unto you, Be not afraid nor dismayed by reason of this great multitude; *for the battle is not yours, but God's.*" (2 Chronicles 20:15) The next morning, after being told they would overcome their enemies, Jehoshaphat sent out singers, *before the battle*, to praise God as they went forth. So they sang a victory song *before* actually having the experiential side of victory. I, too, would be given a victory song before my battle, before the "surgery" of the "cutting away of the flesh." I was quickly arriving at the place where I knew I couldn't bring this on, as much as I wanted it to happen; only God could do this. Thus, the song the Lord gave me in anticipation of the event was called "His Marvelous Grace."

His Marvelous Grace

I came before the Lord, my soul in full distress.
He said, "Oh child, what could it be?"
I cried, "Dear Lord above, my heart pleads for Your rest,"
And these few words He spoke to me:

Chorus:

Oh marvel at the grace of Your Almighty God,
A grace so abundantly free.
Oh cling to the vine of my unfailing love,
I've given so freely to thee.

I said, "Oh Lord, but look, Your laws I just can't meet."
He said, "My truth will set you free."
"But little fruit I bear, my life spells out defeat."
He said, "No child, You belong to me."

Chorus:

Oh marvel at the grace of Your Almighty God,
A grace so abundantly free.
Oh cling to the vine of My unfailing love,
I've given so freely to thee.

He said, "Oh child, stand fast! The yoke of sin is gone.
It's bondage entangled ye be not.
My Son has made you free, it cannot be undone!
Your liberty I fully bought!"

"You see, My child," He said. "My victory is yours.
Ole Satan is beneath your feet.
Just rest your eyes on Me, the battle is the Lord's.
Your sins were blotted out at Calvary!

Chorus:

Oh, I marvel at the grace of our Almighty God,
A grace so abundantly free!
I cling to the vine of His unfailing love,
He's given for you and for me!

I marvel at the grace of our Almighty God,
A grace so abundantly free!
I cling to the vine of His unfailing love,
He's given for you and for me!

Susan (Sperling) Brock, 1984

HOMEWORK:

- Where are you in your spiritual walk with Christ? Are you in the "wilderness"? Have you crossed over into the Promised Land?

- Do you have a slave mentality or a warrior mentality?

- What sin are you having a power struggle with?

- Are you willing to surrender and allow God to bring you into the experiential aspect of Galatians 2:20?

- Are you at rest in God, or are you nearing burn out?

Our Identification with Christ

Today, we don't hear much in church about rededicating one's life to the Lord, the Lordship of Christ, or even having revivals, but thirty years ago, these things were discussed on a regular basis.

The first Sunday after the Lord opened the door for me to go back to church at age twenty-four, I immediately went to the front during the invitation from the pastor for anyone to rededicate their life, and I rededicated my life to God. I didn't know if it would be enough, but it was a start.

I would later hear about the Lordship of Christ, and I learned that, when we become Christians, we are to turn over our lives to God and that we no longer run or direct our lives – He does. This should be understood at salvation, but few explain it this way, and most, like me, didn't hear about it until *after* their conversions. The word picture given at that time was, instead of praying for God to be the *passenger* in your car and to give you direction, you should move over and let Him "drive."

Since I was a tomboy growing up and loved the Dallas Cowboys when Tom Landry was coach, (most likely because my dad loved the Cowboys), I used a word picture concerning Tom Landry and Roger Staubach to demonstrate the Lordship of Christ with my Sunday School class.

Roger Staubach won the Heisman Trophy in 1963 and was drafted by the Dallas Cowboys to play in the NFL in 1964. The Cowboys *waited for him for more than four years* while he served in the Navy and served a tour in Vietnam. He was very intelligent, and as a Heisman Trophy winner, he obviously had a successful history of calling the shots as a quarterback. He willingly did something that no other quarterback in the NFL was willing to do: he took *all* his calls (or plays) from Coach Landry. As we all know, they were an extremely successful team, winning two Super Bowls while

Staubach was quarterback, and it calls this to mind the notion that each of us has a mind and a will and probably a decent amount of good sense, but are we willing to take all of our calls from our "Coach," Jesus Christ, who sees the whole playing field? That is what the Lordship of Christ is about.

I was finally arriving at the place where I could see the general process that the Lord wants to bring every one of His children through in our relationship with Him. It is in transforming our lives from being held captive and in slavery to sin to becoming those that step into the Promised Land by faith and are warriors for Christ. This is what Watchman Nee spoke about that should be the "norm" for every Christian; alas, for most of us, it is not. I simply believe we are not taught these things. We are taught how to share our faith or our testimony and we are taught how to win others to Christ. We are taught how to study the Bible or how to handle our finances in a Christian manner, but we are not taught God's Ways, or abundant living, or this crucified life that Paul speaks of.

When I read the admonition from the Lord to "*be still* and know that I am God" (Psalms 46:10, KJV), I could see that one application could be like Moses told the Israelites as they stood before the Red Sea with their enemies at hand to "*stand still* and see the *salvation of the Lord.*" There was nothing they could do but look to God for deliverance. I could see now that there was no physical, mental, or spiritual effort that I could do to bring about this experiential aspect of being "crucified with Christ" and "entering into rest," except to look to God. It is He who tells us that, "He who hath *begun* a good work in you, will *carry it on to completion* until the day of Jesus Christ." (Philippians 1:6, KJV) It is God who begins this work, and it is God who will complete it. We are simply to remain still in His hands. The Israelites came across the Jordan River in the same manner as the Red Sea, and so it is as we move from salvation and seeing Christ dying on the Cross for us to seeing ourselves on that Cross with Christ and raised up and seated in heavenly places in Christ Jesus, according to Ephesians 2:6.

When Jesus states that He has come so we will have life and live more abundantly (John 10:10), it is interesting also to note that we find that it is *in Him* that this abundant life is found: "I am the way, the truth, and *the life.*" *(*John 14:6, KJV) We also see the same concept repeated in Colossians 3:4 (KJV): "when *Christ who is our life....*" For our salvation, Christ is the way to eternal life; for our daily walk in Christ, He is to be our life, and one day in Heaven. "When Christ, who is our life, shall appear, then shall ye also appear with him in glory."

Throughout this entire "process," we continually do what is called "identifying with Christ." This implies being identified (see myself with Him) with His death, burial, resurrection, and ascension and seated in heavenly places (Ephesians 1). It is walking through life every day with His strength and power (Galatians 2:20). It is for each of us to discover as the *active realization of His grace through us.* It begins with our salvation, where we see Him not only as our Savior, but also as our Lord, the Lord and Director of our lives, who brings us to the end of ourselves in order that we may have life. It is an all-inclusive, paid-for gift from God that provides us freedom from sin, liberty in loving God and our neighbor, and life everlasting with the down payment of that eternity being the Holy Spirit within us as God's adopted children, whereupon we receive the full inheritance upon our arrival in Heaven. That inheritance and the rights as adopted children belong to us now where we have been given not *some* of God's blessings, but, according to Ephesians 1:3, *all spiritual blessings!*

I could understand the concept of adoption, as I had been requested for adoption at age twelve by that couple who lived at the end of our block in Waco, Texas, and who counseled me to make amends with my grandmother. I called them Uncle George and Granny. This couple who had become like grandparents to me were the grandparents of Randy and Dennis Quaid, the movie star brothers who came from Houston, Texas. Randy's and Dennis' mother and older sister also had four brothers who were, at that time, all in their late thirties to mid fifties in age, and here I was at age twelve! The offer of adopting me created major strife within the family. In 1968, adoption in America was based on the *Biblical form of adoption*, which meant that, as an adopted child, *I could never be disowned* (even though a child by blood relationship could be disowned), and the adopted child came first in the inheritance! When I heard this, it became easy to understand why there was such a commotion. Because I came from a family that lived in daily strife and conflict, I did not want to step into another family knowing I would be the cause of all the strife and conflict there, thus I did not accept the offer, and no one approached my family about it. I had turned down the offer of adoption to accept a spiritual adoption that same year (unknowingly) into the Family of God, as I was saved that year. I also turned down that potential inheritance along with the one that should have later come through my father's side of the family and could have been pursued when my dad and both his parents died shortly thereafter and everything went to my second and third cousins. Because I became a Christian that same year, I would later understand that I had entered into an inheritance I never have to walk away from.

Incidentally, when I was thirteen, I had a crush on Dennis, who was sixteen at that time. Dennis couldn't have cared less about me, but he had a crush on my oldest sister, Monica, who was also sixteen at the time. Monica couldn't have cared less about Dennis. Years later, when I was working at the Dallas Police Department as a civilian, one of the sergeants I worked with came by and said that Dennis, who was famous by that time, was making a movie in Dallas, and the sergeant would be doing security at the film site. I asked him that if he actually ran into Dennis, would he tell him hello from the girl who lived down at the end of the block from his grandparents in Waco, Texas. He said he would. When he returned the next night at work, the sergeant said that Dennis had remembered me and immediately asked, "How's her sister, Monica?" That blew the wind out of my sails! I thought to myself, *She's married! Did you tell her she's married?!*

In continuing with our identification with Christ, just as we have to become convicted of *sin* in order to see the need of a Savior, we need to be convicted of *self,* with the realization that self-effort has only brought failure in trying to live the Christian life (Galatians 3:3 and Romans 7). This brings forth a thirst for that abundant life spoken of in John 10:10 with the realization that our Christian life up to this point may or may not have been *successful in our understanding,* but in reality, is very unsatisfying, often leading to burnout or despair. At this point we must surrender the self, and we realize, as I did at this time, that we cannot bring on death of self – only God can, because the Bible makes it clear that self will not cast out self. We give God permission as we remain still to bring us through His processing. Listed below are the steps of this process:

The Process of Identifying with Christ:

1. Instead of conviction of *sin,* it is conviction of *self.* The realization that self-effort has only brought failure in trying to live the Christian life. (Romans 7 and Galatians 3:3) We see that there is nothing good about the fleshly or Adamic nature within us all. We can't offer it as a sacrifice to God, even though we desire to please God. God refused Saul's sacrifice of Agag, King of the Amalekites, because He is at war with Amalek, who represents our fleshly nature, from generation to generation. In order to arrive at Roman's 12:1, and present our bodies as a living sacrifice, we must first pass through the process outlined in Romans 6-8.

2. Instead of desire for eternal life, it is a thirst for the abundant life (John 10:10) – desire for more, as our current walk is *not* satisfying, and for many there may be complete burnout in their Christian walk.

3. Surrender – At our *conversion,* it is the realization that we cannot do anything to bring about salvation, as it is a gift of God. As we *identify* with Christ, it is the realization that we cannot bring about death to the self; only God can.

4. The Cross – At our conversion, we see Christ dying on the Cross for our sins. In our identification, we see ourselves on that cross with Christ. We are shown that the only way to make it through to a victorious life is "death." What dies? We are to see that our "old man," or Adamic nature, or "fleshly" or sin nature has been crucified with Christ and that we are not held captive by the power of sin anymore. Now we have a choice: will we walk after the flesh or after the Spirit? At our conversion, we choose by faith to accept what Christ has done for us, not what we can do for Him, as there is nothing we can offer that is worthy of what Christ has already paid. At our identification, we must choose by faith to accept His life lived through us by grace and not by anything we can do. This is the process in Ephesians 2:8-9 (KJV), but carried out at a deeper level. Instead of "For by grace are you saved through faith; and that not of yourselves: it is the gift of God: not of works, lest any man should boast," it is now thus: *for by faith are you identified with*

Christ, and that not of yourselves; it is the gift of God, not of works, lest any man should boast.

5. Some experience denial; just before conversion, there is a grasping for the past, and even though that past was a place of imprisonment of our soul, at least it was something we knew, something comfortable. There could be a crisis experience brought on by personal failure as we are ever pointed to the cross and the offer of forgiveness and new life. For some, just before our identification, we are as the Israelites were – fearful of the unknown and grasping for everything on the way to Canaan. Longing for Egypt, which was a place of slavery, we may have a shrinking back from the cross and the impending sentence that goes with it. There could also be a crisis experience brought on by personal failure as we, too, are ever pointed back to the cross, our cross. We then go back to the previous step.

6. Assurance – After conversion, we need the assurance of our salvation to know that the greatness of God is not our faithfulness or ability to do or keep anything (rules, regulations) for God, but the greatness of God is His faithfulness to keep us. After our identification with Christ, we need the assurance that God will complete this work (Philippians 1:6), and that we have entered into a work, our co-crucifixion, that, just like our salvation, is a work that was really completed two thousand years ago. Now, instead of begging and pleading in our everyday walk, we are giving thanks and appropriating by faith.

7. Rest – At our conversion, we respond to Christ's invitation to all who are weary and heavy laden as He knocks at the door of our hearts and asks to enter in. The heart of mankind is the only place in the universe where God is denied access, as He never forces Himself on anyone. It is by invitation only as we choose to invite Him in.

At our identification with Christ, we realize that we now walk by grace and the Spirit of the Law instead of attempting to live by every jot and tittle of the Law. We realize that, just as much as we want to rest in God, He wants to rest in us, and it is in the heart of the person with a contrite spirit where He finds His Rest. Now our works are by faith, our labor from love, and our endurance from hope. We have proper motivations, and we realize that most of our Christian life is spent discovering. This is like that old Prego commercial in which they were asking where all the great ingredients were, and the response was, "It's already in there"; it's already in our salvation, and has been in there all along!

Thomas Merton said, "The man who does not permit his spirit to be beaten down and upset by dryness and helplessness, but who lets God lead him peacefully through the wilderness and desires no other support or guidance that that of pure faith and trust in God alone will be brought to the promised land."

"The steadfast love of the Lord never ceases. Therefore, we are not cut off from Him. His mercies never come to an end; they are new every morning. Lord, how faithful You are! I say to myself, 'The Lord is my inheritance,' so I will put my hope in Him." Lamentations 3:22-24 (ESV)

HOMEWORK:

- Have you asked Christ to be the Lord and Director of your life? Since He sees the whole playing field called life, can you trust the calls He makes on your life?

- Child of God, do you live each day with the active realization of His grace through you?

- Are you thirsting for the abundant life?

- Do you understand your co-crucifixion with Christ?

- Is your life one of begging and pleading or giving thanks and appropriating?

Entering In — from Crisis and Captivity to freedom

In August 1984, a month before my twenty-eighth birthday and after three and a half years of searching, God would use a crisis of faith to finally bring me through to victory, while at the same time, (unknown to me until later), literally saving my physical life.

After two years of separation and my husband living with my friend Walt, the most optimistic Christian I've ever known, my husband came to me and stated that we were getting a divorce. We had been married four years and separated for half that time. He told me he liked what my going to church was doing for me, but it was not for him, and it was obvious that I was not going to return to my old way of life. He said he was moving back to the Dallas area, and either he would file or I could. I told him I would take care of it if that was what he wanted. He told me it would be uncontested, and he would not show up for any of the court dates. Even though we had been separated for so long, this decision still hurt me very deeply. I felt it was my responsibility to inform the pastor and his wife what had occurred, as I was still teaching Sunday School, and I didn't know how they would deal with this news about me. Never could I have been prepared for their response. The pastor didn't say much, but even though I thought that I was through with those old negative messages, due to the raw emotions of three and a half years of searching and now being informed that a divorce was imminent, I wouldn't be able to handle what his wife had to say to me.

Hiding my feelings was something I've never been very good at, and of course I was depressed and discouraged from what my husband had said, but her words ripped every last ounce of emotional strength away from me that Sunday morning: "Your life over the past three plus years that we've been around you has been a constant roller coaster of emotions, and now you are filing for divorce. God may just have to kill you because you are so rebellious. It may be the most merciful thing He could do for you." I was shocked speechless.

I went home and I stewed all afternoon about what she said, until that evening, I fell prostrate on the floor and cried out to God: "Lord, for three and a half years I have searched and searched and searched for You. I have *tried* so hard to live this Christian life, but obviously I am an absolute failure. I have nothing left to *try* with. After all this time, I don't have the abundant life Your Word talks about. Although I have the assurance of my salvation, I don't have the peace that surpasses understanding, and I don't have that rest that Your Word speaks of. I can't handle it any more. Your Word says that to be absent from the body is to be present with You, so if You have to kill me, then it's okay, and this will be a win-win situation, because I will get to be with You. If this is what You choose to do, then I will ask to sit in Your lap, and ask You why I couldn't get it. If I wake up tomorrow and I'm still here, then I'm not going to *try* anymore."

Emotionally exhausted, I went to bed and fell into a deep asleep. The next morning when I woke up, I was very surprised to still be alive. It was like a ton of weight had been lifted off of me during the night. I didn't have to *try* anymore. I was free!! Although I hoped to live to see the Lord rapture us, if for some reason that doesn't happen, my epitaph was written that very morning:

Susan Sperling _____ (whatever my last name would be)
Born: September 26, 1956
Died: (Day, Month, Year)

She tried... She trusted!!

I was a new woman! I felt that I understood how the Israelites felt as they encamped at the first place after finally crossing that Jordan River after forty years of waiting. The place was called Gilgal, and it meant *the reproach has been rolled away!* (Joshua 5:9). I felt so wonderful, and I wanted to tell Walt. I saw his car at the donut shop.

As I walked in, he took one look at me and said, "What has happened to you!?"

"I found it, I finally found it!" I exclaimed to him. We both rejoiced in my new-found freedom.

Attending church the following Sunday, I tried to explain to the pastor's wife what had transpired, but she told me she didn't know what I was talking about. She said it was obvious I was much happier and left it at that.

About a week or two later, my ex-husband stopped by the little house where I was living. We visited very briefly and he left and went back to Dallas. I thought the visit was a little strange, but it had been pleasant, and I just dismissed it.

Seven years later, something happened that brought me back to this very time in life. My sister Julia called me and told me that a man from my past who had kept up with me through her for years was asking to see me. She said he had heard that I was finally living in a log house (which had been a secret dream of mine for years) and just wanted to see it and see how I was doing. I reluctantly agreed to see this man. A couple days later, he called and asked to meet with me. He said he had something he wanted to confess to me. When he arrived, he looked around at the log house I was living in at that time, and then we sat down for a cup of coffee. That's when I got the surprise of my life.

"Do you remember the last time I saw you?" he asked.

"No, not really," I replied.

"I came by that little house you were living at with that pond and it was right after you had filed for divorce," he continued.

"Okay..." I hesitantly replied, not sure what he was trying to say.

"Did you know I came *to kill you?*"

"What!?" I cried out in shock.

"I had the gun in my pocket and I intended to start an argument with you and shoot you," he replied.

"Why would you want to do that?" I replied with a shaking voice, realizing that most women are killed by their husbands or boyfriends.

"I thought you were already with someone else," he responded.

"No, I never even looked at a man for the entire two years my husband and I were separated," I replied.

There was a heavy silence that lasted for about a minute.

"What stopped you?" I quietly asked.

"I don't know," he responded while crossing his arms. "There was something so sweet about you, and you wouldn't argue with me. I couldn't do it," he replied. We both breathed a sigh of relief as we realized how close we both had been to devastating and life-transforming events.

Our "visit" did not last very long, and he went his way and headed back to the Dallas area where he lived. As he left, I thought about it for a long time, and then it dawned on me... I understood why he couldn't shoot me.... When I thought about the time frame of when he came, it was about two weeks after I had discovered the answer to my "Why." You can't kill a *dead* person! I am crucified with Christ, nevertheless I still live!!! So my premonition *did* come true, but instead of physical death, God delivered me through a different form of "death" in Galatians 2:20! Every day since then, I have recognized that I am only living by grace. I have not seen this man or my first husband in over thirty years. My ex-husband went back and remarried his first wife, and I pray they have been happy.

For personal reasons, I stayed one more year at that small church and to finish out a teaching commitment to the adult Sunday School class. During that year, the desire grew strong within my heart to seek out a deaf ministry. I had taken one sign language class as an elective course at a junior college in Dallas before moving to Tyler, and it really captured my interest. Although I would have loved to go to the church of Pastor Paul Powell, author of the book, God Loves Divorcees, his church did not have a deaf ministry at that time. As the year came to a close, I bid goodbye to the church and to a few of the people who I had come to love during the four and a half years I attended, especially some of the older ladies, along with Walt's daughter, Jackie, and another girl named Lori.

The parting remarks of the pastor's wife didn't bother me at all: "We never understood you."

"That's okay," I responded. "They never understood Jesus either," as I walked away.

I am very thankful I went to that church, and I'm thankful for growing up in the family I came from (and I think it is clear through this story as to why), because of all that the Lord taught me through that time. I truly don't think I could have had the relationship with God that came through such tribulation otherwise. I tell people upon looking back that I may have academic degrees from the University of Texas at Tyler, but the degree that really counts is the "Master's" degree I received from the USAF – the University of Suffering and Affliction Furnace.

"Behold, I have refined thee, but not with silver: I have *chosen thee in the furnace of affliction.*" (Isaiah 48:10, KJV)

For thirty years, I have carried in my billfold these verses from Isaiah 38 that remind me that it really wasn't my mother, or father, or my husband, or the pastor's wife, or anyone else who was responsible for all that transpired, although I sure would have liked it to be a little easier for them to have been more tender. They all have been forgiven as I am reminded of the tenderness of God:

"But what can I say. *He* has spoken to me, and *He, Himself has done this.* I will walk humbly all my years because of this anguish of my soul. Surely, *it was for my benefit* that I suffered such anguish. *In Your love,* You kept me from the pit of destruction." (Isaiah 38:15-17, KJV)

I recall the one year during which I taught the fourth and fifth grade classes at church. That was where I met Lori Haynes. She was nine years old and was rejected at birth by her mother because one of her arms and both legs were deformed. She was raised by her grandparents. Her grandfather was a Shriner who was able to get multiple surgeries performed for her at the Shriner's Hospital to enable her to walk. She walked for many years with braces on. I've shared her story of this young girl (who is now in her forties) with the adult classes throughout the years, and I ask them this question:

In order to see things from God's perspective, it might help if we take a stance as a parent. If you were faced with putting leg braces on a child, knowing it would be painful for many years, in order for her to ever be able to walk, and during that time, the child cried out to you again and again wondering why you were hurting her, what would you do? What would love do? Of course, we all agree that we would put the braces on the child, understanding that the child would never "get it" until the day the braces came off and they took their very first steps... into your arms.

Are you wondering why you are going through what you are at this time in your life? Does God have His braces on you? Can you rest your eyes on Him while He brings you through to victory as well?

Oh, and as to that deaf ministry? When I completed the final Sunday of the church year, I showed up the very next Sunday at that church downtown that had a deaf ministry. Unfortunately, there was no one there. I asked where everyone was, and was informed that the deaf ministry had ended... *the week before.*

Discouraged, I headed out the door after class. The teacher chimed in, "Oh, by the way, the deaf ministry really didn't *end*... it just *moved.*"

"Where did it move to?" I asked.

"Green Acres Church where Pastor Paul Powell preaches," he responded.

"Thank you, Lord," I replied as I walked out the door. You know where I attended the following week...

The table below sums up what the Lord taught me about the difference between our ways and God's ways:

Man's Ways	God's Ways
Suppress Sin (Try not to fulfill the lust of the flesh in order to walk in the Spirit.)	Remove the sinner "I am crucified with Christ..." Gal. 2:20 "Walk in the Spirit and you won't fulfill the lust of the flesh." Gal. 5:16
Victory is a Reward	Victory is a Gift Provided at Salvation
Victory is Attained Gradually	Victory is Obtained Instantaneously. "Ye shall know the truth and the truth shall set you free." John 8:32
Our Victory Over Sin Is in the Future	Our Victory Was Already Won In the Past "Stand fast therefore in the liberty wherewith Christ *hath made* us free..." Gal. 5:1
TRY	TRUST
A Changed Life	An Ex-Changed Life "Not I, but Christ..." Gal. 2:20
Begging, Pleading	Giving Thanks, Appropriating

Struggling	Resting
My Faithfulness to God	His Faithfulness to Me "Being confident of this very thing, that He which hath..." Phil. 1:6
I Must Try to Cast Off Self	Holy Spirit Will Deal With Self – I Surrender to a Work that Was Performed 2000 Years Ago. God Brings it to Pass.
Christian Life Lived by Obedience to Law	Christian Life Lived by Faith - Law Fulfilled by Being in Christ
Holiness Comes as a Result of Obedience	Holiness is a Result of Death
Acceptance with God is through Obedience	Acceptance with God Comes by Being in Christ

The Lord also gave me a second song during that last year of attending the small church. It was a song in reference to the victory the Lord had brought me through Galatians 2:20. The song leader from the church who wrote down the notes I was singing from the previous song, wrote these down as well. I noticed that, many times in Scripture, God's people sang victory songs after going through a time of battle or warfare, such as Miriam leading the Israelites in a victory song after God delivered them through the Red Sea, but I did not see the Israelites singing a victory song after they crossed the Jordan River. The people's final test before entering the Promised Land was crossing the Jordan River by faith.

The Promised Land

Verse 1:

Forty years of wandering,
Never knowing rest.
Before them stood the Jordan,
The people's final test.

Thirsting for the new life,
The manna soon to go.
With triumph over Amalek,
Their spirits no more low.

The people waited three days
For Joshua's command.
As the flooded waters parted,
They came on in the land...
Singing:

Chorus:

He brought us out to bring us in,
The place of victory over sin.
Come on in, we're in, bring them in.
Come in the Promised Land.

Verse 2:

For years I too was wandering,
Wrecked by sin and strife
Seeking Heaven's answer
I gave to Christ my life.

Craving the abundance
He promised in His Word.
His Spirit's holy presence
In my heart was stirred.

My quest for peace near over
His answer to my "Why?"
Sin's grip has no dominion
With Christ you're crucified!
He said:

Chorus:

I brought you out to bring you in,
The place of victory over sin.
Come on in, we're in, bring them in.
Come in the Promised Land.

Verse 3:

Now we are appointed,
To preach among the meek.
Bind up the broken-hearted,
Lift up those that are weak.

Standing with God's armor,
Each piece put on with prayer,
For the pulling down of strongholds,
Victorious in warfare.

To him that overcometh
A new name you'll receive
With power over the nations,
If only you'll believe.
He said:

Chorus: twice

HOMEWORK:

-   - Have you ever been ripped apart by someone's words, only to discover it was used by the hand of God to later deliver you?

-   - How long have you been *trying* to live the Christian life? How's that working out for you? Are you tired of trying yet? Are you ready to *trust,* just as you did in your conversion experience?

- - Are you understanding more clearly now, the reason to give thanks "in all things" as you see Him working it to your good?

- - Have you experienced a time in your life where God had His "braces" on you? What was it like? How did you respond? In looking back, what did you learn?

Part II

The Pathway to Emotional Rest and Healing

Down for the Count

Life became peaceful for a time, and I really fell in love with the deaf ministry at Green Acres. There were about forty deaf members of the group, with half a dozen interpreters and teachers. It was great fun working with them. Since I was not able to interpret any sermons, as that level of skill usually takes years of practice to develop, I asked to be part of the song service and eventually would lead the song service after a few months. It was an awesome sight to see forty plus people all signing to songs together, as this is how the Deaf sing, and I noticed that it was very moving and touching for the hearing people to watch them.

I thought it might be even more worshipful for the hearing if the Deaf would sign the words at the same time as the hearing, rather than exhibiting the typical delay just after the words have been sung, so I asked the choir director if I could come in and practice with the choir so I would know exactly what words would be sung, which verses of each song, etc. In this way, the Deaf wouldn't have to wait until I heard what was sung and then sign that to them, but both deaf and hearing performers would sing and sign the exact same words at the exact same time. Many of the hearing members commented on how beautiful some of the signs were, finally having seen them signed along with the words as the hearing people sang them. It also led more hearing people to volunteer to be part of the deaf ministry as well, especially when the Deaf and the hearing would do song specials together.

I also got to attend a ladies Bible study that was held in the home of one of the ladies from church. It was so nice to be with a group of ladies and not be the only single person there and to have so many who were close to my age. I met a lady there named Latricia Jones, and we became fast friends and have continued our friendship for almost thirty years.

Trish – as I would call her – was the one I would later sell that beautiful piano to for her kids and, later, her grandchildren to learn to play on.

About a year after my divorce was final, one of the ladies I worked with at the Post Office told me she wanted to introduce me to a friend of hers who attended the same church she went to. This man had been through a divorce about the same time I had and was not currently seeing anyone. After being married to someone who wanted nothing to do with God, being introduced to someone who regularly attended church sounded great. I knew now that, if I ever remarried, I needed to be with another Christian.

This man and I met and immediately hit it off, and he later told me he wanted to be a pastor someday, even though he had a good full-time job at the time. I told him I didn't know too many divorced pastors, but he told me of several he knew. I was hopeful for him and thrilled that I had met someone who seemed so serious about his faith. He had a fifteen-year-old son and a twelve-year-old daughter, who were great kids and with whom I got along wonderfully. Although this man was ten years older than me, he was extremely fit and could run circles around me. I felt I had waited a reasonable amount of time to be emotionally free, so we began to date. We dated for seven months and then married. Walt gave me away at our wedding. Trish and her three daughters were there, as were Walt's daughter, Jackie, and Lori Haynes. Several of the deaf couples from Green Acres also attended as well as several of the older ladies from the small church I had attended before, and one young couple came from that church as well.

Just three weeks after we married, a different side of this man came out. First, he insisted that I leave Green Acres and the deaf ministry that I had grown to love and that we start at a different church. I hated to leave but felt it was my responsibility to go where he wanted to go.

Secondly, after only three weeks of marriage, he quit his full-time job and never went back to work again for more than a few days for the next five years! He claimed that his shoulder hurt and he couldn't work. He went from doctor to doctor trying to get one to operate on him until he found one who would. Most of the doctors could find only minimal issues, and I would watch him use his car with a chain to pull out two to three hundred pound boulders so he could till up a small garden (yet he claimed he couldn't work!). Within six months he had gained fifty pounds, and within another year, he had gained an additional fifty pounds. He seemed to thrive on having surgeries.

What was worse was the verbal and emotional abuse that began as well. The angry control freak that had been hidden so well while we dated and from all our friends and family now appeared. I was constantly being accused of being unfaithful, and he would time me from when I would leave work until I arrived at home. To punish me – for who knows what – he slept on the downstairs couch for three years! I got on the overtime desired list within a month of being married and stayed on it for seven years, trying to keep all the bills paid. This included his child support as well. He isolated me from my own family and from even receiving phone calls. Unknown to me, he would contact my oldest sister who was a nurse and ask for some hardcore drug samples for free. She declined.

Although I hated to leave the deaf ministry at Green Acres, when we started attending a church called Southside, I came to love the people there as well. On the first Sunday, I attended a ladies' class led by the pastor's wife. This woman was completely different from the pastors' wives I had met before; she was an absolute sweetheart and was very warm and friendly. I offered that day to be a substitute for her any time she would like to have a break, and she took me up on it the following Sunday. For the next three years, I "substituted" for her class every Sunday. She would open the class with prayer requests and announcements, and I would teach.

Southside would later come under the umbrella of Green Acres as a satellite church, and one of the associate pastors from Green Acres that we had grown to love named Ron Wells became our interim pastor. He and his wife, Beth, lived not far from our house in Lindale, Texas, and Beth became a part of our ladies' Sunday School class. It was a joy to have her as a part of the class. My husband later asked Ron and the leadership at Green Acres if he could pastor and start a house church under Southside's and Green Acre's oversight. They agreed on a trial basis, and he insisted then that I quit teaching and "follow" him. He refused to allow me to teach at the house church, as it was too distracting from his "ministry," so he requested that I take care of the two children who came.

On the more humorous side, these two children were girls, ages three and one. Of course, the one year old was in diapers, and I quickly discovered I was way out of my league and had to be trained in changing diapers. On the first morning alone with them, the one year old needed her diaper changed, so I thought to myself, *It can't be that difficult, right?* When I put the diaper on her, the three year old quickly piped up, "You have her diaper on backwards."

"How would you know that?" I responded, not thinking anyone could know the difference.

"Because I watch Mommy do it every day and you've got it backwards." "Are you sure?" I replied.

"Yes!" she replied emphatically.

So I changed the diaper and turned it the other way, and what do you know, the three year old was right – I did have it on backwards! I hugged her and thanked her for teaching me how to do it right. She replied that she would be watching me very carefully to make sure I didn't put her sister's diaper on incorrectly again! I left her in charge of supervising me in the diaper-changing division, and she checked me every time from that day forward.

In 1990, at age 34, after three years of marriage and my husband still not working, I had to have a hysterectomy. I had been having some serious problems for over a year, and the doctor knew I had never had any children. He told me that it might be possible to put the surgery off for perhaps long enough to have a child but that I would have great difficulty in the birthing process. I had known for years, deep inside, somehow, that it would probably be unlikely that I would ever have children of my own. I told the doctor that our marriage was not going well, and if things got better, we could adopt, so we went through with the surgery. The doctor would later ask if I made the right decision.

"Yes," I replied.

The very day I came home from the hospital, two things happened. First, my husband announced, "God has told me that I don't need to work."

"That's funny," I replied, "God told me you *do* need to work. I'm only supposed to be a helpmate and not do it all." That seemed to have zero impact.

Secondly, my husband accused me of having an affair with the choir director from Green Acres because he had stopped briefly at the hospital to see how I was doing. With that accusation, I had had enough. When I offered to call the choir director and for him to talk with him, he backed off and said that if I hadn't been *sexually* unfaithful, then I must have been *spiritually* unfaithful. (What in the world did that mean?) I insisted we get marriage counseling or I would leave, and he reluctantly agreed. We went back to see my friend and counselor, John Morris.

After seeing John Morris for *eighteen months* of marriage counseling and still being accused of being unfaithful, and even with the help of my friend Walt, nothing had changed. My husband still refused to work and insisted that I wasn't being submissive enough. By that time, working overtime had not been enough, and I was literally selling my own plasma to help ends meet. I was physically, emotionally, and spiritually exhausted, and I knew something had to give soon.

I then found a book called Men Who Hate Women, and the Women Who Love Them.[15] I was absolutely shocked. There was also a Christian version, called Christian Men Who Hate Women, [16] by Margaret Rinck. I could hardly believe what I was reading. It described our marriage to a T. I learned two words I had never heard of before: my husband was a *misogynist* and I was *co-dependent*. I underlined passages and wrote notes as I had with many of the study books previously, and I took the book to John and asked him just to look at some of the underlined areas of the book. I told John it described clearly what I had been unable to explain for eighteen months. Although I could be assertive and responsible at work, when I was at home, I was an absolute doormat in the relationship. I was always walking on eggshells and simply could not win with him. It was like I had returned home all over again with another angry, controlling person.

From what I was reading, the misogynist hates women but is completely dependent upon them. In order to keep the woman from leaving, he controls and dominates her while battering her psychologically and emotionally, including subtle attempts to both confuse her and make her think she is losing her sanity. At the same time, he thinks everyone should focus on him and on his needs, as he has a sense of entitlement for special treatment due to his grandiose sense of importance. Although these men are typically intelligent, they believe they are unusually intelligent and deserving to be noticed as someone special, although deep inside, they are filled with shame and a fear of abandonment. *Their goal is to destroy the woman so she is physically and emotionally unable to leave him.* The book made it clear that less than 1% of misogynists ever change, and I knew I couldn't last much longer.

The term *co-dependent* was first coined after studies on recovering alcoholics and their spouses revealed an interesting conundrum. In almost every case in which an alcoholic stopped drinking, within one year, the non-alcoholic spouse would leave and the marriage would end. Researchers were confused until they realized that the alcoholic was addicted or dependent on the alcohol, while the spouse was addicted or co-dependent on the alcoholic's behavior. When the alcoholic stopped the addictive behavior, the co-dependent's care-taking or overly responsible behavior was no longer needed, which created a crisis during which the relationship usually ended. The co-dependent either had a history of excusing the alcoholic's behavior or would directly step in and take charge of the finances, etc., removing the natural consequences for the addict, while the addict was overbearing and abusive. The co-dependent's inability to stand up to the emotionally abusive behavior was typically a result of growing up with the same verbally and emotionally abusive behavior themselves, in which environment their needs and feelings were ignored.

Well, that was certainly how I grew up, and it was frightening to see that I was simply repeating the same pattern in my relationships. Psychologists refer to this as "learned helplessness," in which case the person believes they have no way out, no choice in the matter ('til death do us part), and no control over their destiny except to keep submitting and accept the abusive behavior far beyond what any emotionally healthy individual would permit. I would later come up with my own definition of codependency after much study:

A co-dependent is an *unwilling* participant in an addiction to non-nurturing relationships who is compelled to repeat those learned destructive patterns from childhood in his or her current relationships unless there is some form of intervention that will break this consumptive pattern.

One thing that became very apparent was the need to stop rescuing everyone whenever something happened. One day, I actually drew a banner and hung it on the wall for my husband and his children to see. The banner read: "The Susan Rescue and Loan Corporation Has Filed Bankruptcy and

Is No Longer in Business." Although the children had not been a problem in any way, it was obvious what was being modeled before them, and that example needed to be changed. My husband laughed when he read it but soon realized I was serious. When the only television we owned broke down, he asked what I was going to do about it.

"Absolutely nothing," I told him. "If you want it fixed, go get a job."

He never did get a job, and the television was never fixed while we were married.

I knew I couldn't "fix" my husband, I could only work on myself. My family had wanted me to end the marriage during the first two years, but I could not gain any peace about it and refused to leave. It didn't matter what anyone else was saying; I only wanted to be okay between me and God. It finally came to a choice between maintaining the institution of marriage or maintaining my life, and I believed God would be in favor of my desire to live, so after five years of marriage, I once again filed for divorce. Immediately thereafter, women started coming out of the woodwork to tell me that my husband had been pursuing them while I was at work. The kindest thing that happened was when Ron Wells, our interim pastor, saw me and told me that he and Beth did not know how I stayed as long as I did, so it had been obvious to others what had been occurring, even though I didn't know others were so keenly aware.

It also became apparent that my husband had *planned* to quit his job *as soon as he married me*, and after our divorce, he later went from person to person for a couple of years, trying to find someone to take care of him. When I saw John Morris years later, after my ex-husband had passed away, John told me that, since he knew that he had passed away, he could tell me that my ex-husband had come for counseling once again. Sadly, I was told, my ex-husband went to his grave "a raging tyrant." I could only wonder, like before, "What happened??!!"

HOMEWORK:

- Are you currently separated or divorced? If separated, you are encouraged to *not* seek any type of relationship with the opposite sex until your divorce is final in order for you to heal emotionally and be reconciled, even if only to maintain a civil relationship with your ex-spouse, especially if children are involved. (Reconciled here does NOT mean re-married; it simply means the ability to talk, at least in a civil manner, with your ex-spouse or perhaps develop a friendship.)

- If divorced, are you seeking a relationship with another, in the hopes that if he or she is Christian, it will be the answer to all you desire?

- Have you discovered in looking back that your relationships demonstrate a repeated pattern? Although you may be attracted to a different person, do the same issues arise in your new relationships as they have in the past?

- Do you understand that, in order for you to be attracted to a healthier individual in a relationship, *you* must become more healthy emotionally? Can you see that, if you don't grow and change, you will repeat the same pattern again and again, with no change in the outcome?

- Are you suffering verbal, emotional, and/or physical abuse in a relationship? If so, seek *immediate* intervention. Please contact your pastor, the police if necessary, and any local authorities as needed. It is imperative that you and your children find a safe refuge and help.

- Are you demonstrating co-dependent behavior? Do you need to "raise a banner" in your home? The <u>Your Name</u> Rescue and Loan Corporation Has Filed Bankruptcy and Is No Longer in Business.

My "Picker" Is Broken

Although there was a sense of relief that the marriage was over and I didn't have to live with any more abuse, I was heartbroken over my seeming inability to have a healthy, loving relationship. I was also heartbroken that I had failed God. I knew I hadn't left God, and He surely hadn't left me, but I was convinced that my "picker" was broken, and I had picked an unhealthy relationship with an angry, controlling, abusive man more than once, and I couldn't understand why. I was almost killed when my first marriage was ending, and care-taking and enabling in the second marriage almost killed me. The following truths became apparent:

1. Time did not fix or heal what was wrong. Even though I had been alone for three years between my relationships, I had still entered into unhealthy relationship.

2. Marrying a Christian did not fix or heal what was wrong with me. I was a Christian and obviously was still very carnal or driven by the flesh in my thinking to be attracted to a man like this. My husband said he too had become a Christian, but struggled in his spiritual life and appeared to be very carnal or driven by the flesh as well. I would learn later, "like attracts like." In thinking I was marrying the opposite of what I had married in the first marriage, I simply married a person with anger issues with a different last name.

3. The duration of the dating stage did not impact the decision-making process. Although in this second marriage, we only dated seven months, in the first marriage we dated *five years*. In both cases, the dark side of the man did not manifest itself until *after a commitment was made*.

4. I needed assertiveness training. I then asked the Lord to take up my training in this area, as I had never learned this in a relationship before.
5. I needed to learn about boundaries. What in the world was that?
6. I needed to regain a sense of competence, achievement or self-mastery, and self-worth.
7. In any church, there will probably be someone you will have a problem with at some time or another, so you need to ask yourself, "Is it worth it to leave the church over this problem, or is it possible to work it out?" We are all sinners who were saved by grace, thus none of us are perfect. We are called by Christ to forgive one another. If our focus is on other people and what they may or may not have done to us, we may miss the message or call from Christ on our lives.

One of the best things that happened to help rebuild my confidence and self-esteem right after the divorce was over was that I took up ballroom dancing. When I lived in Dallas, right before moving to the Tyler area, I had watched some beautiful dancing called the Dallas Push, which was really a form of what is known as West Coast Swing. I had never danced before and didn't even go to the high school senior prom, but thought I would try group lessons. On the second group lesson, I was singled out by the instructor.

He pointed his finger at me and said, "Go home. You will never dance. You are entirely too rigid." So I gave up on the Dallas Push.

Shortly after moving to Tyler, I got the wild notion that perhaps I could try Country Western dancing.

When I showed up for a lesson, the receptionist took one look at me and said, "You don't have a dance partner! You'll have to dance with the dance instructor."

Well, just throw me in the briar patch and make me dance with the dance instructor! was my immediate thought. Unfortunately, when the dance instructor arrived, I saw that he had a broken leg, so there went my Country Western lessons.

Years later, after the second divorce, in the fall of 1991, my mother and her last husband, Ed, told me I should come with them one Saturday to hear the Tyler Big Band. One of the guys I worked with played in that band, so I thought it might be fun. I always loved Big Band music, and believe it or not, the number one song in 1974 at my high school was Glenn Miller's "In The Mood." My mother told me there was a dance instructor that would be coming with his girlfriend, and so I thought if I saw them dancing, I would stick my foot out, stop them, and ask what kind of dancing they were doing. So I did go and did stick my foot out, and when I caught them and asked them what kind of dancing they were doing, he replied, "We're doing ballroom dancing. If you want to learn, just show up next Thursday at the dance studio and you can have three lessons for $5.00."

Well, I could afford that! I showed up. My dance instructor had not arrived yet, and apparently the instructors would pull pranks on one another. The other instructors thought I was the dance instructor's girlfriend, and I quickly told them I had just met him and his girlfriend on Saturday night.

"Yeah, right," they replied.

"No, really, I just met them and I don't know how to dance."

"Yeah, right," they replied.

One of them, Joe Ornelas, decided to start the lesson until my instructor arrived. He wasn't going to let my instructor pull a prank on him if he could help it. He said we would start working on what was called a Foxtrot. He said they would show me a few steps, then play a little music as we danced. I asked if that wasn't too much too soon.

"Right..." he replied. "Now, don't look down," he instructed me.

"Where am I supposed to look?" I replied.

"Try looking over my right shoulder." I thought I was supposed to look to the right to which he replied,

"My *other* right shoulder." He showed me the timing of the steps and said they were, "Slow, slow, quick, quick." So I replied,

"Slow, slow, quick, quick, look to the left over your right shoulder."

"Right...."

When he asked my name, I replied,

"Quick, Quick, Susan."

"And what do you do for work, Susan?" he requested.

I was so befuddled I threw my hands up, stepped back and said, "Can you just hush so I can look down and see what we are we are supposed to be doing!"

"You really don't know how to dance, do you?" he laughingly replied.

"I don't know how to lead, follow, or get out of the way!" I responded. My dance instructor then showed up, and we completed the lesson. After three lessons, I was hooked. I took four more lessons with them after that. Learning to dance was absolutely joyous. It was so fun that I would shout out while we were practicing:

"More *boogie*, please," to which the instructor would reply, "More *basics*, please."

For the first time in a long time, I felt so alive and carefree. I wasn't able to afford private lessons but for just a short time, but I found a lady named Betty Duff who taught group lessons out of her home.

After a month of dance lessons at Betty's house, I felt brave enough to go with my mother and stepfather back to listen to the Big Band. I brought a notebook with me, just in case someone asked me to dance and I could quickly look in the notebook to see which quick, quick, slow, slow, I should do to a song, and whether it was a Fox Trot, Waltz, Rhumba, or Swing.

After sitting there for a couple of hours and enjoying watching everyone else, my friend from the band walked up and told me he noticed I wasn't dancing. When I told him that no one had asked, he asked if it would be all right if he "helped" me. I didn't know what he meant by that, but said that would be okay. He immediately walked back to the band, waited for the song to end and got on the microphone.

"We need one gentleman to volunteer to dance with this beautiful young lady who's sitting off in the corner over here," he shouted over the loud speaker. There was dead silence in the whole room. I thought I would die.

"Gentlemen, we need one man to volunteer to dance with this beautiful young lady sitting off in the corner over here," he repeated. There was dead silence on the floor.

My mother later told me that the man in front of her told his date, "Oh, we all know she's going to be some fat cow of an old woman. Who's going to want to dance with her?"

The third time my friend came out over the loudspeaker, I guess they all figured that someone better volunteer to dance with the old hag, or none of us are going to get to dance at all.

One hand went up, and a man's voice softly said, "I'll dance with her."

"Susan, will you please step out here now?" my friend at the microphone replied.

When I stepped out to the front, my mother said she could hear the guy in front of her say, "Well, if I'd known she looked like that, I'd left you at home!" he responded to his date.

"What dance would you like to dance to, Susan?" my friend in the band replied.

"A waltz would be great" I replied. "I think I know the basic steps for that one." So the band started playing a waltz. My partner told me his name was Jeff Kamel, and off we went. He was my mother's age, and he soon began to tell me he had taken lessons for twelve years. I was really struggling with the box step we should have been doing but was doing the best I could. I told him I had only been taking lessons for a little over a month or so and was taking them at a lady's house. When he told me he took all his lessons at a lady's house as well, I asked him what her name was.

"Betty Duff," he replied.

"You're not doing the box step she teaches!" I instantly responded. We both laughed, and he told me he had changed things up on his own and probably needed to refresh himself on some of the basics. He told me this was the first time he had been out in over six months, as his girlfriend and her mother had been murdered six months before by her ex-husband who had been released from prison and had killed her the same day he got out. That took my breath away, as I was reminded of how close I'd come to such tragedy as well.

We became fast friends from that night forward, and Jeff called Betty to ask if he could come back to her beginner class, which she called her "Clunker" class. Jeff helped me with lessons, and we both helped others learn. Jeff was like the father I never had. When I did start dating again, we would double-date together, and we remained friends until he passed away in 2012.

Jeff taught me everything I knew about being part of a dance club and helped sponsor me with another one of our friends to start a ballroom dance club which puts on dinner dances at one of the local country clubs every other month. I've been the president of that dance club from its inception twelve years previously and have been ballroom dancing for more than twenty years now. I wonder what that dance instructor from the Dallas Push group would say about that now!

When some at church would ask me about my dancing, suggesting that it might be something bad, I tell them what I told the high school Sunday School class I taught for one year when they asked the same question.

"How many of your parents have forbidden you to attend your high school prom?" Not one of them had been forbidden.

"They realize there will be dancing at your proms, right?"

"Yes," they all answered.

"So, the problem then, is not the dancing, but perhaps *where* dancing might occur and *what* occurs at some of these other dances. If your high school prom had drinking, fist fights out in the parking lot, etc., your parents would rightfully have a problem with that, so the thing to do is to stay away from events or places that involve such behavior."

When speaking to those from church, I would add that, with ballroom dancing, all dances are at a country club where there is no smoking, fist fighting, infidelity, etc., and it's like attending the high school prom I never went to, six times a year – and you wouldn't believe what it does for your self-esteem! We also have several pastors and their wives who have danced with us through the years.

Even the Bible tells us in Ecclesiastes 3:1, 4 (KJV), "there is a time and a season for everything... there is a time to dance." In the Psalms we are told, "He has put a new song in my mouth" (Psalm 40:3, KJV) and "He has turned my mourning into dancing." (Psalm 30:11, KJV)

Although I felt like I was back in another wilderness experience, this time to learn about those horizontal, → ← human relationships instead of the vertical, spiritual ↓ ↑ relationships, ballroom dancing was one of the first steps of regaining self-esteem and joy back in my life as there would be much to learn in the coming years.

HOMEWORK:

- Do you have a pattern of picking unhealthy relationships?

- Do you wonder where God is or why He could allow such a thing to happen in your life? Does it seem to occur again and again?

- Is there a pattern of thinking that if you could just pick the right person, everything would be fine?

- Have you learned and expressed emotional and physical boundaries? Do you cross other peoples' boundaries and allow them to cross yours?

- Do you have a tendency to base your worth on what you do or what position you hold, such as father, mother, husband, wife, or what you do for a living? If these titles were removed, could you still maintain your self-worth?

- Do you run from relationship to relationship or from church to church because someone has offended you?

Who's Responsible For Your Happiness?

It was obvious that I had a lot of homework to do if life was ever going to change; if *I* were ever to change and be attracted to a good, decent, and kind man. So, once again, I went back to the Lord to request that He take up my training again, this time with those earthly, horizontally linear relationships. For some people (and it's usually a small minority), the effect of Christ in and upon their lives at their conversion is somewhat like a fireworks explosion, and the transformation in their lives is immediate and overnight. For the vast majority of us, the Holy Spirit does "house cleaning" room by room in our hearts and lives, and for me, it was obviously the latter.

A word picture to explain what many of us who come from deeply dysfunctional backgrounds think when we look upon a potential mate or spouse would be like this: "I'm half of a whole and you (the person we are attracted to) are half of a whole, and maybe, if we can just get together, we can be one complete whole." In other words, "I have what you're missing and you have what I'm missing, and if we can get together, we won't be missing anything."

Unfortunately, instead of a full whole, we both end up with a "flat tire," unable to move forward or backward. In looking to that other person to complete me or supplement my "whole" (which is actually the "hole" in my heart), they will invariably disappoint us, and there is no amount of pushing, prodding, manipulating, tantrum throwing, etc., that we can do to get them to give us what we need. In doing this, we are essentially saying, "I need you to do _____ or give _____ in order for me to be happy." The Lord would show me that this was an inordinate amount of power that we are expecting the other person to have and that these expectations are unrealistic. He would show me that it was even more dangerous than this. Adopting this much focus on and expectations for another human being was to:

1. Relinquish personal responsibility of my own life *and my happiness* over to the other person, who invariably would become a tyrant who would mistreat me and lose respect for me, but even more importantly,
2. To focus so intently on anything or anyone except Christ, Himself, is the sin of *idolatry*, because I was making *them* the center and focus of my life. (*That* realization took my breath away!)

God's Word says, "Ye are *complete* in *Him*" (Colossians 2:10, KJV), meaning to be replete – abundantly filled, *stuffed, crammed full,* perfectly supplied, accomplished, furnished. Now how often are we attempting to *stuff* ourselves with food, activities, relationships, even drink, or drugs, or anything, to fill that aching hole or incompleteness in our hearts rather than with Him?

God wants us to be two complete wholes who together become more than we can be alone. This is called "synergy"; we increase each other's effectiveness. In this way, we become more effective together than we can alone. Just as we look to God first for *love*, and not to our neighbor, in the same way we look to God first to *complete us*, and not our neighbor or love interest. Therefore, since it is not my responsibility to bring about change in any other person but myself, as that is God's responsibility, it is also not their responsibility to make me happy or complete me. When you look in the mirror, you are looking at the person responsible for your happiness – you!

Happiness is taking charge and responsibility of my own life through God's direction, not waiting and expecting another human being to do it for me!

In many of the "vertical line" lessons, I was beginning to see that those that were learned spiritually would now need to be repeated in a mental and emotional association in order that my horizontal, earthly relationships with my neighbor, which in this case would be my spouse or love interest, might be healthier. If "like attracts like," then I need to be healthier if I want a healthier relationship with someone else. Just as I had longed for a restful relationship with God, I also desired a restful relationship with a husband. Just as I had been held captive by the sin nature within, I was being held captive by the wounds of childhood. Just as I had to "die" to the "self," I would discover that I would need to "die" to my old way of relating and to the selfish desire to have the other person complete me. I determined right then that I would never remarry again until I had become healthier not only spiritually, but mentally and emotionally as well. I wondered with seeing who I had been attracted to in the past, could I even be attracted to Mr. Nice Guy.

I had a discussion with my younger sister, who was having similar issues in her relationships and I asked her this question: "Penny, if Mr. Nice Guy came along and was interested in you, what would you do?"

Her answer both astounded and jolted me into reality. "Oh, I wouldn't want to be with him... he'd be too *boring!*"

"Oh, Penny!" I responded. "Pray for the day when Mr. Nice Guy comes along that you will find him to be the most interesting and exciting person you ever met!" That prayer went for me too.

Obviously, even though I had forgiven my mother and both husbands, there were still raw wounds from childhood that still needed healing, as they were influencing and impacting the choices being made of who I was compatible with and attracted to. I would soon discover that, even though it was terrifying to even think of the idea of facing my childhood again, God's way of healing would be to take me back to the "scene of the crime" where I had been wounded in order for Him to walk me through each wound and respond differently this time. Now, I would have an *adult* response instead of a childlike response which, although at the time it helped me to *survive,* was now impairing my ability to move beyond mere survival to abundant living and a peaceful relationship with others.

Since the Lord had shown me that intently focusing on one person and my expectation that this one person would bring me the happiness that was missing in my life was a form of idolatry, I thought it would be healthy to write down a comparison of when I put someone other than Christ as the center of my life versus what it would be to have Christ as the center of my life.

When I Put My Spouse as the Center of My Life:

1. I desire and seek the constant affirmation of my spouse's love, acceptance, and approval, and I'm on a vigilant watch, which keeps me walking on eggshells if I see any clue of their loss of love, acceptance, and approval.
2. Thus, the foundation of our relationship is built on the "shifting sands" (Matthew 7:24-27) of *their* moods, *their* thoughts, and *their* behaviors, which will only crack and break until I build that foundation on Christ.
3. Instead of focusing on who I am in Christ, my identity becomes enmeshed with that of my spouse, and I *lose personal goals and direction*, as the only goal I have is to identify with my spouse.
4. We become tied up in knots, tripping one another in life as though we are tied at the waist and struggling to get free; thus we would pull one another down rather than enhance one another through our gifts, talents, and abilities.
5. As we struggle to regain our previous freedom, we wonder how we lost it in the first place. We become angry and resentful towards our spouse and desire to blame them for taking away our freedom when we were the ones to relinquish responsibility for our lives, our freedom, and our happiness.
6. This focus demonstrates that I love my neighbor *more* than myself rather than *as* myself through the overflow of God's love to me which is contradictory to God's command.

When I Put Christ as the Center of My Life:

1. Because I know God's love, acceptance, and approval of me *never changes*, I can relax and *rest* in the constant affirmation of His love. His Word says I am "accepted in the Beloved" (Ephesians, 1:6, KJV); therefore, I not only can accept myself, but I also don't have to be fearful of how my spouse may or may not feel. This helps me to rest in their love as well, because God's love for me is what really matters.

2. Because Christ, the Chief Cornerstone (Ephesians 2:20), is my foundation, we are free to have both personal and joint goals and direction as we have "synergy," where "two are better than one" (Ecclesiastes 4:9-12, KJV). I can support his goals and he can support mine as we are now free to support and enhance one another rather than be tangled up in one another.

3. I am free to focus on who I really am, my identity in Christ, because "for me to live is Christ" (Philippians 1:21, KJV) and Him living through me, "Christ in you, the hope of glory" (Colossians 1:27, KJV).

4. Now that we both enjoy this new freedom, our love grows for Christ and one another as we are no longer a source of irritation but one of growth and refreshment. We are now free to share the overflow of what we've been given to others and our ability to enhance one another in our completeness in Christ, not *trying* to make each other complete.

5. Because God is teaching me how to love Him as well as teaching me how to love myself and the overflow of that love, my neighbor (who, in this instance, is my spouse), I am in obedience to His Word that commands me to do so with all my heart, mind, and soul.

I saw a 20/20 ABC News Special documentary about what happy people have in common. I wrote down the eight characteristics of generally happy people and put it on the refrigerator as both a goal and a way to measure and mark my progress. Seeing this on a television show was very surprising, yet I think the network was more surprised at the results than their viewers).

Some Aspects Happy People Have in Common:

1. Spiritual faith – it provides purpose in life.
2. Social involvement – it provides support and aids our immune systems.
3. Productive work – is linked to our self-esteem.

4. Satisfying sleep – also aids our immune systems and demonstrates emotions at rest.
5. Satisfying love relationship – the best indicator of happiness and best protection of the immune system from stress.
6. Control – of their own life versus being controlled by others.
7. Optimism – the ability to treat failure as a challenge.
8. Sense of humor – the ability to laugh at ourselves.

As the months went by, I would periodically check the list and ponder as to where I was in my own measure of happiness. I could see that the more I grew spiritually, the happier I was. The more I see God's hand in my life, the happier I am. As I take charge and responsibility for my life and my happiness, I am happier. I am happy when I teach, help others be successful, make others laugh, help others see God's hand and purpose in their life and situation. I am happier because I have a support system of friends like Walt, Trish and Jeff, and my family. Learning to dance has been a source of joy, as it has helped bolster my self-esteem and has been an outlet for expression as has learning sign language, writing, and speaking. I am happier as I pursue my dreams and goals.

HOMEWORK:

- What is your self talk or explanation of how a potential mate fits into your life? Are you consistently disappointed?

- Are you guilty of relinquishing personal responsibility for your life and happiness over to others? If so, do you now realize this is unhealthy and God calls it idolatry?

- How would you respond right now if "Mr. Nice Guy" or "Ms. Nice Girl" *did* come along?

- Who do you put at the center of your life?

God's Assertiveness Training
Part I – Identifying the
Source of the Drama

In learning that I had been more or less a doormat in my personal relationships, it became necessary for me to learn to be more assertive. This is one of the things that I had asked God to begin teaching me, and today my friends and associates can hardly believe that I was ever less assertive.

Now if you are a person who carries a lot of anger, this is *not* for you. This didn't mean to be aggressive or mean, but because I was so out of balance, I needed to learn that it was okay and sometimes necessary to demonstrate anger. With my ex-husband, even when I did express anger, there was never any resolution or a response. As a child, I was not "allowed" to be angry, so I hid those feelings and stayed in a low-grade depression all the time. This led to my attraction as an adult to men who were angry enough for the both of us. These types of men would need to learn to manage and put away their anger in order to be more balanced, but I needed to learn to stand up, set boundaries, and remain steadfast by those boundaries by becoming more assertive and occasionally demonstrating anger.

I needed to learn that, when a man won't negotiate or compromise with you while dating, then he will also be unyielding in marriage. I'm not referring to compromising one's standards or values, but to negotiating and compromising in such things as choosing activities, hobbies, interests, etc. I would later date a guy for two months and after two months he informed me that I needed to quit church, school, dancing, and my job. I informed him that the only thing I would be quitting was him! This type of man would never be concerned about my feelings, needs, or desires, and I needed to be able to recognize this quickly in a relationship in order to either deal with it, or if that is not possible, to decide to walk away, which is what I did.

The word picture I had for boundaries was this: Every one of us is given a piece of "land" that is ours to take care of. For whatever reason, all of these people in my life had walked all over my land and ravaged it, destroying much of it, and there hadn't been anything I could do about it for most of that time. My plot of land faced erosion, and it had gotten worse each year. Finally, I had had enough, and I stood on my land with a shotgun, staring down anyone who might even try to touch my land. I knew it would take this just to get the land cleaned up and to have time to heal. It would be a long time before I would or could allow anyone back on my plot of land.

God's Word in Ecclesiastes shows that there is a time for everything, and that includes anger. Ephesians 4:26 (KJV) tells us to "be ye angry and sin not: let not the sun go down upon your wrath." So, obviously, we *can* be angry and it is not sin. The Lord would give me an unusual verse to incorporate for this training. That verse was Psalms 144:1 (KJV): "Blessed be the Lord my strength which teaches my hands to war and my fingers to fight." I made a wall plaque out of this verse with the silhouette of a Roman soldier and put it on the dining room wall. I determined that each "battle" the Lord would bring me through concerning assertiveness would be commemorated and hung on the wall next to that verse. There would be four such major incidents or battles. Although the majority of the training was done outside of marriage, it still was a tremendous influence on later relationships, as I struggled greatly with the tendency to be a doormat with authority figures, as I was terrified of my mother as a child and my father seemed to be indifferent, unavailable, and detached. When someone in authority said, "You can't, you shouldn't, or don't," I would cower down and believe them and never put up any kind of a fight.

That was, unless it was for someone else. When I took Lori Haynes, as a nine year old girl, out to lunch one day to a Dairy Queen, there were two very tall and strong young men sitting in the next booth from us who began to curse like sailors. At first I got up and stood at their booth and quietly asked them to not curse as there was a child in the next booth from them. They stopped for a minute or so, and I sat back down. Then they started up again. That was when I became like a mother bear protecting her cub, and I leapt to my feet and stood nose to nose with both young men and insisted that they stop the cursing or I would call both the manager and the police. I was like Dirty Harry with his 357 Magnum, just daring them to "make my day." They decided it was best to quiet down, and shortly thereafter they left, yet if I had been alone, I don't think I could have stood up for myself.

Several months after the divorce was final, the first "battle" began. I met a guy who seemed nice and was very interesting. Before police officers wore radios clipped to their shoulders, my friend invented a radio clipboard for the Department of Public Safety officers to use when they would stop vehicles and had to step away from their patrol cars. Although he was also an airline pilot for a cargo transport company and was gone a lot, on the side, he also assisted in teaching and setting up security surveillance on rare occasion for some of the local or federal police agencies. During the short time we dated, my life became like a made-for-TV movie. All of a sudden, the house was being broken into on a regular basis. I notified the sheriff's department and they suggested it was most likely the guy I was dating. I told them he had no motive to be doing such a thing. I told my mother what was happening, and she began to think it might be someone she knew.

As I lived alone and was working overtime, I couldn't be home to protect my home twenty-four hours a day. The house was a two-story log home sitting on the top of a hill with six acres surrounded by one hundred acres of our neighbor's land which he used to run longhorn cattle. What was strange was that things weren't taken, but I would see that the furniture had been moved a few inches and the dog was on edge. I even decided to hire a security guard from time to time when I was gone, but it didn't seem to do any good. When I came home one evening and saw a car parked on the road below the house which quickly drive off as I neared, I decided to go through the house and try to figure out what was happening. That's when I discovered a listening device behind the dresser in my bedroom, and that's when I called the Sheriff's department and the FBI. The FBI determined that the device was a home-made version made from a baby monitor. I even had the telephone company out to the house, and they informed me that extra wiring had been installed in the attic that was not Southwestern Bell wiring material. I believe my phone was being tapped. The sheriff's department continued to point a finger at the guy I had been dating. I could not believe it was him. When I found a second listening device under the couch in the living room I confronted him, and he showed me the types of devices that the state and federal agencies were using, and I can assure you, they were *not* made from baby room monitors!

When I came home from work one evening, I found one of the upstairs doors had been kicked in where someone had climbed up on the deck by one of the bedrooms. This time they left something in the house. There were cotton balls with something gooey on them stuck all across the downstairs ceiling, across the living room and into the dining room. Someone had also tried to steal the riding lawn mower that was chained to a tree. After reporting it again, I asked the neighbors if they had seen anyone around the house, and two neighbors had seen vehicles that matched a vehicle driven by a man my mother knew. I was told that the cotton balls were incendiary devices to help a fire, once started, to quickly engulf the house. I was being terrorized. The Sheriff's Department did come out, and they had a couple of officers sit outside the house for several hours, but no one came that night.

I decided to end the relationship with the guy I was dating for other reasons, and we did remain friends and stayed in contact for over twenty years. It would take me three years to figure out what really happened, but we were never able to prove it in order to press charges. Some of the drama from my mother's life and her past relationships was now impacting me.

When I finally sold the house and moved to a much smaller house, the break-ins continued, so it was obvious it was someone who knew me. Since I lived outside the city limits, I never could enlist the local police department, and neither the sheriff's department nor the FBI, to my knowledge, ever solved it. It would take the three years of break-ins at two different residences and the threat of it following me to a third residence before I finally got enough gumption, self-esteem, and anger to decide I was worth defending and purchased a 38 caliber Smith and Wesson handgun which I kept by the bed. It helped me become capable and willing to take a life if necessary to defend my own, which I had never been able to do before. "Blessed be the Lord my strength which teaches my hands to war and my fingers to fight!"

The second battle in learning assertiveness was in selling the house my ex-husband and I shared. Although I listed it with several realtors, because it was a log home it was extremely difficult to sell. After two years with no success and no offers, I decided to try to sell it myself. After several months, I finally got an offer on the house, and I decided to call one of the realtors and offer them 3% if they would handle the sale for me. I refused to provide any owner financing nor any assumptions and insisted that the buyer obtain their own bank financing. It took three months for the bank to finally approve the sale and to obtain all the inspections. The realtor called and told me to meet her at a lawyer's office with the buyer.

When we all sat down, the realtor handed me the multiple page contract and told me to start signing. I wanted to peruse it first to be sure it was what I understood and wanted. We had waited too long for it to be wrong. After reading the first couple of pages, I turned to the realtor and told her that something was wrong with the contract, and that it looked to me that it was more like an assumption than the buyer having their own financing. She looked at it and told me she didn't think I was right and to go ahead and sign. I told her again something was wrong and if I signed, it would leave me liable if the buyer did not make their payments. She handed it to the lawyer, and he looked at it and told me I was wrong. I told both of them I wasn't going to sign and asked them to call someone with the bank financing department and ask them about the forms that I was being asked to sign.

By this time, the buyer was becoming uncomfortable, as they had waited so long to get it approved and it looked like it might not go through. The realtor was very uncomfortable as well and was starting to get a little perturbed. They put the phone on speaker for all of us to hear and called the bank. The first person we talked to said the correct form was sent. I told them I didn't think so and I wanted a second opinion. The second person said I didn't know what I was talking about and to sign the forms. I refused and asked to speak with their supervisor. The third, fourth, and fifth person repeated what the previous ones had said. By that time, everyone was looking at me like I was crazy. I told them I was refusing to sign the papers. The sixth person asked that we fax the first few pages back to them for them to look at and put us on hold. After she looked at them, she told us they looked fine to her as well. I again refused to sign and she got *her* supervisor.

The *seventh* person got on the phone, listened to what I was concerned with, took the fax, looked at it, and said, "Oh my! We *did* send you the wrong forms and yes, you would have been liable if the buyer is late on any of their payments! We will fax you the correct forms immediately!" Both the realtor and the lawyer apologized and told me they had been handling real estate for years but had never seen such a mistake made like this. It was most likely due to it being a log home and all the inspections and extra requirements by the bank; I'm not really sure. The only thing I *was* sure of was that I was no longer liable and the house was sold. "Blessed be the Lord my strength which teaches my hands to war and my fingers to fight!"

The third battle in learning assertiveness was in dealing with a credit card my ex-husband applied for during our divorce that I was totally unaware of. While we were separated and the divorce was pending, he used my credit (as he had none) and applied for a Montgomery Ward credit card. He then purchased $3000 worth of items and never paid for any of them. *Three years after the divorce,* the collection agencies started calling me. I knew nothing about any card or any purchases. They threatened to ruin my credit if I didn't pay and insisted that, because I had not put anything in the papers concerning this particular card to state I wasn't responsible for his purchases, because Texas was a community property state, I would have to pay. How in the world would I know to put anything in the papers about a card I didn't even know existed, let alone never received a bill for? When they told me that *all of the purchases* were made *after* the divorce was final, *that* made me mad. I told them that, even if I had to take it to the Supreme Court, I wasn't paying for it. They did put it on my credit, and that made me even madder. Everyone I knew told me there was no way to win, because Texas is a community property state and that I might as well just go ahead and pay it and move on.

It took eighteen months to fight it, but I called a television station out of Dallas and asked if they still had the investigative journalists that helped people and told them what had happened. They said that particular part of the programming station had been canceled but gave me the number to a non-profit organization out of Washington D.C. that would help. I called and told them what happened. They contacted the collection agency. I also contacted a lawyer I knew and paid him $50.00 to write a letter to the collection agency defending me. All I asked was if they could show where I had applied for a card, received a card, ordered anything, received anything, was billed for anything, that I would be willing to pay. If they could not prove that, than I was not willing to pay.

When they investigated the purchases and verified that all purchases truly had been made after the divorce was final and were shown the divorce decree, they finally relented, apologized, and notified all three of the credit bureaus, and my credit was restored. I took the letter they sent and the ones from the credit bureaus that restored my credit rating and hung them on the dining room wall. "Blessed be the Lord my strength which teaches my hands to war and my fingers to fight!"

HOMEWORK:

- Do you need "assertiveness" training or self-control concerning your anger and a need to forgive others?

- Are you able to be angry and sin not?

- Have you set physical and emotional boundaries with others, and do you honor other people and their boundaries?

- Are you beginning to recognize a pattern in the type of person you have dated in the past? Do they seem to have the same issues again and again? Do they remind you of how you felt when you were growing up?

- Are you beginning to see that *you* may have a part in attracting the drama you see in your life and relationships?

- What steps of assertiveness have you begun to take? If none, are you willing to ask God to teach you to forgive?

God's Assertiveness Training
Part II – Going Back to School

The fourth battle in learning assertiveness was by far the most effective. The station where I worked with the postal service was the busiest station in town. I was a window clerk for approximately fifteen years by that time and worked, by request, the busiest window at that station. Things had gone well until a new manager came in "that knew not Joseph" (like the Pharaoh who took charge years after Joseph, in Genesis, had passed away). After earning four Special Achievement Awards and serving as Officer-in-Charge at two different Post Offices, now, I couldn't seem to please this new manager.

During that time, I had met a man that became one of the most influential persons in my life since John Morris, the counselor. This man, Terry Danielson, had become a good friend as well as advisor, and we stayed in close contact. He had been encouraging me for a long time to go back to school and finish my degree. I went to see Terry and told him about a story I had recently heard from Paul Harvey on the radio.

In Enterprise, Alabama, at the turn of the twentieth century, cotton was the main agricultural crop in the area. And then one year, a foreign visitor came to town. No one thought anything of it, but that year, the harvesting of the cotton crop was half what it had been in previous years. The next year it was half what it had been the previous year. The town people got together and knew they would have to make a decision about the situation. Either they would all have to move away and find somewhere else to raise cotton or they would have to diversify crops and raise other things. The town chose the latter and became the most prosperous they had ever been in the town's history. They chose to erect a statute to commemorate the foreign visitor who came to town and forced them to make the drastic changes that led to the town's prosperity. It was the Mexican boll weevil.

I told Terry that this new manager was my Mexican boll weevil and that I needed to diversify by going back to school and finishing the bachelor's degree I never completed and perhaps pursue a master's degree as well. I figured I needed to make sure I was marketable in case something ever happened. I told Terry that, in order to do this, I was not going to have any school loans but would pay cash for everything as I went, and thus, would need to locate a cheaper place to live. Terry offered the duplex where he had his insurance office located. Half of the duplex was his office, but the other side of the duplex was a one bedroom unit for residential living. Terry offered me the chance to live there for $250.00 per month as long as I was going to school, and I took him up on it. I would have to make major changes at work as well, which included going back to the evening shift and working in mail processing again so I could attend day classes at school. Due to my seniority, I would not have the problem I had encountered before in working that shift, and could still attend church as well. I did everything that could possibly be done to attempt to "count the cost" (Luke 14:26-33) to prepare for this major change while continuing to work full time, but I could never have prepared for what happened on the very first day of school.

Terry had encouraged me to finish my bachelor's degree in psychology, as he believed I was very good with one-on-one counseling and encouragement to others. I had not been to school in fourteen years since receiving an associate degree in postal management at the local junior college. By this time, I decided to jump into the psychology program at the University of Texas at Tyler. The Spring semester was almost complete, and they had what was called a "mini-mester" course which was a complete semester fit into three weeks before the first Summer School classes began. In reading the requirements for the course, which was called The History of Psychology, there was one prerequisite class which I did not have. The fact was, I didn't have *any* hours in psychology, but I would be taking that very prerequisite class the very first Summer session, which would be three weeks later. I decided to go ahead and take the class and signed up over the phone. The recording stated that if the prerequisite had not been taken, there was a possibility that the student *might* be asked to drop the course and take the prerequisite first and then take that class the following year. It would be two years before that class would be offered again, and I didn't want to wait for it as it was required for the degree program, so I went ahead and signed up and decided to take my chances.

Terry stopped by to see me the day before school was going to start and see how I was doing. I had a premonition that something that I could never plan for or prepare for was going to happen the next day, and I was pacing the floor wondering what to do. Terry told me I didn't know what I was talking about and not to worry about it. I told him I had premonitions about school before one other time, and it was about first grade, and it all came true. The only thing I liked about first grade was the bus driver and the last day of school. Second grade was heaven in comparison. Terry told me he wanted me to come by the office after school the next day and tell him about the day as he was sure nothing could possibly happen that I hadn't already done or prepared for.

I arrived at the campus the next morning and found the classroom for the course. I was thirty-eight years old, the exact age of the average student attending U.T. Tyler. It was only a junior and senior level college at that time in the spring of 1995. There were approximately sixty other students for this particular class, and they all looked to be in their late twenties to mid forties in age.

The instructor walked in the class and began to speak. "My name is Dr. Henry Schreiber, and I am the Department Chair of Psychology here at U.T. Tyler. This class is the History of Psychology. Most of you sitting here today will not pass this course, and the few that do will typically have at least fifteen or more hours in psychology. How many in here have fewer than fifteen hours of psychology?" Half the hands went up in the class.

"You can probably see who will not pass." He abruptly continued, "Surely, there is no one here with *twelve* or fewer hours in Psychology?" About a dozen hands went up.

"You can go ahead and leave now if you want to." Half a dozen people got up and walked out of the class.

"Now surely, surely, there is no one in here with *nine* or fewer hours in Psychology?" Five or six hands went up. I was absolutely terrified by then. Here was someone insisting that *you can't, you shouldn't, and don't,* and I thought I might get by missing only *one* prerequisite!

"I don't know why any of you with that few hours think you can pass this course, so if you want, you can leave now too." Three more got up and walked out of the class.

"I want to go on now to question two, but let me be clear, surely, surely, there is no one sitting here today with *six* or fewer hours in Psychology?" Three hands went up. Before Dr. Schreiber could continue, one of the three stood up and walked out of the class and two more from the back joined him.

Dr. Schreiber continued: "I can't believe I'm even asking this, but surely, surely, there is no one in here with *three* or fewer hours in Psychology?" Two hands went up; mine and the guy behind me.

Dr. Schreiber looked at us both in disbelief and said, "I'm not sure why either of you are still here. Surely, surely, there is no one sitting here today with *no* hours in Psychology!?" I was the only one with a hand in the air.

Dr. Schreiber pointed his finger at me and said, "Get up and leave right now! It never *has* been done, never *will* be done!" I couldn't move if I wanted to. I hung on as tight as I could to the chair while Dr. Schreiber abruptly turned to the rest of the class and continued. "Question number two: How many of you in here work?" Two hands went up, mine and the guy behind me. I was incredulous. What in the world were all these people doing in here at their age and *not* working?!

"You cannot pass this course if you are working," Dr. Schreiber continued. The guy behind me stood up and walked out of the class.

"Question number three: Why in the world are *any* of you still sitting here taking this course (because it's going to be so difficult, I was guessing...)? Everyone one in the first and second row repeated, one after the other, "It's required!" I was sitting in the third row.

When he saw that I was still sitting there he said, "Well, I guess since you're still here, I'll *let* you answer." Now that's when I got mad and decided to fight. He had started this in the public arena and I would finish it, whatever came, in the public arena:

"Dr. Schreiber, I took a $5000.00 a year cut in pay so I could sit in your classroom here this morning. I changed shifts from a gravy eight to five job to a shift working evenings so I could sit in your classroom here this morning. I moved into a cheaper place so I could afford to sit in your classroom here this morning. Dr. Schreiber, even though it has been fourteen years since I've been to school, more than twenty years ago, when I changed schools in the second six weeks of the fall semester, I had *three* teachers who told me to drop their courses, and who said it never had been done, never will be done, and I became one of their very best students, *as I will be yours!!!*"

There was dead silence in the classroom. As my sister, Penny, says, you could hear a mouse peeing on cotton! Now *that's* quiet.

After a couple of minutes, a girl in the row behind me who had been the Valedictorian at her school, stood up and said in her East Texas lingo, "Dr. Schreiber, she ain't gonna drop!"

When I got home from school that day and told Terry what had happened, he couldn't believe it. Although those three weeks almost killed me, and I would literally record the class on a tape recorder and play it while I slept, hoping that *anything* would stick, while working full time, I made a "B" for that class and was very happy to get it. The very next week after the "mini-mester" was over, when the first Summer School class started and I sat in the class for that required prerequisite to begin, guess who was the teacher for that class? Yep! Dr. Schreiber, and wouldn't you know it, I would get in trouble again, and once more, on the very first day of Summer School, but for a very different reason.

Many people will tell you that when they went back to school as older adults, they performed better because they were more serious about their studies. Although that was certainly true, I had been serious about getting good grades years before as well, but had lost direction and focus in college when the Dallas Police Department had refused to accept me as a police cadet right after high school. I was not even given a chance to try as they took one look at me when I walked through the door to come take the physical.

"You cannot pass the physical exam," they said as they looked at me.

"You have a lazy eye. You can't shoot. You will just get your partner killed."

"Won't you even let me try?" I replied.

"No. You have no depth perception. You can't judge distance," they replied.

"That's funny," I replied. "I must have amnesia too, because I *drove* all the way down here and I don't recall running over a soul!" They didn't even smile at my humor and I was sent away. That's when I got hired for the department as a civilian. As I look back, it was probably one of the best things that ever happened, although I was completely deflated and disappointed at the time, and I could not get any direction in college hours while in Dallas. After arriving in Tyler, I decided to go ahead and finish my associate's degree for the postal service.

Aside from this, the main reason I was glad to go back to school as an older adult was because of the time that was allotted to be more grounded in my faith. Some of the people I would deal with throughout the time I attended college were non-Christians who were quick to suggest that Christianity was a crutch for the weak and the misinformed, and it certainly could not stand up under the scrutiny of science. That summer in 1995, science and my faith in Christ collided on the very first morning in Summer School.

Although the vast majority of people might suggest that Christianity could never compete with or compare with science, in my humble opinion, the opposite is true. Science, in my view, will *never* catch up with the Bible. After being allowed by that sweet pastor's wife (and every one of the wives I've met since that day were just as sweet and kind) to teach on any subject I wanted, one series I did was on humanism.

Humanism believes there is no God, that we are products of evolution, that there is no right and wrong, thus no moral absolutes, there is no heaven nor hell, and their supposed scientific conclusions come mostly from philosophers as compared with the Bible and true believers in Christ, many of whom were actual scientists such as Frances Bacon, Louis Pasteur, and Isaac Newton.[17]

Just think about it, in a *logical and factual way.* Here are but three examples of why I say science will never catch up with the Bible:

1. Gold – The Bible states that, in Heaven, the streets are made of gold, and *the gold is transparent as glass* (Revelation 21:21). It has only been in the past fifty or sixty years that scientists have been able to see gold refined and purified to such a degree that it gets hot enough in the purification process to appear *transparent or clear.*
2. Mount St. Helens – Most antagonists of the Bible decry the account of the Flood which is responsible for the Grand Canyon.

They say it is impossible for crevices the size of the Grand Canyon to be formed in forty days or less, which is the Biblical account of the length of the Flood. Yet, when Mount St. Helens erupted in 1980, crevices the size of those seen in the Grand Canyon were discovered in *twenty-four hours!*

3. Man on the moon – In 1969, when NASA was preparing for man to land on the moon, they were very concerned with the landing feet of the lunar capsule and how deep it would set in the existing dust. As there is no wind on the moon, and many of the scientists believed in evolution, thus, according to carbon dating, there would be *millions of years* (as compared to thousands of years per the Biblical account) of dust settling there, they decided to build platypus type feet, hoping the capsule would not sink very far. In truth, the capsule only settled in a few *inches of dust*, suggesting that the earth is less than a hundred thousand years old, thus disproving carbon dating for all time, and pointing to the veracity of the Bible. [18]

I could go on and on, but I digress. On that first day of Summer School, we watched a video based on the research done in 1975 comparing human babies with Rhesus monkeys with the question supposedly related to when human beings start having a sense of self. Young Rhesus monkeys were put in cages and temporarily put to sleep while odorless black marks were put above their eyebrows. A mirror was put in the cages as well. When the monkeys awoke, the researchers watched to see how the monkeys responded when they looked in the mirror and discovered the black marks on their foreheads. The researchers determined that, if the monkey reached out to touch the mirror, then they thought it was another monkey in that mirror, and if they touched their own foreheads, than they realized the mark was on their own body, thus they demonstrated a sense of self. It took the Rhesus monkeys until the age of eighteen months to stop reaching for mirrors and to touch their own foreheads.

Human babies were tested with odorless marks on their foreheads and were simply played with until they forgot that something had been put over their brows. They were then held and put in front of mirrors to see how they responded. They, too, took eighteen months to stop reaching for the mirrors and to start touching their own foreheads; thus, researchers determined that it takes both humans and Rhesus monkeys until eighteen months to determine a sense of self as distinct from others.

When I watched this, I really tried, but could not contain my laughter. What does the Bible have to say about this? The Bible posits that we have a sense of self *before we are even born!* In the Gospels, (Luke 1:44), Mary, the mother of Christ, meets with her cousin, Elizabeth, who is *six months pregnant* with John the Baptist. When Mary announces to Elizabeth that Mary is pregnant, John, who cannot see, but only *hears* this news, shows through all eternity that he can differentiate between himself and another Person, because instantly upon *hearing* this news, John didn't just move around, but leaped *with joy* within the womb!

Dr. Schreiber looked at me and asked what was so funny. I told him in front of the class, that I thought this was one of the funniest things I'd ever seen supposed scientists come up with. He asked me to describe to the class, scientifically, how I could disprove it. I couldn't simply declare what the Bible *says*, as that would be comparing apples and oranges.

I told Dr. Schreiber, "I know for a fact that this is not true. I cannot prove to you *today* in a scientific manner that this is the case, but let me train under you for one year, and I will prove to you, in a scientific manner, that this is not true." He laughed, and the class continued. I didn't know how I would prove it, and I couldn't prove exactly how old we are when we develop a sense of self, but I did know one thing: I didn't have to prove *exactly* when it occurs, I only had to prove it was less than eighteen months!

I had Dr. Schreiber again for a class in the fall, and one of the class requirements was to complete a research paper that had to earn a passing grade in order to graduate. Although the class only lasted a semester, we were given a year to complete it, with a six-week window before graduation of having Dr. Schreiber review our papers and make adjustments in order to pass. In considering my later pursuit of a master's degree, I also faced the requirement to pass the Graduate Record Exam (GRE) before entering any master's program. I was terrified of taking the test while working and going to school full time, so I looked at the research of who did well and how on that exam and discovered that "older" students as myself did better by taking it on the computer as well as making higher marks if they volunteered to do research with their professors while completing their undergraduate degrees. So that's exactly what I determined to do, and I volunteered with a professor named Dr. Marmion and one of her friends.

Dr. Marmion was my statistics professor for another class I didn't know if I would survive because it was done mostly on a computer with a lab, and I didn't know very much at all about how to use a computer. I thought the term "booting up" was a joke made by a West Texas cowboy for turning his computer on! When Dr. Marmion explained to the class that installing the program was very easy and only involved "double clicking the icon," I raised my hand and asked, "What is an icon?!" Everyone laughed and then cringed as they realized the difficulty I would have passing the class. Her class was extremely difficult, and I would later take a regular math statistics class as an elective just to be sure I understood the material.

After surviving her class, I told Dr. Marmion that she owed me money for a face lift. She laughed and asked why, and I told her that, after taking her class I had developed numerous lines in my face from making the "Huh?" look with my mouth hanging open every time I was in her statistics class!

The research I did with Dr. Marmion taught me *how* to research and *how* to write an effective paper for potential publishing with statistics. I used what she taught me to work on that required paper for Dr. Schreiber. I wanted to prove my theory about the sense of self. I discovered that many of the scientists found "interfering variables" or things they simply didn't account for that blurred the outcomes of their tests. For example, Piaget was famous for thinking that he discovered that it took babies until nine months of age to understand that, when something was moved out of their sight, it still existed. He realized that he had not one, but two, interfering variables. It takes a baby until nine months of age to be able to sit up and also that long to be able to reach around an object, so he used a different kind of test and discovered that, at birth, babies could prove they understood that an object still existed even though it was out of sight.

In the same way, I posited that there were two interfering variables in the research of the sense of self. How long might it take for a baby to understand how a mirror works, and how old does a baby have to be to have the motor skills to touch their foreheads? If I could find *one* baby that was younger than eighteen months who understood how a mirror works, then I could test him or her with the mark or a sticker on their forehead and see what happens. If I could prove this premise, than I could promote the actual testing of numerous babies to disprove what was written in those textbooks and on film. I carried some stickers with me everywhere I went and would ask parents with small children if they had mirrors in their homes and if their babies had played in front of these mirrors.

One day I went into Grandy's to have lunch, and I saw a couple there with their baby having lunch as well. The child was well under eighteen months, and I approached the family and told them about my research. The mother said that her baby was eleven months old and that they had full length mirrors in several rooms of their house that the baby had seen since birth. I was thrilled. I asked if we could take the baby into the restroom after they were finished eating, as I knew Grandy's had a full-length mirror in the ladies' restroom. The mother granted permission, and we took the baby girl into the restroom, where I put a sticker on her forehead and then some on her arms so she would forget about the one on her forehead. Her mother turned her around twice and then stood her in front of the mirror. The little girl did *not* reach for the mirror! She did not have the motor skills to reach up and grab for the sticker on her forehead, but you could see the surprise in her eyes when she saw it in the mirror and she attempted the best way she knew to try to reach up and grab it off her forehead! I was so excited!

I finished both the research for Dr. Marmion and the research paper for Dr. Schreiber and submitted it. He called each of us to come by his office to review what we needed to correct before our final grade. I stood in line that day behind another girl who was a straight A student. She came out of his office in tears with a "D" marked on her paper and had only six weeks to make corrections. I was terrified.

As I walked in, Dr. Shreiber looked up at me and said, "Sit down. I have good news and bad news about your paper. The good news is that you passed. The bad news is," and he hesitated. "The bad news is, it's one of the best papers I've ever seen written by an undergraduate!"

"I told you!" I shouted as I jumped up with joy. "I told you I would be one of your best students!"

"You were really miffed that day in class, weren't you?" he laughed.

"I was more terrified than angry!" I replied.

Dr. Schreiber later wrote a letter of recommendation for me for a scholarship. I ended up with a 3.87 GPA for my undergraduate degree. Current laws forbade testing on babies, so I would not get to prove or publish my theory, but I learned a lot during that time and gained deep respect for the point of view of these instructors. Even though many of the professors were non-believers, I was extremely grateful for the things they taught, especially the overwhelming data demonstrating how environmental elements influence our lives. While doing regular studies, on the side, I had to look at what the research at the U.T. Library showed on several subjects that were of interest to me. Listed below are a few areas that research at that time showed were 100% caused by environmental factors, although we never see this in the news:

1. Dyslexia – Research at that time overwhelmingly showed that dyslexia is caused by one environmental factor, and it has nothing to do with a physical disability. It is caused by trying to learn to read *without using phonics!* Since the early 1960s, the United States started using the Look and Say method, even though phonics had been proved for years as the better method.[19] I personally believe phonics was removed in the United States when we decided we didn't want God in the schools and prayer taken out of school. The books that used phonics were called McGuffey Readers, and they contained numerous references to faith and strong character building. I personally never even heard of the word *dyslexia* until the 1970s, when so many people began to be affected. It was discovered close to the turn of the twentieth century, and when Russia discovered the cause, the Look and Say method was banned from their teaching methods.

2. Anorexia – Research indicated the presence of *both parents* as extremely controlling who refuse to allow the girl to grow up and take on responsibilities. You typically did not see this with boys, or in foreign countries or among Hispanics or blacks. Most cases involved white, American women.[20] The girl feels so controlled that she thinks to herself, "You may make me do everything you want me to do, but you can't force me to eat." After there is

extreme weight loss, brain function is affected to the point that it becomes life threatening, and intervention is required.

3. Autism – Although previous research could not come up with an actual cause, those who suffered from this disorder typically came from the United States and were typically white, *upper middle class,* and the child was often unusually good looking.[21] This strongly suggested an environmental cause.

4. Alzheimer's disease – Research previously had not come up with an actual cause, but autopsies showed a high level of *aluminum* in the brain of those who suffered from them.[22] I surmised out loud in class one time that our parents and grandparents cooked with cast iron skillets, while we now used aluminum pots and pans, aluminum cans for sodas, and the number one ingredient in antiperspirant is aluminum and wondered if it took until we were older in life for the aluminum to cross the blood/brain barrier. That idea was pooh-poohed until a documentary came out regarding a study of an African tribe that had one of the highest incidences of Alzheimer's in the world. The researchers discovered that outsiders had brought in some cheap aluminum pots and pans made in a foreign country with them that the natives were still using twenty years later. When they took the pots and pans away from them, the incidence of Alzheimer's began to drop.

5. Homosexuality in men – Research in 1999 showed a clear *environmental* factor contributing to homosexuality in men *from birth.* 100% of the homosexual men had a weak or missing father and a domineering/critical mother.[23] 85% of men who were criticized by a "nagging" wife would leave; they would leave the room, leave the house, find jobs that kept them away from home, etc. Although the presence of these types of parents certainly did not "cause" homosexuality, in most cases, however, the presence of these types of parents coupled with at least one incident of sexual abuse of the child was often enough to push them over the edge into homosexuality. Typically, such abuse was from a friend of the family or a family member.

One reason I can see that homosexuality is so clearly a sin before God comes from the study given to me by John Morris, my counselor, in Roman's 1:21-32. Just as I would have to deal with a root of bitterness in my own heart and life as well as sexual sin, I could see that the anger and root of bitterness these boys hold towards their fathers for not rescuing them from both a parent and from sexual abuse turns into seething rage and a love-hate relationship for not only their earthly father but their Heavenly Father as well. They are shaking their fists before their earthly fathers and Heavenly Father and saying, in effect, "You will not tell me what to do!" Just as I knew God but was unthankful and therefore began a descent into a pit of sin, they, too, fall into the same pattern, and God's words make clear the end result.

I was also reminded of all those years as a child of constantly being on the lookout for and escaping from pedophiles because the parental safety net was not sufficient for whatever reason. No wonder so many feel they are born with such feelings. Although the vast majority that live under these environmental factors do *not* become gay, the better term would be born *into* an environment conducive to, rather than born *with,* such a condition, as though it is something you catch or develop like a cold or cancer. This argument reminds me of an old Ann Landers commentary called "How to Raise a Juvenile Delinquent," which described the environmental aids parents unknowingly provide that later influence some to become delinquent. It clearly demonstrates why we all have the need to forgive one another, "lest a root of bitterness" well up in us, and "thereby many be defiled." (Hebrews 12:15 KJV)

I was able later to pass the G.R.E. Exam for the master's program by completing it on the computer. I had considered going into a doctorate program right out of the bachelor's program at a different university, but a friend told me about one student who found that it didn't matter what your grades were, what letters of referral you had, or anything else, they would not accept a student into their program who worked. I thought to myself, "Here we go again," and decided to call them. Sure enough, they related that this was the case.

"Pray tell, I am forty years old now! How in the world am I supposed to survive by being in your program *without* working?!"

"You take a five year vow of poverty," the lady from the university replied. "We simply do not accept anyone in our program who works."

"Lady," I replied, "You don't want me, and I sure don't want you or your program!"

By 1997, times appeared to be changing for careers in psychology and counseling. Many were closing up their practices, and jobs were becoming scarce. I figured I really needed to be more diverse in order to be marketable, so I changed directions somewhat and pursued a master's degree in public administration, which could be used later in a position that might be non-profit – a church, hospital, human resources, or even city or county government administration. With a background in psychology, I could help advise people with career choices in human resources, or possibly be a workplace counselor through the Employee Assistance Program with the postal service, etc.

The master's program at U.T. Tyler required comprehensive finals with tests over six subjects, and even if you earned an A in the course for that subject, you still were required to pass the "comps" in order to graduate. I rearranged my schedule so I would have only one class during the final semester, thus freeing my schedule up to study. Since I knew I had memorization skills from learning those 2000 scheme items for the Post Office years before, I typed up *fifty pages* of single-spaced typewritten notes and memorized them during that last semester.

Not long after I graduated with my master's degree, I saw Dr. Schreiber at the Post Office. He came to the window where I was working at a different office (it would take me seven years to get the equivalent of the job I had previously with weekends off).

He asked how I was doing, and I told him, "Dr. Schreiber, I just graduated with my Master's degree from U.T. Tyler and I wanted you to know."

"Congratulations!" he replied.

"I graduated with a 4.0 average," I added.

"That's wonderful!" he replied.

"I was the only one in the entire department who passed the comprehensive finals the first time through." He hung his head and looked at the floor for a moment.

"Dr. Schreiber, you became one of my favorite instructors, but please, *please* don't ever tell another student that it never has been done, never will be done, again."

"I won't," he softly replied. We hugged one another, and he walked out the door.

My mother will tell you that I was a different woman after finishing both degrees from U.T. Tyler. All I can say is that God's Assertiveness Training 101 really works! Blessed be the Lord my strength which teaches my hands to war and my fingers to fight!

HOMEWORK:

- Do you have a "boll weevil" in your midst? Are you able to give thanks, realizing that this may be by God's hand in bringing about change in your life?

- Are you willing to ask God to teach you assertiveness?

- What verse has He given you concerning this area in your life?

Taking a Break

After four years of working full time and going to school year round, it was time for a needed break. I got together with a friend named Norma and took a seven-day cruise to Hawaii for a very reasonable price. I had taken a four-day, three-night cruise the year before starting back to school and had really enjoyed it, so I knew this would be fun, too. On the last night of cruises back then, there would be an amateur talent contest by the passengers. I decided on a lark to try something that I had learned about during my four years of school. It also involved one of the eight items from that list on the refrigerator of things happy people have in common – the ability to laugh at yourself.

One of those environmental influences we looked at, which I thought at first would be something like astrology, truly persuaded me in the veracity of its influence. That environmental influence was birth order, or the order in which you were raised in your family. Although this would not be a significant do-or-die necessity in life to know this subject, because this particular influence affected not only what happened on that cruise, but who I did actually marry later, I would like to briefly share some information on the subject. There are lots of books out there about birth order that you can study for yourself. One of the best that I found was The Birth Order Book by Dr. Kevin Leman.[24]

In psychology, we learned that birth order began to really be studied when NASA scientists noticed that twenty-one of the first twenty-three astronauts in space were firstborns. In fact, all seven astronauts in the original Mercury program were firstborns. Fifty-six percent of U.S. presidents by that time were firstborns, while only four were the youngest of the family. The odds of such a high number of firstborns in one field occurring simply by chance are astronomical. In another example, research unveiled the fact that most stand-up comedians came from one particular birth order than any other, and that is the baby of the family. It became obvious to researchers that some variable was impacting these career choices – birth order. Soon, the reasons became very logical and obvious for all to see. Birth order can affect personality, career choices, and, often, *who we choose as a spouse.* Although you may not have heard of the influence of birth order, many scientific, long-term research studies have been conducted, including one study by a mother-daughter team that spanned a forty-year period.

From a Biblical standpoint, birth order is extremely significant, especially that of the firstborn. The firstborn was the one who received the family blessing as well as a major part of the family inheritance, usually two-thirds. In the Old Testament, the worst plague that befell the Egyptian people occurred when the death angel passed over and all the firstborns died, from the Pharaoh's son all the way through the firstborn of the cattle!

In the New Testament, when a believer enters into the Family of God, he or she is given firstborn status. We are co-heirs with Christ, who is the Firstborn, and who represents the first fruits of our inheritance through the resurrection. The believer is not given only a double portion of the blessing, but, according to Ephesians 1:3, we get *all* the blessings. We believers are all, according to Hebrews 12:23, members of the same church, the Church of the Firstborn!

For brevity's sake, the birth order positions I'll talk about are firstborn, middle born, and baby of the family. Birth order isn't a system that says that all firstborns are equally one way, all middle children are another, and last borns are always like this or that. There are tendencies and general characteristics that often apply, but the main gist is that there are dynamic relationships that exist between members of a family and certain interfering variables which affect each family situation. It's important that you understand these interfering variables, as I am technically a middle-born child, born the third out of four girls, but these interfering variables affected my birth order status, as it could for others as well. These variables are as follows:

Spacing: The number of years between siblings. Research has indicated that when there are five or more years' difference between siblings, the family, for all practical purposes, has started over, and there is a reassigning of birth order. For example, I was the baby of the family for six years, then a younger sister came along. Because there were five or more years' difference, she was the "first" of the "new" family, and thus carried many firstborn characteristics. Most personality is formed by age six, and thus, I carry mostly baby characteristics even though I am technically a middle child.

Sex of the child: You will carry firstborn characteristics simply by being the *first male* or *first female* born in the family, although you may not be the first child. For example, if there are four siblings and the first two are male and the third is female, the female will, like the first male, carry firstborn characteristics, as she is the first female born in the family.

Physical differences or disabilities: Those siblings born with disabilities are usually assigned baby of the family status, as the baby is the one most watched out for and is often considered the weakest in the family, simply by physically being younger.

Blended families and twins: If you grew up with half brothers or sisters, these too would be considered as well as twins. Twins require considerably more attention than other siblings. Twins will be assigned different birth order status, usually by the parents.

If you have figured out which birth order you are more associated with, let's look at each one now:

FIRSTBORN: ACHIEVER

You are naturally goal oriented, ambitious, and a high achiever who generally knows where you're going and how to get there. Firstborns tend to be perfectionists, and because of that, more than any other birth order status, may suffer with the problem of stuttering while growing up. (My mother, a firstborn – only born – suffered with stuttering.)

Firstborns are more motivated to achieve because everything about you is a big deal – even before you were born. Your parents had never been parents before and didn't know what to expect, so they couldn't wait for your first words and first steps; thus firstborns are known to walk earlier and talk earlier than all other birth order statuses. As an adult, you have great confidence that other adults will listen to you and take you seriously, because all adult eyes were upon you from the cradle on up, and you learned well. If you tended to younger brothers and sisters, your leadership training continued. You are attracted to careers that require precision, concentration, self-discipline, and working with data; thus you make great accountants, bankers, administrators, scientists, lawyers, and managers. You are usually more attracted to those who are the baby of the family or middle born, because you tend to be rather competitive with other firstborns. The baby of the family offsets your more serious side, while you influence them in taking charge and taking responsibility for their life.

MIDDLEBORN: BALANCED

Second born or middle children don't possess that driven, compulsive nature one often sees in the firstborn. You are the most influenced by the firstborn, and the second or middle born will often branch out in the opposite direction from the firstborn in interests and careers. As middle kids, you will say you didn't feel that special growing up. In the family photo album, there seem to be many more pictures of the firstborn, than that of the middle child.

Second borns or middle children tend to make the best marriage partners and are the most balanced adults, because in order to gain the reward and recognition that often went to the firstborn, you seek outside the family and create for yourselves a new "family" where you will feel special. While the firstborn typically has few friends, the middle child develops many, and your peer group is usually of much older people, often including adults. Thus, you leave home physically and emotionally much sooner and develop people-oriented socialization skills much sooner than others. You work harder to make your marriages work and are much more accepting of other people. Because you didn't have Mom and Dad all to yourself and get your own way, you learned to negotiate and compromise and thus make wonderful counselors or mediators, consultants, and leaders. The middle child usually marries outside their birth order, as two middle kids would potentially have weakness in meeting problems head on, due to the tendency to avoid conflict.

BABY OF THE FAMILY: PERSUASIVE

Youngest children are typically the outgoing charmers who are affectionate and uncomplicated. Babies of the family tend to be the family clown or entertainer, because you seek attention and you know you have to jump through hoops in order to get it. This is why more comedians are babies of the family than any other birth order status.

Babies of the family are impetuous and brash – you go ahead and do things and worry about the repercussions later, as you may have been a little rebel growing up and gotten away with murder. This could lead to money problems later in life, especially if you pair up with another baby of the family.

Last borns are perceptive people-persons and are extremely persuasive, thus you are good in sales, entertaining, journalism, industrial relations, etc. In order to get someone's attention, you know you have to get their facts right and have your ducks in a row. On occasion, you will "come from behind," and when you do, you will surpass the achievements of even the firstborn. Gideon thought he wasn't qualified to lead an army of three hundred because his family was poor and he was the baby of the family (Judges 6:15). Jesse and his sons didn't even consider the possibility of calling David out of the field for the prophet Samuel to consider for king, because he was the baby of the family. Then there was the oldest sister, Miriam, and oldest brother, Aaron, who ended up serving the baby of the family – Moses.

What absolutely sold me on the power of influence of birth order was that, after I realized I was more associated with the characteristics of the baby of the family whose best compatibility is with the firstborn, I could see how my *unconscious* choices from age five to that day for both friends, male and female, and love interests were *all* firstborns or those who had taken over the firstborn position! The odds that I would do that by pure chance are next to impossible. Moreover, was the explanation of the *type* of firstborn I was most compatible with. Research suggested that firstborn males who had no sisters would be attracted to an Olive Oyl type girl (from Popeye and Olive Oyl) who had tomboyish looks, a straight up and down figure, with very attractive facial features who would mother them unreservedly. They would do best with a baby of the family who had no sisters.[25] This was one reason my relationships with these firstborns were not working! I would add to this my perception that this type of firstborn was also attracted to women whose names were interchangeable with a man's, like Bobbie, Billie, etc. My friend, Terry Danielson, a firstborn with no sisters, broke off the relationship with me to date a woman named Frankie who mothered him unreservedly! Well, those characteristics don't fit me at all! I don't look like that, and I "ain't your mama!"

The research indicated that my most compatible firstborn would be one who had at least one sister! When a friend tried to be a matchmaker for me later, when I discovered the guy was a firstborn with no sisters, I asked if his ex-wife had a name interchangeable with a man's, and he answered, "Jerri – how did you know?"

So you can guess what it was that I did on that cruise on that last night... standup comedy! Since it was on that checklist of what happy people have in common, what better way to laugh at oneself than to laugh at the career I was in. Have you ever heard of anyone working for the Post Office telling jokes about themselves? I didn't even have to make very much up. All I had to do was to tell some of the crazy things that happened while working at the Post Office.

My routine started off like this: "For years my friends and families have told me that I ought to try my hand at standup comedy, so I figured, what the hey, I'd give it a try. I figure the worst you guys can say is, 'Don't quit your day job!' What's my day job? I hesitate to tell you. You see there's three places you don't ever want to confess that you work for – The police department, the Post Office, or the I.R.S. You either wrote them a ticket, lost their mail, or stole their money.

"Well, I will confess that I did work for the Dallas Police Department as a civilian. They told me I couldn't be an officer because I had lazy eye so I couldn't shoot, but I noticed on this cruise that they were doing skeet shooting off the back of the ship, and I wanted to try to see just how bad I really am. When I noticed only guys were doing it, I asked the cruise director if anyone could do it, and she said, yes, but wouldn't I rather join some of the ladies and wear a grass skirt. When I looked at her like she was crazy, she told me I didn't look *that* bad, and that's when I informed her that, back home in Texas, I had shut down three nudist colonies just by *threatening* to show up, but I sure would like to try the skeet shooting.

"When it came to my turn, all the guys backed up to the wall, I'm guessing to watch the dumb broad shoot. The guy in charge asked me if I knew how to shoot skeet, and I told him I had never shot a shotgun before and was told I couldn't hit the broad side of a barn but just wanted to try. He explained how it worked, and would you believe it? I hit the first three in a row!

"All the guys started hollering, 'She's a liar, she's been shooting all her life!'

"The cruise guy looked at me and said, 'Wow, ma'am! You're an absolute natural for shooting moving targets! What do you do for a living?'

"'I work for the Post Office, but I'm not under stress!'

"I never realized how much power I had as a postal employee until I got on the plane to go to Hawaii. There was a guy sitting in my place on the plane, and as I got closer to him, he looked at me condescendingly over his glasses and said, 'Excuse me, ma'am, I realize I'm in your seat, but I'm a lawyer and I need the extra light to see what I'm doing.'

"'That's ok,' I replied. ' I'm a postal employee, and I didn't pass the metal detector!' Poof, he was gone!

"Now, I want you to know that I worked the window for many years as a postal employee and I knew my customers so well, I could even tell you their religious preference. You'd be surprised how many people come to the Post Office that believe in reincarnation. You know how I can tell? I can hear them out there in the line: 'Am I going to be waited on in this lifetime?!'

"You guys are really hard on us postal employees. Why, just the other day, I thought we were getting our first compliment. This lady informed me that the postal service was the first one to hire the handicapped. I told her I didn't know that!

"'Yeah,' she replied. 'It's the only place I know of that you have to have dyslexia in order to get hired!'

"Okay, now that I've told on me, can I ask you a question? Why do you ask the same silly question every time we have a rate change? You act normal on the Friday before all rate changes, but every Monday, when rate changes occur, all day long, twenty times a day, for months, you ask the same question, over and over: 'How much is a one-cent stamp?' You will look at me like a deer in the headlights. I've always wanted to ask you when you ask me that: 'What time is the six o'clock news?' It's not like you *ever* paid tax before on stamps!

"The funniest thing I ever heard a customer say was to one of our carriers. You see, the highlight of a lot of elderly people's day is to get their mail, and this one day, a carrier is walking up a long driveway and there is this elderly lady standing there at her screen door, with her schnauzer dog, trying to get out the door, and you know who gets out first. Yep, down the driveway, up to the postman, grabbing hold of his leg, ripping, snarling, and tearing. Then, here comes the little old lady, running down the driveway...

"'Oh sir, I am *so* sorry! I don't know what's wrong with this fool dog! I just had him *fixed* yesterday!'

"The postman looked at her like she was nuts, and said, 'Fixed!? Lady, you should have had his teeth pulled!! I could tell when he came out the door, that he didn't have sex on his mind!'"

That's a small portion of what I threw together that night, and everyone seemed to have as good a time as I did laughing at the Post Office and laughing at themselves.

There was a comedian from HBO who had been hired by the cruise line who happened to be sitting in the crowd that night. He later came up to me and said, "Lady, you could really do this!" How about that for baby-of-the-family characteristics!

By the way, the incident with the skeet shooting on the cruise really happened just like that, except for the remarks about the nudist colonies (although that part *could* have been true)!

HOMEWORK:

- Which birth order are you associated with? Are you taking into account the interfering variables such as spacing and sex of the child?

- Do the significant others in your life belong to your same birth order, or are they different? If they do belong to your birth order, although not insurmountable, do you recognize any potential weakness which needs to be dealt with, such as competitiveness, avoidance of dealing with issues, or money problems?

- Is there a special inclination associated with your birth order which you have never developed? Why not?

Feasting on Crumbs

Have you ever had incidents in your life in which you *knew* God had intervened or you could see His Hand? As Christians, probably most of us can recount a story where perhaps there was angelic protection, maybe in a car wreck, or God's perfect timing was so evident that you had to give Him the glory for it. I am convinced that, in 1961, when I was a five-year-old child hiding in the bushes in the backyard from that predator, the still small voice within that said to "keep still" was of the Lord. I believe it was heavenly protection as well in getting to come home alive that very same year from the friend of the family who was also a predator. I'm also convinced that the Lord intervened the month before my twenty-eighth birthday, as has been shared previously.

Another incident occurred at age fifteen, when my younger sister, Penny, and I both went to visit our grandmother in Long Beach, California, during the summer of 1972. Our two older sisters, Monica and Julia, had been to visit her the previous summer. Grandmother took us to Disney World, Knott's Berry Farm, the San Diego Zoo, the Queen Mary, as well as other places. One place we also went was to the piers at Long Beach to swim. We went twice. The first day was bright and sunny, and there were hundreds of people swimming. The piers there were the longest I've ever seen in my life, some being three thousand feet long. We came back to the piers the very next day, but no one was swimming, and it was very overcast but still very warm. As we walked along the pier, I asked our grandmother if I could go swimming again, like we had done the day before, and she said yes. Penny didn't want to join me. It was a long walk from where we were back to the beach and then down to the water. I remember getting into the water about chest deep and looking over to all the people walking on the pier. They were hundreds of yards away by that time, and I was the only one swimming. I hadn't noticed the day before that everyone on the pier seemed so far away.

After only being in the water for just a few minutes, I heard a very authoritative *female* voice say, "Get out of the water!" I looked around with great surprise to see who had said it, but there was no one there. I looked up at the pier and no one was looking my way, and I knew it was impossible to hear them, or for them to hear me.

Then I heard that voice again: "GET OUT OF THE WATER – NOW!!!" I didn't need to hear another word. I didn't know where it came from, but I wasn't going to question it. I hurried toward the shore and climbed out, running toward the pier. It seemed like it took forever to get to where my grandmother was. I was shaking when I got to her and kept looking back at the water. She asked me what was wrong, and all I could tell her was that "someone" had told me to get out of the water. As I looked to where I had been swimming, I noticed a large, dark shadow, right where I had been. I thought, maybe there had been a shark or something, but I never saw a fin. I don't know what it was, but there was no question: someone was watching over me.

I've also had the *very rare* and occasional dream through the years. My sister, Julia, has had these types of dreams all her life. On Sunday morning, October 4, 1981, I awoke from a dream and announced, "someone we call President would be assassinated very soon." When asked did I mean *the* President, I said no, it would be someone that we in the United States *call* President that would be assassinated. On Tuesday, October 6, 1981, President Anwar Sadat was assassinated.

While finishing both degrees at U.T. Tyler, there was not a lot of time for socializing, but when it was possible, my friend Trish and I would get together for lunch and discuss spiritual issues. She too had been divorced and was struggling with all the accompanying feelings and hurt, and one day she asked me a strange question concerning relationships, one which obviously neither one of us had any expertise, since our marriages had failed.

"If you ever discover in your studies the reason why men can treat women like dirt and some of those same women will fall all over themselves to be around a guy like that and keep trying to please them, could you let me know?" Now *that* was an interesting question that made me question how guilty I was of just that same type of thing and how many other women are as well.

A few months later, I had a strange dream. I was in heaven in front of a fabulous banquet feast. There were tables so long that you couldn't see the ends of them at which people were seated, with food everywhere. Everyone was talking and having a wonderful time. Christ was there and was laughing and talking. There was joy all around. Every few seconds, I could hear cheering and applause from the adjoining room, as the angels would cheer and clap and the double doors would open to the banquet as another believer who had just accepted Christ was brought into the banquet hall to join the celebration and enjoy the feast set before them. There was only one thing wrong: there was nothing on my plate. As I looked around, an angelic creature flew to me and placed one pea on my plate, looked at me for a moment, and then flew away. All I had to "feast" on was one pea, and I could see that we were intended to enjoy the entire feast, but somehow, I didn't know how. When the flying creature looked at me for that moment, it was as though it were telling me that I needed to learn how to stop "feasting on crumbs" so I could partake of the entire celebration. I then woke up.

I had seen some of the research by then that could be applied to this dream. I wrote Trish a letter so she would have something to look at rather than just hear. This is the letter I wrote her:

Trish, you asked me several months ago to let you know if I ever discovered in my studies the reason why a man could treat women like dirt and they'd fall all over themselves to be around him or to please him. I think I've found it – and it's scientifically backed. In Sperling language, I'll call it "feasting on crumbs." I'm serious now, so hang with me.

Sperling's Law: "It's hard to sit down to a sumptuous steak when you're only used to feasting on crumbs." Too many women, and some men, are habituated to accepting a "meal" of crumbs in a relationship.

Now what this really means, logically and scientifically, is in three parts---Research on rats demonstrates what is known as the *Frustration Effect*,[26] which is an increased vigor following non-reinforcement. Non-reinforcement causes frustration, and that frustration is motivating, or drive inducing.

Rats trained on a two runway apparatus were given four pellets of food at the end of each runway during the training period. After training, conditions changed so the number of food pellets at the end of the runway were either four pellets, three pellets, two pellets, one pellet, or zero pellets. Runway two remained constant with four pellets. There was an inverse relationship between running speed in runway two and the number of pellets in runway one – the fewer the pellets, the faster the running. The animals ran fastest when they received less and less reinforcement. Similar behavior has been found in humans as well.

6. *Partial reinforcement*[27] is behavior that is rewarded intermittently that builds the organism's ability to cope with and ignore frustration for longer periods of time; thus the behavior itself extends for much greater lengths of time. (It's the same principle or theory used in slot machines that maintains the behavior of pulling that arm handle for longer periods of time when usually all you get is just a little "crumb" back.)

Research demonstrates that behavior learned through partial reinforcement is much harder to break then that of zero reinforcement. (When the slot quits paying off, we quit, but as long as it hands out something, even a measly pittance, we'll keep hanging in there. Can you begin to see how this can apply to a relationship, where we stay too long waiting for a pittance of love, acceptance, approval, etc?)

7. *Theory of Transfer*[28] says that we will transfer what we know and understand to what is new and unfamiliar. We will try to recreate that which is familiar. If, during our childhood, we were only given "crumbs" of affection and acceptance, if we have not dealt with these issues and had these needs met, we will seek out the same (familiar) type of relationship(s) in our adult lives. Although it may be painful and is, in a sense, a "prison," there is a sense of comfort in the familiarity of it as *it's the only thing we've ever known*. Without intervention, our self talk is like this:

A. "I can fix it this time if I try hard enough," (in order to gain acceptance), or,

B.   "It's just too frightening to step out of my 'prison,' because what I find may be taken away and perhaps it's best that I never experience it (intimacy) in the first place."

***

One of my greatest weaknesses has been the fear of rejection. I would simply respond in *anticipation* of being rejected as it was familiar. I found that I was attracting relationships that would involve just that – rejection. I prayed about this and begin to write down questions concerning rejection and what God might want us to do in order to change our thinking concerning rejection as well as our habits and, thus, our very destinies.

Why Are We Attracted to Those Who Continually Reject Us? What Would God Have Us Do?

1.   To change our pattern of mere survival to living. "I am come that they might have life, and that they might have it more *abundantly.*" (John 10:10, KJV)

I have a choice – I want steak, not crumbs or leftovers.

2.   To tire of being rejected, you *choose* your own pain. "And you are complete in *Him.*" (Colossians 2:10, KJV)

I don't deserve rejection – I can walk away.

3.   "Love thy neighbor *as* thyself," not *more* than thyself. (Mark 12:31, KJV) To love your self is not a *suggestion,* but a *commandment.*

I must love me as much as him/her.

4.   To "love *as* thyself" (Mark 12:31, KJV) means to help set emotional boundaries or "armor." Without armor, there is no respect from the other person, for they view no armor as no self-respect.

I must demonstrate self-respect.

5. To allow him/her the freedom of choice, I need to back off and away and let him ask for me. (King David knew what he was made for, yet he waited until he was called for, and he never usurped Saul's place.)

    "And he said unto his men, The Lord forbid that I should do this thing unto my master, the Lord's anointed, to stretch forth mine hand against him, seeing he is the anointed of the Lord." (1 Samuel 24:6, KJV)

I must not manipulate (through weakness) or pursue.

6. "Wherefore take unto you the whole armor of God that ye may be able to withstand in the evil day, and having done all to stand." (Ephesians 6:13, KJV)

I need God's strength to withstand.

7. "Above all, taking the shield of faith, wherewith ye shall be able to quench all the fiery darts of the wicked." (Ephesians 6:16, KJV)

    "And we know that all things work together for good to them that love God, to them who are the called according to his purpose." (Romans 8:28, KJV)

I must believe it will work out to my good.

8. It's not my responsibility to *make* him/her see the truth, change, or find truth. It is only my responsibility to *tell* the truth. He/she must be seeking truth, otherwise it is valueless.

    "And ye shall know the truth and the truth shall make you free." (John 8:32, KJV)

I am not to rescue or enable him/her.

9. The jealousy, insecurity, anger, etc., you see in him/her was there before you met him/her.

"For from *within*, out of the *heart* of men, proceed evil thoughts, adulteries, fornications, murders...etc." (Mark 7:21, KJV)

I cannot *cause* jealousy, insecurity, etc., I can only *reveal* it.

10. I am not to give away the most important or precious thing(s) I have to someone who will not appreciate or cherish it. If I would not give a valued family heirloom to a two year old for fear that they would break it, likewise, how can I give my body, heart, love, etc., to someone who will break me? I won't be happy with someone who simply wants a painting to cover the wall. I need someone who recognizes that I'm a Rembrandt and who appreciates that about me.

"And whosoever shall not *receive you*, nor *hear your words*, when ye depart out of that house or city, shake off the dust of your feet." (Matthew 10:14, KJV)

I deserve to be valued and appreciated. I show this by demonstrating emotional boundaries.

11. It's more important to see the hand of God in this than to feel I manipulated others through the power of my love.

"Be still and know that I am God." (Psalms 46:10, KJV)

12. By facing my fear of rejection, I am growing and will later be attracted to a more emotionally healthy person, because I, too, have become more emotionally healthy.

"For God has not given us a spirit of *fear*, but of power, and of love, and of a *sound mind*." (2 Timothy 1:7, KJV)

I need to put away dependent behaviors.

13. I am to take charge and responsibility of my own life rather than waiting for someone to come in and do it for me. I am not to surrender that responsibility to others.

"Ye are *complete* in *Him.*" (Colossians 2:10, KJV)

Happiness is taking charge and responsibility of my own life, not expecting someone else to do it for me.

14. God's purpose is *not* to "win" that person over, but to *win me through.*

    "How can you say to your brother, 'Let me take the speck out of your eye,' when all the time there is a plank in your eye?" (Matthew 7:4, KJV)

    "When you pass through the waters, I will be with you." (Isaiah 43:2, NIV)

I need to gain mastery in my own life.

15. I demonstrate self-love by not allowing or enabling him/her to put me at the bottom of his/her priority list. I may *lose them*, but it's better than *losing me. (*Mark 12:31, KJV)

Am I demonstrating self-love?

16. This is about learning to meet my own needs rather than seeking someone else to meet them for me. My need for self-love and self-respect is greater than my need for a physical and emotional relationship. My relationship with me must be right before I can have a happy and healthy relationship with another.

    "Ye are complete in Him." (Colossians 2:10, KJV)

When I take responsibility of my own life, my life will <u>command</u> respect – not <u>demand</u> it.

17. This is about realizing that someone who rejects you cannot claim to be in love with you. There is nothing wrong with the love I offer or with who I am; the problem lies within them. A child does not comprehend that there is something wrong with the parents – the child only thinks that the reason love is withheld is there is something wrong within him or herself. Facing this

person is finally arriving at the place where the "old self" or "old brain" is finally able to realize that there was nothing wrong with the child – the problem lay with the parents, who were incapable or unable for whatever reason to meet that child's needs for love and acceptance. This will bring freedom of not "performing" for crumbs of affection.

"...*He* hath made us *accepted* in the beloved." (Ephesians 1:6, KJV)

The problem of lack of love lies with them and not me.

18. This is a lesson to teach me to not allow others to make my choices for me; that is my right and, more so, my responsibility. In longing for someone to come in and take care of me, I have given up that right and responsibility and landed in prison with a taskmaster.

"Therefore they did set over them taskmasters to afflict them with their burdens." (Exodus 1:11, KJV)

I don't want another person making my choices for me; I want mutuality, not Adolf Hitler.

Goal: Become self-confident and assertive in the
relationship as you are in the work place, school, etc.

HOMEWORK:

- Are you guilty of "feasting on crumbs"? Isn't it time for abundance?

- Do you spend an inordinate amount of time concerned with the fear of rejection? Does this cause you to "walk on eggshells" around others? Isn't it time to set emotional boundaries?

- Are you guilty of manipulating others through weakness? Can you step back and allow the other people in your life the breathing room to make their own choices regarding a relationship with you or the amount of time they spend with you?

- Are you an enabler?

- Are you consistently told that it is *you* that is responsible for the fits of jealousy, rage, etc., in others? Do you understand now that you cannot *cause* this; you can only *reveal* these things?

- Do you know in your heart that you deserve to be valued and appreciated? You are so valuable that God sent His only Son to die on your behalf so you might live!

- Are you demonstrating self-love?

Why We Are So Attracted to Certain People

During that last year of my master's education, although I didn't have much time to read for fun, there were two books that I found that were as influential on those horizontal, emotional relationships as the book on Job and The Ins and Out of Rejection had been for my vertical, spiritual relationship with God. They were both written by the same author; one was intended for singles while the other was for those already married. They were written by Harville Hendrix, Ph.D., who was a pastoral counselor, who, himself, had experienced divorce. He was a faculty member at the Perkins Divinity School at Southern Methodist University in Dallas, Texas, for nine years before moving into private practice. After having a divorce in 1975, he was led to study marriage with a focus on marital therapy, and this study produced his two books, Keeping the Love You Find,[29] for singles, and Getting the Love You Want [30] for those who are married.

According to Hendrix, we unconsciously want to be whole and heal our childhood wounds, and this is what "chemistry" is based on. Hendrix posits that we are attracted to the person who carries both the positive and negative characteristics of our primary caretakers, hoping that this person we are with will meet those unmet needs of our childhoods. According to Hendrix, that person we have "chemistry" with was also wounded in their childhoods, but responded in an opposite manner than we did. For example, if both were ignored as children, one will more than likely jump through hoops to get attention and run over other peoples' boundaries and allow that to happen to themselves, while the other decides they don't need people and sets up very rigid personal boundaries that are almost impossible to break through.

At first, those things we like about a partner seem wonderful, until a commitment takes place. After that, those same things lead to a power struggle. For example, if while dating, your partner appears to be very gregarious while you are shy and quiet, after a commitment, they seem to pressure you into coming out of your shell, now, in your eyes, they talk too much. You feel that if you give in to them for whatever it is they are calling out in you, somehow you feel like you would rather die than give in to it; hence, the power struggle.

According to Hendrix, the power struggle in the relationship is God's way of leading us back "to the scene of the crime," where we were wounded, in an attempt to work through and put away our old responses and to respond with a more emotionally mature response. We do this when we arrive at the place where we realize that, although we chose a partner to fill in what is missing in ourselves, that partner is not capable of giving us what is missing. When we stop looking to that other person and choose to develop those lost strengths and abilities within, then we are able to enter into a more intimate and restful relationship with that other person.

Hendrix calls this process finding your true self, which occurs when you enter into a conscious relationship in which both partners become conscious of what is really happening in the relationship and help one another rather than continue to wound one another. He breaks down the process into understanding this attraction by showing that the *negative* things you dislike in your partner are really mirroring truths about yourself. He calls this our "disowned self." For example, those angry, controlling men I had been attracted to were pointing the finger back at me. At first, I thought, "well, I'm not angry," until I recognized that depression is just swallowed anger. I was not allowed to show anger as a child, so I suppressed it, and it came out as depression. Thus, I was attracted to someone who reacted in an opposite manner as I did, a man who could be angry for the both of us. That's why I needed to learn to become angry and sin not. I has been attracted to someone who was controlling because I had refused to take charge and take responsibility for my life and my happiness, which the Lord had also been dealing with. It was very eye-opening to realize that what I disliked in both husbands was really true about myself.

According to Hendrix, the *positive* things we like in our partners are really the things we had to put away in our childhoods in order to survive, and he calls this our "lost self." I was attracted to men who were intelligent, influential, and resourceful. Looking back, I realize that, just like my mother wanted to prove to *her mother* that she wasn't dumb, I had some homework too. I felt pretty dumb as well, due to the constant negative messages that "no one wants to hear your opinion," and "children are neither to be seen *nor heard*." I felt dumb, because it appeared that nothing I could say had any value to anyone growing up, although school seemed to fix that issue, as well as understanding that the baby of the family is the least likely birth position to be listened to growing up, due to their lack of experience compared with other family members. Also, as a child, I felt I had no influence on what happened to me, let alone had any influence on what happened to others. I stayed quiet in order to survive and didn't ask questions to stay out of trouble.

According to Hendrix, what we did in order to survive caused us to develop what he calls our "false self" and dictated how we responded in our relationship as a child and how we respond in our adult relationships in an unconscious relationship. As a child, I would withdraw, become sad, depressed, compliant, a chameleon, trying to be whatever it was I thought the authority figures wanted and would repress personal needs, as I knew they would not be met. This led me to be a caretaker and enabler as an adult.

Where Hendrix and I differed was that, although he strongly encouraged that, while single, we learn how to live with ourselves, be content being alone by ourselves, and learn to take care of ourselves, he insisted that the only way to truly heal was to be in a marriage relationship and go through that power struggle where both enter into greater intimacy by both becoming conscious of what is transpiring and helping one another through. Thus, he encourages us to go ahead and follow our heart as it leads us to that person we have chemistry with, because as long as there are no such things as arranged marriages in the United States, the chemistry will only lead us to continue doing the same thing, and marriage is the only way to break through as we "die" to our old way of relating.

After being married to a controlling, angry man and realizing that less than 1% of misogynists ever change because they are simply *not interested in working with you*, I knew there was no way I would accept marriage to another guy like that, as it would be impossible to ever break through the power struggle into intimacy with that type of person. At least this explained why my "picker" was broken, but I was determined there had to be another way of becoming healthy without actually marrying. I believe Hendrix's theory would work well within a less dysfunctional partnership than what I had experienced, but when it's life and death (and especially for some women who are attracted to men who can and will actually beat them to death), this simply will not work. Yet I couldn't dismiss much of his theory, because it was too good. I prayed about it and came up with a way to add to what he had used without being married.

Since I was living next door to Terry, why not explain some of this to him and ask him to assist with his thoughts and views? The thought the Lord put on my heart was this: the one you have chemistry with is the only one who can "push your buttons," which causes you to relive those negative messages from childhood. Even though Terry and I were just friends, there was a kind of chemistry in the relationship. What if our relationships were designed to "conform us to the image of God's Son" (Romans 8:29 and 2 Corinthians 3:18) and, in doing this, we discover there is man's way which is counterfeit and defeating, versus God's way, which truly does lead to intimacy. What if God does want to bring us "back to the scene of the crime" or wounding, and the way to win us through is to relive those negative messages with that person, but now with a more mature, adult response, rather than how we did as a child? Although I had already gone through that list of negative messages once, the first time worked more on the *vertical* relationship between me and God, but now, I needed to go through it again, this time through the *horizontal* relationships. This time, I could use what I had learned from the Harville Hendrix books.

A few days later, before that final spring semester had started, I popped in to Terry's office to ask him something, and he looked up at me and said in an agitated voice, "When does school start back for you?"

I was heartbroken. I went back to the duplex and started crying. Then I realized, "Hey, silly, he just *pushed your button!*" So I got a pad of paper and a pen out and began to write.

> What did he actually say?
> What did I "hear," the negative message from childhood?
> What was my survival response?
> What does God want me to do?

Negative Messages Relived...

Statement: "When does school start back for you?" (I wish it would hurry up.)

Message: "Go find someone else – I can't and don't want to meet your needs... **you're a burden**."

Survival Responses: Withdraw; feel sad, depressed, and hurt; repress needs; be a chameleon; be whatever he wants in order to try to please and be at peace.

What God wants me to do: "When I was a child, I spake as a child, I understood as a child, I thought as a child, but when I became an adult, I put away childish things." 1 Corinthians 13:11 (KJV)

When I was a child, I survived through my false self and lost my true self. Now that I'm an adult, I will *put away the survival mechanisms of my childhood* and learn a new way of relating by letting my true self come out. *Who we are* is quite different than *what we did to survive*. We must choose, and just as there was a power struggle between the spirit and the flesh, there is once again a power struggle and we must choose which one will prevail – who I am (my identity in Christ) or what I did to survive.

How I do this:

1. Forgive your parents: They could not give you something that they may never have received themselves. If you don't, "a root of bitterness" (Hebrews 12:15) may come up whereby many are "defiled."
2. Allow God to take you back "to the scene of the crime" by reliving your negative messages – this time, *consciously*, by asking your partner to help you:
    Write down:
    What did my partner actually say that pushed my button.
    What did I hear - a negative message from childhood.
    How did I respond? (Survival mechanisms – (false self)

What could they have really been saying? (Die to self).

Possible Answers From Terry's (and God's) viewpoint:

1. Develop your own identity.
2. Don't make Terry the center of your life.
3. Take responsibility for your own success.
4. Give Terry space.
5. Ask for small things that Terry *is* willing to give – a hug, a few minutes a week, etc.
6. Realize that the power of his influence is not the same as him being the center of your life.
7. Fill intimacy needs through others.
8. Look at the situation from his point of view; did I violate his personal boundaries?
9. Ask for specific boundaries – once a day, twice a week, etc. He was not saying don't *ever* come over, he was not rejecting you, he may have been saying "Ouch! You've stepped into *my* space and are violating *my* boundaries."
10. Realize that he is not your mother/father, and he does not have the same motives.

After realizing that I may have overstepped Terry's boundaries, I went back next door to ask for sure and to apologize. Sure enough, that was *exactly* what had happened. He wasn't rejecting me, he was simply saying "Ouch," and wanted to re-establish his boundaries, which was obviously something new for me to realize.

Terry "pushed my button" a total of thirteen times over the next few weeks and months, and each time, I would do as I had done before, writing down what he said, what I "heard," how I responded, and then prayed to ask God's wisdom as to what really was being said. After the thirteenth time, when all those negative messages had been gone through, something happened. There was a realization that, even though my dad had been dead for many years, I was carrying some issues I had had with him that needed to be dealt with. So I had an imaginary conversation with him as though he were sitting in the room with me.

"Daddy, there was nothing wrong with the love I had for you as a five- or six-year-old child. It was a perfect, childlike love. Your inability to love me in return was not my fault. The problem was on your side."

Suddenly, it was as though a weight was lifted off of me and another shackle released. Although I lived in that duplex next to Terry's office for nine years, from that day forward, from that very moment, I was no longer attracted to angry, controlling men.

Man's Ways	God's Ways
"You make me complete."	"You are complete in Him." Colossians 2:10
"I need you to fulfill my needs."	God will supply all your need. Phil. 4:19
"I need you to make me happy."	Happiness is taking responsibility for your own life and happiness through God's direction.
Goal: To win them over	Goal: To win you through and conform you to the image of Christ. Romans 8:28,29
Intimacy is obtained through sex	Dying to self as answer to power struggle results in greater intimacy Gal. 2:20/I Cor. 13:11
Marriage is a picture of convenience.	Marriage is a picture of Christ and the Church, His Bride – Ephesians 5
Marriage is a contract that can be broken.	Marriage is a covenant that must not be broken.

HOMEWORK:

- Do you understand that there is partial truth in the criticism(s) from your partner concerning you? The reason you feel like you would almost die if you gave into them is because you are hearing a negative message from childhood, when you were physically, financially, and emotionally helpless and completely dependent on your caregivers.

- You are no longer that helpless child. You are an adult now, with the capacity for adult responses. If they have "pushed your button," then they simply reminded you of one of those negative messages from childhood. They are NOT your previous caretakers, and they do not have the same motives. Knowing this should free you to open up and become more vulnerable to what they are *really* trying to say to you.

- Write down what they said, what you emotionally "heard," how you responded, and then what God through them is trying to say to you to help you respond in an emotionally adult way. Your tendency is to respond the same way you did as a child, and that is the only way you were able to *survive,* but God is calling you to *abundant living,* not merely *existing.*

- Child of God, if there is only one thing you get out of this book, it is this very truth. Try it! Taste and see that the Lord is good to you!

The Blessing

I met a few great guys to date after that second divorce, and with two in particular I maintain a close friendship with today. The first was Richard, with whom I have been friends for more than twenty years now. Richard was the second of four brothers and is one of the smartest and funniest guys I've ever met. Although we only dated a short time, I introduced him to ballroom dancing and taught him how to dance, which he took to like a duck to water. He was an airline pilot and lived in Jacksonville, Texas, just south of Tyler, where I lived at the time. He flew 747s and was gone at least seventeen days every month. This made it difficult for him to develop any close friendships, let alone develop any love interests. He really seemed to enjoy the ballroom dance atmosphere and the people there he met, so in the end, he became one of my very best friends, and I became like the sister he never had. It seemed that everything Richard touched in the business world turned to gold, and thus, he was able to retire early from the airlines and invest in businesses in the Jacksonville area. He became my mentor in business and encouraged me for years to go into the rental business as a landlord as he had done, which I finally did for more than ten years a few years later. I would walk with him through his relationships and become the best friend his dates never knew they could have. We would both teach any girl he would be interested in how to dance and we would often double date. Richard would be the one who would help Jeff Kamel and me to start up our own ballroom dance club, and Richard and I currently lead that club, called the Venetian Ballroom Dance Club.

Once Richard left the airline and became established in Jacksonville, he joined the local Rotary Club, where he met a fellow named Jerry. Jerry was divorced, and Richard suggested that we meet. When I first met Jerry, I really didn't have any interest in him. A couple of years later, though,

Richard suffered a relationship breakup and really seemed to slip into a temporary emotional slump, and both Jerry and I came to his side to walk with him through those few months. I spent a lot of time getting to know Jerry as we helped Richard during those few months, and that was when I really became attracted to Jerry. He was the firstborn in his family and he had, not one, but *three sisters*. I would really get to see if any of that birth order business about a firstborn male and the influence of sisters had any veracity or not. Jerry was very smart and just as funny as Richard, and between the two, they kept me in stitches laughing.

Jerry was completely different from either of my two husbands and was and is a very nice guy. I could tell that I was finally becoming compatible with someone who was really easy going and who didn't have anger issues directed toward me. I could really see the difference that growing up with sisters made in his life as compared with the two men I had married; it was night-and-day different. Jerry and I discussed at length the things I had been learning about chemistry in relationships, and we talked about our marriage failures and things we had learned while dating. I shared with Jerry what my previous pattern had been, and he shared his. Jerry's pattern had been to rescue women, but I didn't need rescuing. So Jerry would be the first guy I dated who had sisters and was not like my previous husbands, and I was the first girl he dated that didn't need rescuing and was not like his previous relationships.

Jerry and I would date off and on for *six years,* until June 2004, which was a longer relationship than either of my marriages lasted, but in the end, he simply could not give me what I wanted most – his heart. I could not fault him for that and realized that, just as my sister, Penny could see she wasn't ready for Mr. Nice Guy, Jerry's heart wasn't ready for a woman who didn't need rescuing. I could see my own homework would include more time and work in healing over the influence of my father who was not emotionally available to me. I told Jerry to pray for the day that he could be attracted to a woman who didn't need rescuing and I would pray for the day that I would be attracted to another Mr. Nice Guy with sisters who would be able to be more emotionally vulnerable with me. I am happy to say that all three of us – Richard, Jerry, and myself, came out winners in the end, although it would be another six years before I would marry.

Richard later married a fantastic, incredibly smart woman named Nancy, whom I told him was the most compatible woman I had seen him with during the more than twenty years I have known him. They were married in September 2012, and she has become a wonderful ballroom dancer as well as a fabulous cook and friend.

Jerry met an awesome woman named Carol, who is one of the most vivacious women I've ever met, and she *doesn't need rescuing!* When he told me about her and how he was attracted to her, when he introduced me to her, I jumped for joy, because it was obvious he had finally completed his homework too. She is smart, happy, and full of joy and is the life of the party wherever they go. They have been dating since January 2012, over two years now, and we are all hoping for the very best for them.

We are all part of a Tuesday night dinner club that meets every week at a different restaurant in Jacksonville and thus, we plan to remain in contact and as close friends for years to come. The dinner club started with some of the couples that Richard and Jerry met through Rotary and has included other couples in the Jacksonville, Texas area we have met through the years. Although Richard, Jerry, and I were single, there were four other couples in the group that had been married for years:

George and Jean had been married for fifty years, Raymond and Cindy had been married for forty years, John and Luz had been married for over thirty years, and Dick and Debra had been married for sixteen years. I really got to have a good look at the men who were devoted to their wives and how they interacted, and it provides a great example for me, even to this day. I watched George as he would take months to search for just the right gift for his wife, Jean. I watched John's devotion to Luz as she endured months and even years of health issues. I watched Dick's adoring eyes toward Debra and her devotion to him in return. I'll never forget the night that Cindy was fifteen minutes late for our weekly dinner and Raymond threw down his napkin and ran out the door with great concern on his face to go search for her. Cindy would later report that she had locked herself out of the house and thus had no key or phone and was sitting at the next-door neighbor's house, knowing Raymond would look for her, which he did.

I figured it would be a good thing to bring any guy I would date to the Tuesday night dinner club, as it would be helpful to undergo the scrutiny of our friends to determine how compatible we would be, and it turned out to be very helpful.

During the time I was dating Jerry, I was still living in the duplex next to Terry Danielson, and Terry's assistant was a deacon at his church and invited me to attend. It was a non-denominational church, and I thought it would be interesting to check it out. I was still rather dejected by the fact that I had failed God and didn't think I could ever again have anything of value to offer God's people. As I walked into the service, someone was giving a "word of knowledge" from the Lord in a deep booming voice that burrowed into my heart.

He repeated again and again, "I have not disqualified you... *I* have not disqualified you... I have *not* disqualified you..."

Suddenly, I could contain it no longer, and tears began to stream down my face as I whispered, "Lord, is it *really* possible that I'm not disqualified? Is it really possible that You can *ever* use me again? Will You *ever* get a return on Your investment?" I visited that church a few more times and enjoyed the people I met but continued on with the search for a message and a place where I would really fit in and be an asset and encouragement to others. My desire was to attend a church that didn't necessarily have any Deaf that were attending, but who were open to how signing songs in sign language could enhance the worship service.

In the summer of 2003, the year before I would move to Jacksonville, I started attending a church in downtown Tyler, Texas, that had a nice-sized singles group. It was led by a wonderful woman named Pat Mallory who is precious to me for many, many reasons. On the very first morning I met her, I volunteered to assist in any way I could. We had lunch together that week and shared our backgrounds, and she asked me to begin teaching again. There were three or four other teachers who would take turns each week, thus you would only teach once a month, so it became a great way to ease back into teaching as well as an opportunity to hear the wonderful teaching that these other gifted leaders provided.

In the fall of 2003, many of the churches in the Tyler area were offering the 40 Days of Purpose small group Bible studies incorporated from the book, The Purpose Driven Life,[31] by Pastor Rick Warren. It was an extremely popular Bible study that was being done nationwide, and it was so well received at the church I was attending that they decided to incorporate one of the Bible study sequels in the spring in lieu of Sunday evening services. Pat Mallory asked all of the teachers in the Singles Department to be facilitators along with most of the other Sunday School teachers in other departments throughout the church.

The Sunday we were going to begin the Bible study sequel in early 2004, I was sitting in the pew before the morning service started, thumbing through the hymnal, looking at the songs we would sing during the service. The hymnal opened to one song that brought me to a sudden stop. It was called, "Pass It On" by Kurt Kaiser.

Boy! That sure takes me back, I thought. I had a memory from 1969, when it was written, of my seventh grade choir teacher from junior high in Waco, Texas, who introduced it to us, the very year it was written! I hadn't seen the song in all those years, nor Mr. Harding. Marveling as I looked, I could still remember those words:

> "It only takes a spark to get a fire going.
> And soon all those around, will warm up in its glowing.
> That's how it is with God's love, once you've experienced it.
> You want to sing, it's fresh like spring.
> You want to pass it on." [32]

I remembered that this teacher, Mr. Harding, was the only person in my entire childhood who had shared Christ with me, and because of his influence, I accepted Christ as my Savior early the next fall after seventh grade. As I wondered how he was doing, the service started, and I closed the hymnal and forgot all about it – until that evening at the Bible study.

That night, the very first question we discussed was: Who have you influenced for Christ? Of course, we all thought about 1 Corinthians 3:7, referencing one who plants and one who waters, but God gets the increase. We all wondered, as we discussed, if we would ever know, this side of Heaven, who we may have influenced for Christ and what a blessing it would be to know.

Then, His gracious Holy Spirit laid upon our hearts this thought: *Instead of seeking the blessing of knowing who you influenced for Christ – why don't you seek to thank the one who influenced you for Christ?*

"Wow!! What a great idea!" we surmised. Instantly, I remembered that morning and thought, *Okay, Lord, that's twice today. I get it. Once again, that would be my seventh grade choir teacher, Mr. Harding! It will be great fun to try to find him. This will be a nice way of saying, "Thanks!"*

That very evening, I went home and got on the Internet. Sure enough, there was no Claude Harding in Waco, Texas, but there were three in the state of Texas – one in south Texas, one in west Texas, and one who lived just north of Houston. I thought I'd try the one closest to Houston, as that was closer to Waco than the other two.

I dialed the number and a man answered, "Hello?"

Hello, is this Claude Harding?" I responded.

"Why, yes it is," he replied. I felt chills, because I actually felt like I was recognizing his voice – one I hadn't heard in over thirty-five years, but I wasn't sure.

"Well, I'm not sure if I have the right Claude Harding," I replied, "but if I do, then this is a voice from more than thirty five years ago!," I gleefully added.

There was dead silence on the other end of the phone.

I continued, "Now, the Claude Harding I am looking for used to be a seventh grade choir teacher at Tennison Jr. High in Waco, Texas, and the reason I am calling is that I wanted to thank..."

He interrupted me before I could finish the sentence.

"This is either Felicia Mouldin, Susan Sperling, or Janice Turnbaugh," he replied. Now there was dead silence on my end of the phone.

With a trembling voice, I responded, "Mr. Harding, this is Susan... but how could you possibly know that? It's been more than thirty-five years, and hundreds of kids went through that school, and Lord only knows how many years that you taught!"

"Oh no, Susan," he responded. "I only taught *one year,* and then I served in Vietnam, and during that one year, the Lord laid on my heart three little girls to pray for, and I've wondered *all these years,* what became of you girls!"

I was filled with chills, then amazement, and then tears of joy as I shared with Mr. Harding that I indeed had been saved that very year, and that Felicia had been my best friend during junior high. I explained that we moved away to Dallas when my dad died the following year, and I had lost contact with everyone from school. I could only wonder who got the blessing that day – it went *both ways,* and on *this* side of Heaven!

I went to see Mr. Harding that summer to thank him in person for his influence for Christ upon my life. He was the song director at a small church just north of Houston. As I walked through the doors of that church after not seeing him for all those years, you will never guess what song he was leading the choir to practice for the morning service....

> "It only takes a spark, to get a fire going.
> And soon all those around, can warm up in its glowing.
> That's how it is with God's love, once you've experienced it.
> You want to sing, it's fresh like spring.
> You want to pass it on."

HOMEWORK:

- Isn't it time for you to thank the person who influenced you for Christ? Who knows? Maybe you, too, will be blessed on this side of Heaven.

Rejoicing in Heaven

Through the summer of 2003 and into the spring of 2004, I could tell that changes were coming. Terry Danielson moved away to Arlington, Texas, in the early fall of 2003, after selling his business and his home. He offered to sell me the two duplexes where his office and the portion I lived in were, along with the one next door, but after praying about it, I decided against it. I did begin to get into the rental business, however, with the influence of my friend Richard. I bought a couple of small, two-bedroom single-family rental homes in Jacksonville, just south of Tyler, and rehabbed and rented them to help towards retirement. In January 2004, I only paid six months of renter's insurance where I was living in Terry's duplex with the thought on my heart that I might not be there much longer. Sure enough, in late May, a great buy on a small three-bedroom house in Jacksonville came on the market, and I pounced the morning after it was listed and made an offer. So, in June 2004, after nine years of living in the duplex, I would now own my own home and would be close to the other two to oversee these rentals and two others I would later purchase. My friend, Terry, would later pass away suddenly of a heart attack, on December 26, 2004. He was a dear friend who would be greatly missed.

Although I hated to leave the singles ministry and Pat Mallory in Tyler, I knew I would need to find a church home in Jacksonville and began to visit different churches during the summer of 2004. When I walked through the doors of the third church I visited, I knew I was home. There was such a sense of freedom and warmth present, and their singles department was pretty similar to Pat Mallory's. When I walked into the sanctuary for the first time, it was as though I was sitting in a miniature Green Acres which I had not been in over twenty years, and during the song service, I felt led to freely sign a couple of the worship songs in the pew

196

where we stood and sang together just to joyfully worship God. The pastor, Brother Bruce, was a dynamic preacher, and his message was inspiring.

On the Thursday following that first visit, I received a phone call from the choir director who had searched for the visitor card I had filled out. His name was Kelvin and he was a marvelous choir director, and the music that morning (and every Sunday afterward) was just the best. The words he spoke confirmed what I had already sensed when I first walked through the doors of that church, the words that I had been waiting for twenty years to hear, and they sealed my decision of where my church home would be in Jacksonville from that day forward.

"I saw you Sunday morning out in the sanctuary signing to a couple of the songs we were singing during the service, and they really made the songs more worshipful. I know you were just a visitor, and we don't have any deaf that attend our church, but would you *ever* consider coming and signing a special with our choir some time?" It was music to my ears. I joined Central in September 2004, after completing the church year as a teacher for Pat Mallory in Tyler.

The rest of 2004 and all of 2005 were filled with joy and peace and some truly strange yet wonderful events. After seeing Mr. Harding, my seventh grade choir teacher, in the summer of 2004, I ran into many of the wonderful Christians who had influenced my life so profoundly over a two-year period, including John Morris; Lori Haynes, the nine year old who had worn braces during her childhood who had moved away and then moved back to the East Texas area; Eva Aills, a girl who had been in the high school Sunday School class I had taught at that first church; and several others. I could sense that these were happening to remind me and prepare me for something to come, some kind of test in which I would need to be reminded of God's faithfulness in the past. I wasn't sure what that would be, but I reveled in one divine appointment after another of running into these old friends and a chance to say thanks to those who had meant so much and to catch up with what God had been doing in their lives. During that same time period, a different kind of divine appointment occurred through the singles department at Central, right in the middle of all the destruction and heartache between two hurricanes on Labor Day weekend 2005.

Hurricane Katrina occurred on August 23, 2005, and Hurricane Rita occurred on September 18, 2005. Our singles department had been scheduled for months to attend a singles retreat at Alto Frio, just west of San Antonio. As the weekend approached, news accounts were coming in daily of the New Orleans Superdome overflowing with victims and the Houston Astrodome filling to capacity. It would only be a matter of days before new sites would be needed to help with the overflow, and the Alto Frio retreat had several hundred beds which could be used.

Our church had already sent numerous groups of men to New Orleans with chainsaws to help clean up in the aftermath of Hurricane Katrina, and the church was also housing dozens of refugees with cots in the family life center. Our singles group offered to surrender our beds at the retreat for those potentially overflowing from Houston, but the leadership at Alto Frio told us that half the facility would be donated on the following weekend after we left and that the singles retreat would meet as scheduled.

I still felt somewhat guilty for going to have fun when so many were suffering, and we had no idea what was planned or who would be speaking during the three-day event. I asked the Lord to make it clear to us that it was His will for us to be there.

The morning we were to leave, I went to Wal-mart to see if there might be any interesting books to read on the way down there, as it would be a six- to eight-hour drive. I figured we would all visit awhile and then settle in, where some would nap, which would be a great time to settle in and read.

There was one book that kept grabbing my attention as I perused all the different titles. I kept coming back to it and finally went ahead and picked it up and took it with me. After we all loaded into the van and took off, we visited awhile, and then I settled in to read. After about an hour, my roommate asked me what I was reading. I told her it was a very interesting book about a pastor who lived close to the area we were passing through and how he had been driving from a pastor's conference and was hit by an eighteen wheeler crossing a bridge, where he was pronounced dead at the scene.

The Lord led another pastor who had been at the same conference to stop and pray for the "dead man." After some time of prayer, the man came to, and later recounted what he had seen during his death experience. I told her the name of the book was 90 Minutes in Heaven,[33] by Don Piper.

Jackie, our singles director, told us that this name sounded really familiar for some reason. She thought about it a minute and then pulled out some paperwork and exclaimed, "Good grief, he's the keynote speaker for the entire weekend at the retreat!" Wow! What a confirmation! Obviously the Lord *did* want us to attend that conference for a specific reason.

When we arrived, we met Don Piper that very evening and told him what had transpired concerning his book and he was just as excited as we were. All weekend, we felt that something special would happen, but were not for sure what that would be.

We were all invited to join a group going to the local state park on Sunday afternoon to minister to the local residents with face painting, Frisbee toss, hot dogs, and a gospel survey. Those of us doing the questionnaires went out in groups of twos. When the Lord said that "the fields are ripe unto the harvest" (John 4:35), we had no idea we would see this firsthand.

When we walked over to the very first family camping next to our group, less than one hundred yards away, we realized why the Lord wanted us there this particular weekend. It was a Hispanic family of five, with three women and two men. Two of the women were in their twenties and the third was their grandmother. They spoke in broken English and we spoke in broken Spanish, but when we completed the survey, the three women wanted to know more. We shared the plan of salvation and *all three women prayed to receive Christ as their Savior!* One of the younger women stood there with tears streaming down her cheeks.

They were tears of joy as she shared in her broken English, "I come to United States few weeks ago from Central America to see family. It took many days to get here. After I get here, I hear Christian radio station for first time. I've been listening every day. It do something in my heart but I not know what to do about it – until today. Thank you for coming today and telling us about Jesus."

When we left the park a couple of hours later, the grandmother was still studying the Bible study pamphlet in Spanish we had left with them. When we got back, we shared with Don Piper and the entire group what had transpired, and others shared their stories of what happened with their surveys, and we rejoiced together as we learned of the numerous people who were led to Christ that Sunday afternoon in the state park.

Whenever I am tempted to think that our God can't possibly take the time to consider the trials and tribulations of just one of us and to commune with us, especially in light of what is happening in a world filled with a war in Iraq and Afghanistan, threats from North Korea, earthquakes here and there, etc., I pause and remember how He brought five singles from Jacksonville, Texas, between two hurricanes, just to share the love of His Son with our three new sisters in Christ. His Word will not return unto Him void, but will accomplish His purpose, and so we can be assured that the new Word for all those others that day as well as that which was hid in these sisters' hearts will also be carried back to Mexico and to Central America and beyond, to be planted and sown into the fertile ground of waiting hearts.

HOMEWORK:

- Are you aware of the opportunity to witness through divine appointments set before you by God? Are you willing to be used in this manner?

- What great story is there to be told about the divine appointments in your life?

What Is Your Name?

The year 2006 was one of the toughest years I went through. I've never passed any of the Lord's tests with flying colors, and this certainly would be no exception. It was the year I had my fiftieth birthday, and I was tested physically, emotionally, and spiritually, all at the same time. At work, I was offered a job promotion to become an instructor for the postal service in Norman, Oklahoma, but after much prayer, I turned it down because the Lord laid on my heart the need to remain close to my mother to take care of her, as I lived the closest to her of all six of her children. She lived only twenty-five miles away in Frankston, Texas. She had suffered a stroke, and although she had recovered about eighty-five percent of her physical movement, I knew it was very comforting to have someone close by who checked on her on a daily basis.

Health wise, I also suffered some setbacks. In 2004, I had fallen off a chair, broken a rib, and bruised a kidney. Then, I unknowingly got into a hot tub that was infected, causing me to get pseudomonal folliculitis. It created such a shock to my body, I then contracted a light case of shingles. The doctors could only figure out the broken rib and bruised kidney and could see the shingles, but didn't know what was causing the continued welts all over my body, but my younger sister, Penny, who had previously worked as a respiratory therapist figured it out and told me it was the hot tub. I then was able to get the proper medications to treat it.

Unfortunately, the condition had caused a different problem that didn't show up until 2006. Every time I got my teeth cleaned, I would be ill afterward for weeks. When I talked with the dentist and hygienist, they thought I was crazy, but it was logical to me that the hygienist was so thorough and would cause all my gums to bleed that it was stirring up something that was making me sick, but I just didn't know what or why. I decided to start looking for a hygienist who was gentler in cleanings.

When we had a family reunion that year, about a month after one of those teeth cleanings, my oldest sister Monica, who was an RN, saw just how sick I was. The doctors had tested me for all kinds of conditions but couldn't figure out what was wrong. During the reunion, I became so weak, I could barely walk. After watching me for two days, Monica suggested that I get tested for H-pylori, which doctors at that time believed was caused by drinking impure water in third-world countries. When I was tested, I tested positive, and the doctor figured it was most likely a lingering consequence from that infected hot tub. Needless to say, I don't ever get in hot tubs anymore; hot tubs are just huge petri dishes of bacteria unless extremely monitored for cleanliness. Also, since that time, dentists and hygienists are trained in most of the larger cities to watch for these types of symptoms in their patients as they are clues to other health issues, especially before doing major dental work. I was given a three-fold group of antibiotics and later recovered. However, I was still very wary about having my teeth cleaned.

I was also tested emotionally and spiritually, as during this same time period, I saw two relationships end. One was with a girlfriend that I had known briefly and one was with a guy I dated for a short time who was the brother of one of the most awesome families in our church. At the same time, the teaching ministry I was involved in suffered a drastic change due to a decision that took me almost a year to make but had became absolutely necessary, and I later changed departments and teaching assignments. Later, in the fall of 2006, I was asked to lead the Ladies' Bible studies on Sunday evenings, which I absolutely fell in love with, but our beloved pastor, Brother Bruce, accepted a call to another city, leaving a huge hole in all our hearts later that year. Thus, spring and summer and into the fall were times of tremendous testing. While none of these events by themselves were insurmountable, when added together, they brought a serious time of self-examination and crying out to God for greater intimacy with Him. It led to an even greater depth of hunger and seeking that I hadn't experienced since that three-and-a-half-year quest when I first started back to church at age twenty-four. It was here that the Lord began to show me more of that progressive revelation of our relationship with Him.

As new Christians, we obey the Lord simply because He is our Lord, or Master. As we go through our wilderness experiences, (which we've learned are the places and circumstances that God uses to create the opportunity to get to know Him and His Ways more intimately), we see in the New Testament that this greater intimacy, *which He pursues in us,* leads Him to no more call us slaves, but friends, according to John 15:15. When mere friendship does not satisfy our soul, for many of us, we may become like John, who sought an even closer friendship to the Lord and referred to himself as the "disciple whom Jesus particularly loved" (John 13:23, Complete Jewish Bible translation). We then discover as many before us have discovered, Christ, the Bridegroom, our Heavenly Husband. As my earthly father was unable to show and teach me about men and relationships, the Lord would use this time in my life to continue His training to help me understand a clear and healthier view of marriage by looking again vertically at our relationship with Him. Here I could gain a better perspective for a later, horizontal relationship with another, one who would be emotionally available to me.

It was here that, first, I would look back again on my favorite Bible character, David. Specifically, I looked back to the time when he sat in the Cave of Failure, the cave of Adullam. He had been anointed as king years earlier and had been waiting on God for his time, had also killed a giant, married the king's daughter, and was serving the current king, Saul. All of a sudden, David had almost everything stripped away from him. David had to run for his life from Saul's jealousy, and in doing this, he lost his job and thus his income, he lost his wife as Saul married her off to someone else after David left, he lost his spiritual mentor, Samuel, who was too old to leave with David and who later died, and he lost his best friend, Jonathan, the king's son. He went to the cave of Adullam, where it appeared that all his dreams had died. Bill Gothard would call this spiritual event the "death of a vision." It seemed to me that all my dreams and desires were at an end as well. However, it was here that David would write Psalm 142, through which he cries out:

"I cry to You, O Lord; I say, You are my refuge, my portion in the land of the living. Listen to my cry, for I am in desperate need... set me free from *my prison,* that I may praise Your name." (Psalm 142:5-7).

It was here that the group of misfits formed around him who later became a great and mighty army. It was here that David saw and I saw that, even when everything is stripped away from you, when you have God, that is enough. Even though my heart's desire was for marriage, having God as my Heavenly Father and Christ as my Heavenly Husband would be enough.

It was the place where I could sit quietly and say, "Lord, I love you, and even if I never have the opportunity to marry again, I will still love You."

The Lord began to show me more of what He intends as our Heavenly Husband. Due to being married to an emotionally distant, yet verbally abusive man, I hated the words "submit" or "follow." Those words were something you did only out of fear, and they led to resentment and rebellion from being imprisoned. The Lord had shown me that it was the goodness of God that leads us to repentance (Romans 2:4). This was why I was able to submit to Him, not out of fear and terror, as had been the case when I was growing up, but because I was *loved* into submission and I *desired* to follow One who would demonstrate such love for me. The Lord reminded me of this as I was led to read Isaiah 54: 4-6 (NIV):

"Do not be afraid, you will not suffer shame. Do not fear disgrace, you will not be humiliated. You will forget the shame of your youth... *For your Maker is Your Husband*, the Lord of Hosts is His name... The Lord will call you back as a wife distressed in spirit, a wife who married... only to be rejected."

The Lord began to show me that just as our Heavenly Father desires and pursues a place to rest in us, and we in Him, as our Heavenly Husband, He pursues us with the desire to cleave to us. I was dating men who were unable to "cleave," so the Lord took me back to the beginning, to Genesis, to show His intent. In Genesis 2:18, the Lord said, "It is not good for a man to be alone. I will make for him a companion suitable for helping him." But God didn't create Eve right after that. He did something rather odd. Instead of creating a helper, companion, God created all the animals and birds and paraded them before Adam. In doing so, it is noted that once they were all paraded before Adam and Adam gave them names, God says, "but for Adam, no suitable helper was found." (Genesis 2:20, NIV) Is it possible that God was awakening Adam's desire for a helpmate by having him see that none of the rest of creation was suitable? Is it possible that God was "freeing me up" for a more suitable and intimate relationship with Him, by having the doors close to so many areas of my life that year? Was it His way of awakening my desire for greater intimacy, by showing me that none of those things were suitable?

When Adam sees Eve and understands she was taken from his rib, he says, "*At last!* This is bone from my bones and flesh from my flesh. She is to be called woman because she was taken out of man." (Genesis 2:23 Complete Jewish Bible) Now I don't know about you, but I've always figured it would have made more sense if the next verse said, "This is why a *woman* is to leave her father and mother and *follow* her husband, and they are to be one flesh," but it doesn't say that at all. I mean, we live in a patriarchal society, and it certainly was that way in Biblical times as well, so it comes across to me as somewhat odd when God says, "for this reason a *man* shall leave his father and mother and *cleave* to his *wife,* and they are to be one flesh" (Genesis 2:24, KJV). Not only is Adam's desire for a suitable companion awakened when Eve is presented to him after viewing all of creation, but he also exclaims, "At last!" So, from the *beginning,* except for God, Himself, this woman who is presented to him is seen as someone the man forsakes all others for and *cleaves* to for the rest of his life!

So what does *cleave* mean? To find out, I brought out the old faithful Strong's Concordance, and was I ever enlightened! To "cleave" means "To impinge or have an effect or impact; to *make steady inroads,* to cling to or adhere, *to catch by pursuit,* to abide fast, hold fast together, follow close or *to be hard after,* be joined, to glue to, to be in motions toward, to keep company."

Now this doesn't mean a man merely pursues a woman until she marries him; no, these words are said about a man and his *wife.* He is to cleave to his *wife,* to be in constant pursuit of and keeping company with his wife. Well, no wonder I was still having trouble locating a suitable companion; the ones I had been looking at, for whatever reason, did not have the capacity to cleave to me. I would need to learn to be able to recognize men with the capacity to cleave, as this is what our Heavenly Husband does with us! How can you *not* submit and follow a God who is in constant pursuit of you, who is hard after your heart and desires to keep constant company with you!! We are the Bride of Christ and He is our Heavenly Husband!

The Lord would add even more to this to increase my (and your) desire for Him. In Hosea 2:14-16 (KJV), it says this:

"Therefore *I am now going to allure her*; I will lead her into the *desert* (there's that wilderness again!) and speak *tenderly to her*. There I will give her back her vineyards, and *will make the Valley of Achor (Trouble) a door of hope*. There she will sing as in the days of her youth, as in the day she came up out of Egypt. In that day, declares the Lord, you will call me '*Ishi*'; you will no longer call me '*Baali*.'"

The word "Ishi" is seen only twice in Scripture. In 1 Chronicles 5:24, it is seen as one of the names of the sons who were descendants of the half-tribe of Manasseh who were mighty men of valor. The only other time this word is seen is when it is used here, in Hosea. According to the Strong's Concordance, "Ishi" means "To be extant or still in existence, a *husband* in the flower of his age, a champion, a worthy, and great and mighty man."

We will no more call Him *Baali*. "Baali" in the Strong's Concordance means "One who has dominion over you; one to whom it is due, your master." Tears began to stream down my face as I began to see how the Lord was revealing Himself as our Heavenly Husband. "Baali" was who I had been married to in the past; men who sought to only have *dominion* over me, to *boss* me and show me *what was due to them*. That is *not* what God intends for us! He doesn't want us to view our relationship with Him in that way or our relationships with one another in that manner. He is our "Ishi," our husband in the flower of his years who is *our* great and mighty champion!

In the fall of 2006, a couple of days before my fiftieth birthday, I received another surprise, one that seemed to be the culmination of all the previous months, if not *years* of testing. I was watching television on Sunday morning while getting ready for church. I usually listened to either Charles Stanley, David Jeremiah, or Jentezen Franklin. That morning, one of the sermons was about Jacob and the struggle he had all night with the Angel of the Lord from Genesis 32:24-32. What grabbed my attention was when the pastor suggested that the biggest test for Jacob was *not* the struggle that lasted the entire night. The test for Jacob was at daybreak the next morning, *after* wrestling with the Angel of the Lord and *after* having his hip socket dislocated.

Jacob's biggest test was in the form of a question: "What is your name?"

In the Bible, a person's name was extremely significant. Often, a person's name was viewed as the equivalent to the person, himself, describing his character and reputation as well as his *future*. The name Jacob meant "heel catcher" and was given during Jacob's birth as the second of two twins when he grabbed hold of Esau's heel (Genesis 25:26). It also meant "supplanter" (to take the place of, as through force or scheming); thus, to take by the heel to circumvent as if tripping up the heels or to restrain by holding by the heel. This would very well describe Jacob's life, one of trickery, scheming, and deception, until he was "tripped up" by the Angel of the Lord that night. God could see different potential within Jacob, who would be in the lineage of Christ, but it would take a holy wrestling match to bring him to the place where Jacob was willing to make a confession. That confession came from the realization Jacob had of who he was wrestling with and the refusal to let go until he received a blessing. Jacob knew it was the Angel of the Lord, because in verse 30, he names the place where this occurs, Peniel, as he had seen the Lord face to face and still lived. The blessing Jacob would receive was the result of his confession to the angel's question: "What is your name?"

"Jacob," the supplanter, one who schemes to trip up other people through deception. That's who and what he had been. That was the greatest test – owning up to who he really was. After fifteen years of singleness and all the struggling, hearing this brought me to my knees in tears and conviction.

"Lord, my name is Quitter!!" As the tears streamed down my face, there was relief in truly owning up to what my life had previously spelled out. I knelt there for several minutes, weeping and confessing, and weeping once more.

Then you have the giving of a new name. In most instances, this was used to establish authority over a previously given name and to indicate a new beginning or a new direction in that person's life. Examples would be Abram to Abraham, Sarai to Sarah, Cephas to Peter, or Saul to Paul.

For Jacob, his name was changed to Israel, which, according to the Strong's Concordance, literally means "he will rule as God," but comes from two other meanings, strength and mighty as in the Almighty, and to prevail or to have power as a prince. Genesis 32:28 (KJV) confirms this when the Angel of the Lord says, "for as a prince hast thou power with God and with men, and hast prevailed."

Later that afternoon, I was reading in Isaiah again, and was looking again at those verses from chapter 54:4-6 where it says, "You will forget the *shame of your youth...*" and "The Lord will call you back as a wife distressed in spirit, *a wife who married... only to be rejected.*" The Lord continued on in Isaiah 61:7 (KJV): "*Instead* of their *shame,* my people will receive a *double portion,* and *instead* of *disgrace* they will rejoice in their *inheritance;* and so they will inherit a *double portion* in their land, and everlasting joy will be theirs."

I just love those "instead" verses in the Bible! There is a principle that is very clear which says, "As ye sow, so shall ye reap" (Galatians 6:7, KJV), as well as the verses which indicate that the sins of the fathers can become a curse that extends to the third and fourth generations (Numbers 14:18, Exodus 34:7). Then there are those words of grace – "Instead"; Instead of what was planted, instead of the expected consequences, sometimes, in grace, consequences can be changed.

"Even now, declares the Lord, *return to me with all your heart*, with fasting and weeping and mourning. Rend your heart and not your garments. Return to the Lord your God, for he is gracious and compassionate, slow to anger and abounding in love, and *he relents from sending calamity. Who knows? He may turn and have pity and leave behind a blessing*"
Joel 2:12-14 (KJV)

Instead of the thorn bush will grow the juniper and *instead* of briers, the myrtle will grow..."
Isaiah 55:13 (KJV)

In those verses in Isaiah 61 were those indications again of a "double portion" and an "inheritance." I knew God was and is our inheritance and my portion, and I had been seeing those verses for years about a double portion and remembered that Job received "double" after going through all his testing.

It was when I arrived at Isaiah 62:2-5 (NIV) that I gasped as His Holy Spirit caressed my bruised spirit. I would even be reminded of the word picture concerning boundaries by which we are each given a portion of land, and my land had been desolated in the past. Yet, more importantly, what brought tears of joy and wonder was the prospect of *a new name*. It was as though the Lord was saying, "Your name will no more be called 'Quitter' because:

"... you will be called by a *new name* that the mouth of the Lord will bestow. You will be a crown of splendor in the Lord's hand, a royal diadem in the hand of your God. *No longer will they call you Deserted, or name your land Desolate.* But you will be called *Hephzibah (my delight is in her)* and your *land Beulah (married)...* as a bridegroom rejoices over his bride, so will your God rejoice over you."

I began to shake all over. I whispered out loud to the Lord: "Is this really You, Lord? Do I really get a *new name?!* I'm not a "Quitter" anymore in Your eyes?! Are You really saying some day I will be *married??!!!*"

A peace came over me that I hadn't experienced in years, and that's when I got up and started doing house cleaning, going through dresser drawers and closets, to make sure there was room for whoever was to come. Then the idea hit me – wouldn't it be a great idea to have a wedding right in front of our ballroom dance group and surprise them! What fun!

HOMEWORK:

-   What is your name? What meaning has that been in your past? Do you desire a new name from the Lord? Are you ready to "own up" to your past? Have you experienced Christ as your Heavenly Husband? Isn't it time you did?

The Two-fold Dream

The year 2007 brought a new interim pastor to our church who was a kind, fatherly pastor named Brother Pete. I was enjoying being in a ladies' Sunday School class led by an awesome teacher named Pat Socia. Her father had been a pastor, and she was well-versed in the Bible, and probably the best Sunday School teacher I ever sat under. She asked me to be her substitute when she was out, which was a great honor to me. I loved being in this class, as she was and is a dynamic teacher, and we learned a great deal under her tutelage. It helped make up for how much we missed our beloved pastor, Brother Bruce.

One of the other "leading ladies" in the church was Lynda Sanderson, who was the director of the ladies ministry. She, too, was an awesome, loving, caring woman, and was very close to Pat Socia. Lynda had welcomed me the very first morning I had visited Central and had sat with me to make me feel at home. She approached me in late 2006, since I was only substituting at that time, and asked me to lead the Sunday evening ladies' Bible studies for the church starting in January 2007. One study would be on Wednesday mornings and the other on Sunday evenings, before the service. These would typically be the Beth Moore studies or something similar. I readily accepted.

A few months after Brother Pete had been there, he came to me with a surprising request. He had seen me signing an occasional song during the worship service and asked if I would consider starting a deaf ministry in the church. I told him that would be impossible, as I had not even been part of a deaf ministry in over twenty years and could only sign a few of the *slower* worship songs and that it takes years of practice to become an interpreter. Nonetheless, he wanted me to be in prayer about it and consider it. I felt honored that he had asked me, but didn't think there was even a remote possibility of doing that.

At that time we were doing a Beth Moore study called "Stepping Up,"[34] based on the Psalms. One of the daily homework studies was about sowing seeds and persevering until we see the harvest. Beth Moore noted that, when she had gone to Africa, although many of the people were given seeds to sow, a lot of the seed was merely eaten, thus they had nothing to plant for a later harvest, and thus, they remained in the captivity of poverty and hunger. She suggested that, as Christians, many of us do the same thing and do not apply God's Word into our realities, remaining in spiritual captivity or bondage. One way she suggested that we apply God's Word to our situation *or our desire* was by personalizing Psalm 126, and in that way, we were sowing God's Word into our lives. So my homework assignment went like this where I expressed the *dream of my heart*:

"When the Lord brought my *captive* soul to victory, I felt like I was in a *dream*. I was filled with laughter and joy. Others looked at the husband by my side and the joy in my heart and said to themselves – God has done great things for her! Your goodness flows like streams in the Negev, Oh, Lord! You have restored the years the locust hath eaten – our end is like Job – a *double portion* is our *inheritance*!! The tears You had me weep, watered the *harvest* that You have brought forth."

Psalm 126 (Personalized)

Six months went by, and Brother Pete came to me again about the deaf ministry. Again, I told him that I thought it was impossible, because I had never interpreted someone preaching and didn't know enough words to be able to do such a thing for five minutes, let alone for an entire morning service. Then Brother Pete told me he desired to have a deaf ministry in place before the next pastor came in. Once again, he asked me to be in prayer about it, and I said I would.

We were in a Beth Moore Bible study at that time, in the Book of Daniel.[35] When we got to the fourth chapter in Daniel, where Daniel tells the king in verse 27, "Renounce your sins by *doing what is right,* and your wickedness by *being kind to the oppressed.* It may be that then your prosperity will continue," (NIV). Those verses grabbed my heart. Beth

Moore suggested that these were two warning signs to us as Christians of being corrupted by the "Babylons" in our lives. One is losing touch with the poor or oppressed, and second is losing touch with our own poverty of spirit. Those verses really struck a chord in my heart. I could see that, in order for our spiritual prosperity to continue, we can compare that to the degree that we remember the oppressed as well as never forgetting our own capacity for spiritual poverty. In the New Testament, we see the same admonition when the Lord says in Matthew 25: 34-40 (NIV):

"Then the King will say to those on his right, Come, you who are blessed by my Father; take your *inheritance,* the Kingdom prepared for you from the founding of the world. For I was hungry and you gave me food, I was thirsty and you gave me something to drink, I was a stranger and you made me your guest, I needed clothes and you provided them, I was sick and you took care of me, I was in prison and you visited me. *Then the people who have done what God wants* will reply, Lord, when did we see you hungry and feed you, or thirsty and give you something to drink? When did we see you a stranger and make you a guest, or needing clothes and provide them? When did we see you sick or in prison, and visit you? The King will say to them, Yes! I tell you that *when you did these for one of the least important of these brothers of mine, you did them for Me!*"

I added that verse from Daniel 4:27 to the refrigerator door at home, to be a checkpoint to periodically remind me of our accountability to the Lord concerning this, but what could I do for the poor or oppressed? The thought of a deaf ministry came to mind as the deaf are certainly some of the oppressed in our society, but once again, I couldn't see a way that it would be possible to start such an endeavor, and I really loved leading the ladies' Bible studies and substituting for Pat Socia.

Later in the year, we studied in Genesis about Joseph. Even though God had a call upon Joseph's life, it seemed that everything went poorly for Joseph. He was sold into slavery and later wrongfully imprisoned for something he didn't do, and yet this was exactly within God's providence in preparing Joseph for the future, not only for him, but also for the salvation of many others. If anyone had something to complain about in life and what life had dealt him, Joseph did.

I happened to watch a movie that came out during this time in 2007, with Sylvester Stallone called *Rocky Balboa*, with Sylvester Stallone once more playing the part of Rocky. There is a scene in the middle of the movie in which Rocky's son gets in his father's face about how the son's life has been so unfair and that his father was ruining it for him. I'll never forget that scene because of what Rocky says to him:

"Let me tell you something that you already know – the world ain't all sunshine and rainbows. It's a very mean and nasty place and I don't care how tough you are, it will beat you to your knees and keep you there permanently if you let it. You, me, or nobody is gonna hit as hard as life, but it ain't about how hard you're hit, it's how hard you can get hit and keep moving forward, how much you can take and keep moving forward. That's how winning is done.

Now, if you know what you're worth then go out and get what you're worth but you gotta be willing to take the hits and not pointing fingers saying you ain't where you want to be because of him or her, or anybody. Cowards do that and that ain't you! You're better than that!"

Rocky Balboa [36]

In moving forward with God, one of the things you see about Joseph in his prison is that he has finally learned empathy. When he is with his brothers, he tells them of *his two-fold dreams,* of how they will all bow before him, which incites strife and jealousy. He is then thrown into a pit and then sold into slavery. When he is wrongfully imprisoned, and we see a different Joseph, one who notices the heartache and sorrow of those around him. Joseph is put in charge of attending the king's cupbearer and the king's chief baker who have offended the king and have been thrown in prison with Joseph.

One day, he notices both of these men with dejected looks on their faces and asks, "Why are your faces so sad today?" (Genesis 40:7, NIV). One wonders if he would have ever noticed before, because he seemed to be indifferent to the hurt his brothers felt knowing that he was his father's favorite. Not one word is said about noticing their wounded hearts, where a root of bitterness arises, leading to envy, jealousy, and murderous thoughts and intents.

When Joseph notices the sad faces on these two men and asks what is wrong, they inform him of the two dreams they have, which he knows he can interpret for them. So he is faced with a choice: *Do I help someone else with their dreams while I am waiting on my own?* The Bible study we were in brought us face to face with this question: "Who's dream are *you* helping?" Joseph would help a cupbearer, a baker, and two years later a Pharaoh with their dreams before they were used to help him with his.

That brought me back to Brother Pete and his desire – *his dream* – for a deaf ministry. Could I help someone else with their dream before God brought my own dream to fruition? Could I, in doing this, also be helping the oppressed? In early 2008, I approached Brother Pete, who asked me again if I had thought any more about the deaf ministry. This time, I told him I was willing, but the only way I could possibly think of having success was in not only knowing what every song would be, but knowing exactly what the sermons would be – word for word. It would also mean I would not be able to lead the ladies' Bible studies or substitute for Pat Socia, as it would take a lot of time in order to work on the signs, and thus, I asked Brother Pete if this was what he really wanted. Again, he told me that, yes, he wanted a deaf ministry in place before a new pastor came. Brother Pete got back with me a few days later and suggested that it might be possible to provide me with his sermon notes before every service. I told him I would need them as early in the week as possible in order to work on them to learn the signs for the words and practice them. He said he would do that. He asked if I knew if there were any Deaf in Jacksonville. I told him the only Deaf I had ever met were a couple who were both profoundly deaf who had come three years previously to look at one of the rent houses I had, but I didn't have a fenced yard for a dog, so they had gone elsewhere. I told him I would try to ask around and see if they still lived in the city.

When the deaf couple had come to my house, at that time, they lived on Brookside Street in Jacksonville, so I took a chance, thinking that perhaps they may not have moved after all and started knocking on every door on Brookside, asking the residents if they knew this couple. The street was only about four blocks long, so it didn't take but a couple of hours, and sure enough, one of the neighbors told me they still lived there toward the end of Brookside. I knew it was James and Pamela Johnson's house when I saw the sign on the door that said to press the doorbell four times as it would make a light come on in the house. They remembered me, and I told them that Central was starting a deaf ministry and I would be leading it. I invited them to come, and they said they would. They are both in their early sixties today, and except for the people at James's work, we are the only friends they have, as both their families live in Missouri.

For the first year, it took forty to fifty hours a week to prepare for each Sunday, and I was able to find a sign language dictionary online called ASLPRO.com on which people would actually video each sign in a short video dictionary, which was very helpful. Thank goodness that Pamela has always been kind enough, as well, to help me to learn the correct signs. There are really two kinds of signing in this country: American Sign Language and the older version, which has only been in existence since the late 1800s. James and Pamela prefer the older kind, although most churches use ASL. Each year they have been attending has become easier and easier to interpret, and now it only requires a few minutes each week to prepare, although, in reality, I'm probably only on a grade school or junior high level of proficiency. What you discover with the Deaf is that, just like with any other language barrier, the people are usually thrilled that someone is attempting to learn their language and converse with them.

Most people don't realize how the Deaf have impacted our lives in even the smallest ways. How many know that, every time you watch football and you see men stand in a huddle, it was created by the Deaf? When a hearing college played the Deaf from Galludet University, some of the hearing players knew sign language and thus could "read" the plays that the deaf players were planning. So, the deaf players decided to stand in a circle so the hearing players couldn't see them signing to one another what the next play would be, hence, the huddle was formed in football.

As for the sign language being interpreted at Central, I noticed that the hearing at our church are also influenced not only by the signing, as it truly does enhance the worship service, but the deaf couple themselves influence us all, as it helps us all to remember to "do what is right and remember the oppressed."

For Joseph, it was two years after he helped the cupbearer and baker with their dreams before his dream began to be realized. As I helped our interim pastor fulfill his dream, mine would begin to be realized two years later as well when the Lord would give me a new verse.

HOMEWORK:

- Are you ready to apply God's Word to your situation or desire? Take the verse or verses the Lord has put on your heart and personalize them.

- Do you need to stay in touch with the oppressed as well as be reminded of your own spiritual poverty? Is there something the Lord would have you do concerning this?

- Do you have a tendency to approach your Heavenly Father and complain that life has been unfair to you?

- Are you able to notice the hurt and needs of others? Have you learned empathy?

- Can you help someone else with their dream while waiting on your own to come to fruition?

Know When to Hold 'Em, Know When to Fold 'Em

In the spring of 2008, the Lord would give me more verses to muse about as I looked toward the future. Once again, I was taken back to Isaiah 54, this time, to the very beginning of the chapter:

"Sing barren woman who has never had a child! Burst into song, shout for joy, you who have never been in labor! For the *deserted wife* will have more children than the woman who is living with her husband, says the Lord. *enlarge the place of your tent, stretch your tent curtains wide, do not hold back; lengthen your cords, strengthen your stakes. For you will spread out to the right and to the left...*"

Isaiah 54:1,2

This one made me sit up and think for a minute.

"Lord, You really have a sense of humor. Now I'm either fixin' [that's good East Texan for "getting ready"] to gain a whole bunch of weight – 'you will spread out to the right and to the left' – or my family is fixin' to be increased. I sure hope You mean the latter!"

I began to ponder on what the Lord might do, and in looking back at almost seventeen years of singleness, I noticed that where I *lived* seemed to lead to a more and more remote possibility of meeting someone. I started in Dallas, an area of more than a million plus, then moved to Tyler, an area of 85,000 people, and was now living in Jacksonville, Texas, a population of about 14,000 people. A job had come open at work as the postmaster in Gallatin, Texas, whose population was just barely 400. It would be only nine miles from my house instead of the thirty-five I was driving one way each day from Jacksonville to Tyler, and I wondered if the Lord would want me in an even smaller place to prove and show his glory, so I decided to "throw out a fleece" (Judges 6:36-40) and put in for the job. It would not be a promotion, as it was the lowest-level postmaster position there is, but it would be so much closer to home, and as I'd learned before, a title or promotion really didn't mean much to me anyway.

When I got the answer, it was one of those decisions about which you have to decide, *is this really worth fighting over?* It's like that Kenny Roger's song, "You've got to know when to hold 'em, know when to fold 'em, know when to walk away, know when to run."[37]

Often, when I see that something has so many obstacles in front of it, it could very well mean that it is *not* where the Lord wants me, even when it's "unfair." For example, I was asked at work to do a three-month internship as a customer service representative during one summer working with Express Mail sales. The supervisor was a wonderful woman to work for, and I was given free rein to go about any way I wanted to increase sales. I went to each of the Tyler substations and wrote down the names of the businesses with the largest mailboxes at each station. I then called the secretaries at the businesses and told them I was surveying for the postal service where they might be sending Express Mail in the country, even if they were using other companies. When they told me the cities they were mailing to, I would look up those cities to see if they were sites we guaranteed delivery to. For those that we did guarantee, I would set up appointments with the decision makers at those businesses. When I walked in, already knowing where they mailed to, I offered the proposition of having them test our service while maintaining their current service to prove the quality of our on-time delivery. When they saw the prospect of saving a lot of money if they changed over, once we had proven ourselves, Express Mail Corporate accounts soared. In three months, I had doubled the number of accounts we had from the very inception of Express Mail in Tyler years before.

When the customer service representative position came open full time, I put in for it and thought I would have been a shoe-in for the position. Although I passed the initial interview process, I was not part of the second package, and someone else was selected. I chose not to fight the decision.

One month later, the wonderful woman I would have been working for suddenly announced her retirement and the job situation was changed so dramatically, it quickly became one I would not have enjoyed working in as I had previously. I was very content then that it had *not* worked out!

The answer I got concerning the Gallatin Post Office in 2008 ended up being a consequence and the cost of a battle that, for me, *was* worth fighting, which stemmed from incidents that began in 2001. One of the weaknesses of a Christian with the gift of mercy, according to the Bill Gothard Seminar notes on spiritual gifts, is taking up offenses for others. Sometimes, this can lead us to make unwise choices based on emotions rather than spiritual wisdom. In looking back, I must confess that my emotions were definitely involved, and yet it became a battle I didn't wait to be asked to join. It was one I jumped into with both feet and would have taken on Rocky Balboa if it was necessary!

Now the reason that a gentle-natured person with the gift of mercy who had been through God's assertiveness training class got so riled up and took up the cause of another was because of what happened in the 1960s. I hated the 1960s (well, except for a lot of the music, like the Beach Boys, the Lettermen, and oh, maybe Dennis Quaid, oh, and Saturday morning westerns). The events of those years resulted in so much strife, grief, and chaos, it reminded me of my own home life. I wondered as a child what was going on with our country. Just as there would be a war over my childhood innocence, I watched from age seven to eleven as our nation lost its innocence, as we shut God out of our schools, lost a president, and drafted our boys into the military and sent them off to Vietnam. How logical is it to scare a kid into practicing hiding under their desk because of Mutual Assured Destruction (MAD) and the possibility of nuclear attack, but let's not talk to God about it! No, just have your folks dig a bomb shelter and hope for the best.

I didn't know God, but I knew there was a God. And let's get real, we all know in our hearts that there is a God. The Bible tells us we all know this. "The fool says in his heart there is no God" (Psalm 14:1, NIV), and if you're reading this book this far, you're no fool! According to Psalm 19:1 (KJV), even nature declares the presence of God: "The heavens declare the glory of God and the firmament showeth His handiwork." You can walk into any grocery store and see there is a God by the orderliness in nature.

Every striped watermelon has an even number of stripes; every orange has an even number of segments, I can go on and on. If you don't believe, you can ask Him and He'll reveal Himself to you. There was even a man who owned a chain of 7-11 convenience stores who was a Christian and who required a lie detector test for all prospective employees in the 1970s before such a test became illegal. He discovered that, at the end of the interviews, when he asked did the person believe there was a God, 100% of the time, when they said, "No," it showed they were lying.

At that time, although I didn't know His Word, it was as though I could hear a great door in Heaven close, leaving a huge vacuum in its place, and in looking back, I wonder if it was as though our nation was entering into the first stages of Romans 1:21-32 just as I had, when we knew God, we did not glorify God as God, we were not thankful, and our foolish hearts became darkened, and then we were given over. God never forces Himself on anyone, especially His own people, and we can see the historical precedent for that in the Old Testament in Ezekiel 10. His Shekinah glory departs hesitantly from His people who don't want Him, withdrawing to the Temple and hesitating again. We see how He pauses, again and again, and then departs, leaving man to his own devices.

When I saw the Beatles for the first time on our shores, my reaction was the opposite of all the screaming girls; I was grief stricken. When I saw Twiggy for the first time, I felt the same. It's not that the Beatles or Twiggy were bad or evil, and I'm not a psychic or spiritualist, but I could, as an eight-year-old kid in 1964, sense *what was coming behind them* – that loud, pulsating, hard, raging music that we've been listening to for the past almost fifty years. There's nothing *gentle* about any of that. I know many love it, but in my wildest imagination, I cannot see heaven filled with these sounds, or should I say, for me, the *noise* of this type of music.

You don't typically see Black women or Hispanics with bulimia or other eating disorders, but since Twiggy came on the scene, you see young white, American girls trying to get thinner and thinner to be "beautiful," not realizing it started with Twiggy.[38] Was that Twiggy's fault? Of course not! Yet one must ask the question: how's all that working for us after all these years? When we said we didn't want God, what did we fill that vacuum with? Although all the boys I knew carried rifles to school back then in the backs of their pickups, today, we have kids killing one another at schools at an unprecedented pace, gangs, drugs, eating disorders, poor education, etc.

The one thing I think that bothered me the most about the 1960s was how our country treated our soldiers from Vietnam. Most of these guys didn't want to go – they were drafted! They did what their country ordered them to do. I had two brothers who served, and one was spat upon in an American airport! Yet I think the incident of Lt. William Calley stood out for me as the epitome of the craziness our country was wrapped up in. During the spring of 1968, I didn't and don't know what exactly happened, but I could see the impact it had for all of the other soldiers who were serving over there and the treatment they received when they came home. It was a travesty. I determined at that time as an eleven-year-old kid that, although I was too young then to do anything about it, if there ever came a day when I could do something for one of those Vietnam vets on a personal basis, I would. Lt. Calley's words at his court martial still strike a chord in my heart today as do the words of the song written about that incident a couple of years late, named "Battle Hymn Of Lt. Calley" by Terry Nelson and C Company.

"Yesterday you stripped me of all my honor, please by your actions that you take here today, don't strip future soldiers of their honor – I beg you."
Lt. William Calley [39]

In the Battle Hymn of Lt. Calley, he speaks about being a little boy who wanted to grow up to be a soldier and serve his country – how he would play "soldier" by wearing a saucepan on his head for a helmet and waving a wooden sword in one hand and the American flag in the other.

As a soldier in Viet Nam, he felt he was just like any other soldier of that era – forgotten, while life went on stateside, and people were marching in the streets in protest, which simply aided in defeat. Soldiers were being ambushed on the left and right and it was difficult to determine who the enemy was, whether the VC or the good. Your only desire was to be judged by the question of whether you fought or whether you ran – to be counted as a soldier who never left his gun and the only prize won was that of serving one's country.

How did those events from the 1960's impact what happened in 2001? After the tragedy of the September 11 terrorist attacks, there was a major impact on the postal service, and package shipping came almost to a standstill. With mail volumes down all over the country, the postal service started seeking ways to cut expenses until our country could heal. The first choice made in Tyler, Texas, would impact one of these Vietnam veterans.

The postal service allots service members additional points when taking the postal exam, and if they've been injured, they get even more points, but that is it, and once you are hired, you then do the same job everyone else does. This Vietnam veteran was a *three-time Purple Heart recipient,* having been shot twice in the same day and then injured at a later time in Vietnam. His injuries forced him to wear a leg brace, and yet he did the exact same job that everyone else did and never complained for *twenty years.* A couple of years prior to 9-11, he was injured in a car wreck, and those previous injuries were aggravated where he temporarily lost the ability to lean into giant metal containers and pick heavy packages off the floor (those containers would later be replaced, as they were later deemed as a safety issue for *all* employees). This employee had to request to be considered as a light-duty employee only because he simply couldn't lean into them and stand up.

The postal service decided for financial reasons to terminate light-duty assignments, and this veteran was the first person to lose his full-time job. He was only allowed to work twenty hours a week, and his hours were split in such a way that he had to come early in the morning and then late in the afternoon, sometimes on the same days. Other days his schedule was changed, making it impossible for him to even get a part-time job. This impacted not only his pay, but also his ability to take care of his family and his retirement, and that's when I became an advocate for him, writing even the president, trying to get help for him. Although Congressman Ralph Hall had helped me in the past, because this veteran lived in Jacksonville and not Tyler, Congressman Hall couldn't help. The Congressman over the vet's district could not provide any help either, although he was sympathetic.

For *two years* this veteran and I fought the postal service's ruling, with phone calls, letters, etc. Finally, in 2004, right before I moved to Jacksonville, redistricting occurred during which Jacksonville got a different

Congressman. Jerry, the guy I had dated for several years, was the County Chairman for the new Congressman and told me he would be driving the New Congressman to a meeting in Cherokee County as he greeted his new constituents. I asked Jerry to present to the Congressman all the letters and info about my friend, and just two days later, the supervisor and the postal service was ordered to re-instate this veteran to full-time status as well as reimburse him for two years of back pay for the hours he lost!

In 2008, when I put in for that postmaster position in Gallatin, once again, someone else was chosen, and I knew this was the consequence of my decision years earlier to "take up the offense of another." Although I had served as an officer-in-charge at two larger offices, had been awarded four Special Achievement Awards, had a master's in public administration, and had been working for more than thirty years, that day, I chose to "fold the cards" and not take up the fight for that office, as I had only myself to blame. For me, if that was the only cost I would have to pay, it was nothing compared to what this veteran had paid so we could live freely in this country. I knew that God would make His way plain while I was in Jacksonville and not Gallatin, and I couldn't wait to see what would happen next.

HOMEWORK:

- Do you have a tendency to fight every battle or do you know how to choose your battles? Are there instances in your life where you feel you have to push your way through only to later realize it was not of the Lord?

- Is there something happening in your sphere of influence where you should stand up and fight?

How's That Working out for You?

My *spiritual* captivity had been broken the month before my twenty-eighth birthday, when I finally comprehended that the Christian life is not lived by *trying*, but by *trusting*. The Lord had also been working in my heart and life concerning *emotional* captivity by working through those negative messages once more. This also meant understanding that Christ alone should be the center of our lives, and not our spouses or children, or jobs, or anything else, as well as helping me see that we are complete in Him. This included the concept that we are responsible for our own happiness and no one else. He had also been showing me what He really intends for marriage by understanding the concept or ability to cleave and seeing our Heavenly Husband as our "Ishi," our great and mighty champion. I would have two more areas of weakness that had to be dealt with before my captivity would be "turned back."

The first was in dealing with my "broken picker." I asked the Lord to "examine me, O God, and know my heart; test me, and know my thoughts. See if there is in me any hurtful way, and lead me along the eternal way." (Psalm 139:23-24, Complete Jewish Bible)

When I thought about it, although I was no longer attracted to angry, controlling men and the Lord was teaching me that I needed to discern a man's ability to cleave, I had to confess the general tendency to choose men several years my senior. Although I did date a couple of guys who were my age, the majority, and certainly both husbands, were ten or more years older than I was. I'm sure most would say that it was because of my father's absence and that I was choosing a father figure, but I have to confess that the reason the Lord showed me was more base than even that. As I got really honest before the Lord, it was my way of attempting to protect myself from rejection. In thinking that I would always be the younger woman for my husband, I had hoped to increase the odds in my favor that he wouldn't leave me. It was as though the Lord were then asking, "How's that working out for you?" I could see that it certainly had not worked in the past, and because the Lord had been dealing with who we are in Christ – our identity – there was really no need to be afraid. This was just a youthful way I had used to survive in the past and as a daughter of the King, I knew I had plenty to offer a man closer to my age. So I purposed to look for men closer to my age.

Today, with the Internet, there is not a lot of blind dating or having your friends set you up, so I opted to try online dating. Boy, was that an eye opener! It was a good thing I had worked for the Dallas Police Department in the past, because otherwise, online dating probably would have been too much of a shock. Why do men and women put pictures online that show them twenty or more years younger? Do you think we won't notice the very second we meet you? I tried Christian web sites as well as those that match you by personality, but in most cases, the matches would be one hundred or more miles away because I lived in a rural area, and a long-distance relationship usually does not work out, so I used Match.com, as it had many more singles that lived closer to me. I typically would choose to meet at Barnes and Noble for a cup of coffee so it was not difficult to escape if I knew it would not be the type of person I would be interested in, and neither would waste his or her time or money by sitting through dinner before we could get away. If things worked out, you could always go to dinner together later.

I never figured out why, when I said I was the president of a ballroom dance club and I went to church, and showed pictures of our dances with all of us dressed to the nines, so many men seemed to make it their life mission to show me that I needed to change to their lifestyle of sitting in a tree every weekend for six months at a time hunting or riding four wheelers in the mud for "fun." I decided to try in a fun way to deter some of these "East Texas Rednecks" by putting some descriptive words about who I was:

"If a tie is something you only associate with a goat or a calf, we might not be compatible."

"If your 'hot spot' of the places you'd really like to go and see in life are Wal-Mart and the Post Office, we might not be compatible."

"If you'd rather ride a Harley, sit in a tree, or spit on a deer scrape, we might not be compatible."

Still, many were not deterred. Now, why in the world would you say that it is just too much for you to date a woman who owns a cat – a woman who owns her own home, has no children and no bills?? I can promise you, my cat has been more faithful than any husband ever was! So if you want me to choose between you and my cat, guess who's leaving? (It's not her!)

I got really good at these coffee interviews. Having a psychology background, a detective spirit, access to Publicdata.com (which I had learned to use for all of my renters), and even a little experience with some handwriting analysis courses I had picked up for fun on the side, I could tell in five minutes a lot about the men I went out with. This included his birth order, if he had any sisters, where he worked, where he lived, how much taxes he was paying on his house, if he had a house, was he honest, did his public persona match his private persona, was he a convict or a cheat, if he was gay or bisexual, or if he even had a libido! (I told that police department they should have let me try!)

I got so good at discovering things about people that my mother called me one day extremely concerned about a girlfriend who lived in San Francisco who hadn't returned phone calls or letters in several months. This was a friend of hers of more than thirty years who had cancer, and my mother was concerned that maybe something had happened to her, since she lived alone and had no children. Before calling me, my mother had called the non-emergency number to the police department there and asked for a "welfare check," during which the police department goes by to check on the well-being of a person who has not been reported missing.

Although my mother didn't know the name of the apartments her friend lived in, before the police could get there, I looked at a satellite view of the block where the woman lived. I saw the name of a building across the street, looked online for a business there, called the number, and had a man look out the window there in San Francisco to see if there was a name on the apartment building across the street. He said there was no name but personally knew a couple of businesses that were in that building. I found one that would answer the phone, and they went upstairs, knocked on the woman's door, and when she didn't answer he left her a written message under her door to call me and my mother! My mother's friend called me and then called my mother a couple hours later and told her that, between the police and the people from her apartment building, she would never stay out of contact with her again, as she knew Mom would tell me to "sic em," and she would be found.

I did meet a few nice guys online, but the majority were simply not compatible with me. I did date one guy for a few weeks, but, once again, I could see that, although he was very close to my age, he had no ability to cleave and had no real interest in either attending church with me or becoming involved with our dance club, and I walked away. My mother *insisted* that there would be no way I would ever meet a guy who would want a woman who went to church all the time and went ballroom dancing and that I needed to quit both church and dancing. I told her that I'd rather be single. If a guy would not go to church, we would never be on the same page spiritually, and if he wasn't at least willing to *try* to learn to dance once every other month while we are dating, then he would probably not be concerned about anything else after we made a commitment either.

I sat dejected on the couch one evening after that and poured out my heart to God.

"Lord, my 'picker' is still broken, after all these years! It's as though I hadn't learned a thing, as I keep picking the wrong kind of men or there are so few to pick from at all! I can't trust my heart in this. What is wrong?"

As I got still before the Lord, the thought came to me, and it was as though He were saying: "Why not stop doing what you've been doing? How's that working out for you? Aren't you tired of doing it your way?"

Is there some other way, Lord? I thought. We don't have arranged marriages in our country, so I wondered what He meant. The only thing I knew to do was to ask for direction in meeting guys and spend time getting to know them.

Then His Holy Spirit brought to mind a verse: "You did not choose, me, but I chose you..." (John 15:16).

"Okay Lord, that's for salvation," I mused.

"Am I not 'Ishi,' your Heavenly *Husband?*" the thought came to mind. "Your *Husband,* the *Bridegroom* who *chose* you? The *Bridegroom chooses* the Bride, the Bride does *not* choose the Bridegroom," the thought whispered in my heart. "The *man* chooses the woman, the woman does not choose the man."

Good grief, how could I be so dumb? I thought, as it finally dawned on me.

"Okay Lord, then You choose. I give up. I don't know how You're going to do this, as it seems to me to be impossible. How in the world can I meet a guy who is a firstborn, has at least one sister, goes to church, and furthermore is mature in his faith and puts You first in his life, is optimistic with a good sense of humor, lives or works in the Jacksonville, Texas, area, has the ability to cleave, can pass 'muster' with the Tuesday night dinner club as well as my mother, would be willing to try to learn to ballroom dance, and won't ask me to get rid of my cat or sit in a tree, and is not the Pope?"

I determined that I would not renew the Match.com subscription that would end in two weeks and would just be still and watch to see what God would do. I had been waiting for seventeen and a half years, so what's another few months or a year?

Ten days later, on Wednesday, July 1, 2009, I received an email notification that someone was trying to contact me via Match.com. I had put in my profile that I would like to meet a guy who was 5'10" or taller (so I could wear heels as I am 5'7") and a guy named David had responded to me about that.

"I really don't match your height requirement, but I sure do like your profile and your sense of humor," he responded.

Before responding, I looked at his profile, and wow! He seemed like a nice guy! I perused his profile further. He teaches an Adult Sunday School class at his church! He loves Schnauzers. He's slightly taller than me.

I quickly responded: "Thanks for writing! I'm always open to meeting new people no matter the height – the reason that was there is because I dance and didn't want to wear flats. I love your profile, and I have a secret love for Schnauzers. I've always wanted one and fell in love with one in Tyler several years ago. I'd love to meet some time and have a cup of coffee and share. I think we would have a lot in common and, at the least, would walk away new friends. What do you say? I work in Tyler and live in Jacksonville. Maybe one evening after work or something sometime?"

We corresponded for four days. He lived in Tyler and worked *one mile from my house in Jacksonville*. It seemed our lives had been parallel in many ways. We both threw paper routes as kids. We both went to high school in

Dallas. We graduated one year apart and were only eighteen months apart in age. We both worked for the City of Dallas. We both moved to the Tyler area and our parents later followed. We both had three sisters, and he was the only male. He lived in Tyler and worked in Jacksonville, while I lived in Jacksonville and worked in Tyler.

We tried to meet a couple of times, but something came up or we would miss one another, and then, James and Pamela Johnson, the deaf couple, notified me they would not be able to attend church on Sunday. Most of the time they didn't tell me if they would miss, so I always prepared, no matter what, but that particular Sunday they did tell me. Since I didn't have a replacement, any other time I would not have been able to miss, but this presented the opportunity to meet David at *his* church, in *his* Sunday School class, with *him* teaching. That sure beat Barnes and Noble for coffee! So I suggested just that, and David replied, "Sure!"

I met David Brock on Sunday, July 5, 2009. I sat down, and five minutes later, a lady walked into the Sunday School class, looked over at me and said, "Susan, is that you?"

I looked over. It was a lady and her husband who belonged to our ballroom dance club! David's class was wonderful, and he was a very good teacher/facilitator. When we walked into the sanctuary for the service, one of the supervisors that I had loved at the Post Office was there waving at me. I really liked David's pastor, and when he saw me signing during the worship service, he would later come and bring me up to the front to sign for everyone a few weeks later when I visited again. When I visited that second time, weeks later, when the pastor saw me signing during the worship service, he walked all the way to where we were standing, grabbed me by the arm, and escorted me to the front of the church and asked me to continue as they played, "How Great Thou Art." After the service was over, an elderly gentleman walked over to me and started hugging me and kissing me on the cheek, and *wouldn't stop!* He kept telling me how much he enjoyed the signing, and I assumed from all the kissing and hugging that he was some kinfolk of David's.

When David asked me who the guy was, I answered in surprise, "I thought you knew him. I've never seen him before in my life."

David responded back, "No, I've never met him before, either." We both laughed as we walked out of the church.

David and I had a three-hour lunch that first Sunday we met, at Fat Catz, a Cajun seafood restaurant that was a favorite of both of ours in the past. From the moment I met David, our relationship started at a steady, even keel, and it has been that way ever since. There was never the drama-filled, roller-coaster emotional ride that I so often found myself on in too many previous relationships. David had a handsome eighteen-year-old son named D.R. who had just graduated high school and a beautiful fifteen-year-old daughter named Laura who had just completed tenth grade. David had recently divorced, even though he did not want the divorce after twenty-one years of marriage, and his ex-wife referred to David's mother as "the patron saint of all mother-in-laws."

David had not only taught adult Sunday School for years, but had also been a discussion leader for Bible Study Fellowship, a worldwide organization for adults and kids for several years as well as one of the facilitators for Kairos, a men's prison ministry. Although we had much in common, we grew up quite differently, as he was raised in a very warm, affectionate, loving Christian home, with both parents at home his entire life. David had "Mr. Nice Guy" written all over him, *and I was attracted.*

The second area to be dealt with before the emotional captivity would be "turned back" would come next, and it would be the greatest test of all.

HOMEWORK:

- Have you completed your homework on negative messages?

- Is Christ the center of your life?

- Do you truly see that you are complete in Him and you don't need another person to complete you?

- Are you beginning to recognize when someone has the ability to "cleave"?

- Is your "picker" broken like mine was? What is the Lord saying to you about that?

There Is No Plan B

We all know as Christians that God's intent for us, as His children, is to "conform us to the image of His Son," or make us "more like Christ." As you likely have learned in this book thus far, one of the ways He does this is by taking us into our wilderness to be alone with Him, back to the "scene of the crime" of our childhood wounds. This time it is for winning us through by helping us to put away our childhood ways of responding to hurt and using a more adult and mature way of responding.

Another way I have discovered that God makes us more like Christ is by having us face, once again, all those areas where we have failed in the past, by being tested again in that very same area. One of the greatest challenges for man, as seen in the Bible, which is replete with admonitions and example after example of failure and the unintended consequences of failing in this area, is the challenge of remaining sexually abstinent unless married. God's Word makes it very clear that sex outside of marriage is considered a sin, yet how many times do some of us think that this rule should be for someone else or that there will be no consequences? Nothing could be further from the truth. I would probably have to say that this was my greatest area of weakness as well, and it certainly had been the case with both husbands. I had failed miserably both times, thinking all those years before that it didn't make that much difference as long as we eventually married, but I can confess that, if I had exercised more self-control and I *had* waited, both marriages most likely would have never occurred. Of all the challenges in life toward being faithful and obedient to God, this would be the "big one" that had to be faced and had to be won if I were ever to be delivered fully from all my captivity. With God, there is no Plan B when it comes to sex. Instead of "going all the way" with the men in my life before marriage, I wanted to go all the way with God and try things His way.

If I may be frank with you in this area of life, may I just say that my way never worked. The consequences for my disobedience became very apparent shortly after marriage. For some reason, after we said our I-do's, the physical side of marriage came to an abrupt halt. Even John Morris, the pastoral counselor, would shake his head in disbelief as he would hear our story, telling me it was usually the women he had to counsel with concerning the physical side of marriage. For men who have anger and control issues, it appears to be more important to them to have *control* than it is to enjoy that area of marriage which can be explored with freedom without guilt or shame. My second husband purposely would sleep on the downstairs couch for the last three years of our marriage to keep us apart, because control was so important to him. I determined at that time that, if I ever did remarry, the first time a husband even suggested that he sleep on the couch, the next morning that couch would be burned and we would not *own* a couch! In marriage, I had noticed, when conflict arose, the physical side of marriage seemed to be the first thing to go, and the last to come back after the conflict was resolved, but for me, the major conflicts were *never* resolved. If I had been obedient to God's Word and His Ways, I do not believe I would have had to face these issues, as we most likely would not have married.

The Bible makes it clear that, even though this is a difficult area for us to deal with, it is the result of the power of our thought lives. Our thoughts turn to actions, which become behaviors, which turn into habits, which affect our very destinies. If we can control our thought lives and learn to see the consequences of our behaviors, we can impact our very destinies if we so choose.

I'll never forget the year I was teaching the high school class at that very first church. Although I already had one of those "lessons out of the box" prepared, what happened that morning completely changed the class discussion. One of the teenage girls came into class and was telling the other kids in the class before we started about one of her friends from school who just happened to get pregnant. When I asked her about it, she simply dismissed it and said the girl really didn't have any choice, as it "just happened." I asked if the girl had been raped, and she said, "No, it was her boyfriend," and that's when Sunday School became "Truth and Consequences."

"I want each of you to understand something here. This girl did not just "happen" to get pregnant. There's only been one miraculous conception in the history of mankind, and I can assure you, it wasn't this girl. However, this girl did happen to do one thing, over and over and over again: she said to herself the word "Yes," so many times before that day happened, by the time that day came, it was almost impossible for her to say "No."

"How could that be?" the kids replied.

"This girl said yes when she decided to have sex before being married.

"She said yes when she decided *who* she wanted to have sex with."

"She said yes when she decided *where* she would have sex."

"She said yes when she decided *what day* it would be."

"She said yes when she planned what she would *wear* that day."

"She said yes when she made plans as to where her parents would be and where her parents thought she would be that day."

"She said yes when she planned for the time that would *not* be during her monthly cycle."

"She said yes so many times before she ever got to that day, when that day *did* arrive, she probably believed she couldn't say "no!" You could have heard a pin drop in that high school class.

"Now, instead of having our regular Bible study, we will discuss this, and next week, when you come back, we are going to look at two young men, still in their teens, both very good-looking guys, in the Bible, who had the blessings of God upon their lives, but who had to face the very same issue with their thought lives. We will see where one failed and one passed, and we will see the consequences in each of their lives."

The next Sunday, every seat in class was filled. As we started the class, I asked this question of them: "How many of you have heard of David and Bathsheba and what happened between them?" All of the kids raised their hands.

"Okay, then here is my question for you this morning: How many of you think that David's sin with Bathsheba was a 'sin of the moment' which just happened, or was it the result of a lifestyle of years where he repeatedly said yes to one particular sin and no to God?" Every one of the kids thought it was a "sin of the moment."

"Well, let's just see for ourselves by comparing David to another young man named Joseph. I want you first to see how much alike they were in some ways, but how differently they responded because of a decision each made about their thought lives. I want you to see:

THE AWESOME POWER OF OUR THOUGHT LIFE

JOSEPH:	DAVID:
Gen. 39:7 – Well built and handsome	1 Sam. 16:12 – Ruddy, w/fine appearance and handsome.
Gen. 39:2 – Lord was with Joseph and he prospered	1 Sam. 16:18 - …and the Lord was with him.
Gen. 39:3-5 - Things were going well.	2 Sam. 11:1 – Victory over the Ammonites.
Gen. 39:10 - Joseph was tempted *daily.*	2 Sam. 11:2-5 - *One* temptation.
Joseph ran FROM temptation.	David ran INTO the temptation and attempted to cover it up.
Joseph had a pattern of saying "no" in his thought life BEFORE the temptation occurred – "how can I sin against God?" Genesis 39:9	David had a pattern of saying "yes" in his thought life to lust. How do we know this? It begins in Deut. 17:16, 17 – Kings are NOT to multiply: gold, horses, or *wives…*

1. **Thoughts** – Very early in David's life, lustful thoughts were not dealt with. We know this because he had unguarded eyes as well as idleness – "tarrying at Jerusalem" – which led to later seeing Bathsheba and having adulterous thoughts.
2. **Actions – Behavior** – Thoughts lead to actions. David married Michal (Saul's daughter), then Abigail, then Ahinoam.
3. **Habits** - Actions quickly become habits – David took four more wives while living at Hebron.
4. **Strongholds** – Confirmed, well-established habits become strongholds. When David moved to Jerusalem, he took more wives and concubines.

5. **Character** – Total inner or moral qualities that make up a person. Lust was a detrimental factor in David's character.
6. **Lifestyle** – Unconquered lustful thoughts led to a lifestyle of lustful actions, as in his interaction with Bathsheba. Thus, it was NOT a sin of the moment, but a sin of a lifestyle and lifetime.
7. **Destiny** – David faced an affair, pregnancy, premeditated murder, the death of a child, and the sword never leaving David's house; bloodshed; lost opportunity to build a temple for God. His sin affected his children, as they dealt with the same problem. What one generation allows in moderation, the next excuses in excess: 1 Kings 11:1-3, 11: "King **S**olomon loved many strange women... 700 wives, 300 concubines, *and his wives turned away his heart.*"

It was one of the most memorable Sunday School classes these kids would ever have!

As *my* David and I began to date, we both agreed that, from day one, there would be no sex. You cannot imagine how much easier it is when you have someone who is on the same page with you spiritually, and even more importantly, the chance for the man to lead the way by example instead of pressuring for more, and the woman having the opportunity to relax in the relationship and get to know that man instead of being tempted to *try* to create intimacy by manipulating a physical connection. I know that God found David for me, because David had a pattern and a lifestyle of abstinence, remaining a virgin until marrying at the age of thirty-three; thus he had only been with one woman in his life before meeting me. You don't often hear of that today. It removed any hint of pressure.

Shortly after we started dating, we discussed David's divorce and what had transpired as well as my history. We both agreed that David needed to have at least one year from the time his marriage was over before he even thought about what he might want to do in his future. That also removed any pressure from either side as to where the relationship may or may not go. We just relaxed and enjoyed getting to know one another.

Three months after we started dating, David joined a Divorce Care [40] class at our church, where he could continue to heal from the divorce. There had not been one available at the time of his divorce, and Central was offering one, so David decided to join the class, and I encouraged him to do so as well.

Divorce Care is a thirteen-week, non-denominational care group where you can find help, discover hope, and experience healing after going through separation or divorce. It includes a video series and daily home study guide that is hosted by a man who himself suffered through divorce and recovery. David would share with me the things he was learning each week, and I found that they matched many of the lessons the Lord had brought me through in my "homework." I cannot stress more strongly how helpful these sessions can be for men and women as well as your children, from ages five to age twelve, as they have Divorce Care for Kids as well.

We've all been told that more than half of all first marriages now end in divorce. Unfortunately, the statistics continue to climb for each subsequent marriage. According to the statistics in the Divorce Care videos, for second marriages, the failure rate is 76%; for third marriages, the failure rate is 87%; and for fourth marriages, the failure rate is 93%. Obviously, there are a lot of people who don't do their "homework" before they remarry! No wonder my mother could never find success. Thus, later, when the word "marriage" *would* enter the conversation, David and I realized that we potentially had between a 76%-87% chance of failure, so it was important for us to begin with God and His ways from the very onset if there would ever be a chance of having something that would last.

It's important also to note that each person heals on a different timetable than another. You shouldn't compare yourself or be upset with yourself if it takes you longer than other people you know. For me, it would take eighteen years of preparation and determination that I would not remarry until I had become healthy and whole, while with David, it only took one year. I'm sure much of that was because of the difference in our home lives; thus, I cannot overemphasize the importance of having a father present in your child's life and two parents that have the capacity to love, work through conflict, and sacrifice and care for their children. My heartfelt goal for anyone reading this book is that, as your heart and soul are willing, your healing time can, too, be greatly reduced, as you see how another went through what you may be going through right now, applying the principles laid out before you here, and still came out the other side happy and whole.

As I sat in Pat Socia's class in 2006 and 2007, she spoke of a time she used to go all over the country and give a speech called, "Sex, God's Fantastic Gift For Marriage" to high school kids. Pat noted that "Sex is Sexist," in that the woman pays the higher price for failure to abstain, in that sexually transmitted diseases attack a woman quicker and with more vengeance than a man, because her organs are internal; the possibility of pregnancy; and the emotional devastation that accompanies promiscuity for both sexes. She noted that virgins are far less likely to commit suicide than non-virgins; thus sex can be one of the greatest pleasures or bring the greatest pain in life.

She also noted that, in general, most breakups of marriages occur when a woman leaves a man to find another who is more romantic and affectionate, while a man will often leave a woman to find another who is more erotic. Thus, from this preacher's daughter's perspective, from a woman in her seventies, a long hard look at the Bible shows that wives need to learn to be more erotic and put away those grandmother's gowns and stop pulling blankets over their heads while turning off lights, while men need to learn to be more romantic and affectionate. In this way, men, who are by nature fighters, warriors, hunters, providers, as well as erotic, can be "tamed" by the woman and join with her in "nest building" if she will wait until marriage for sex, during which they both enjoy the fruits of sex. Pat also noted that, too often, a woman will try to use sex to get what she wants, which leads to resentment within the marriage; Pat warned that the woman should guard against doing this.

When I looked at David, I could see a "tamed" man, one who had a history of sacrificing for his family, of putting God first in his life, a man who enjoyed the "fruits" of marriage in the past, and who looked forward to someday again being able to do the same thing. When the one-year mark passed from when David's marriage was over, about two weeks later, David proposed. We set the date for three months later. When my next-door neighbor, who was not a Christian, came by one day during that time and found out we were getting married, she was horrified.

"I've never seen this man's car over here all night," she replied.

"That's because neither it, nor he, have ever spent the night over here," I responded.

"OMG, you're going to marry this man and you haven't even slept with him?! What if... What if there's something *wrong* with him, or he's not any *good,* or he's *deformed* or something?!" she exclaimed.

"You know, I've finally arrived at a place where that doesn't matter, because I know it will be okay, and I just want to be with him," I replied.

After being married for more than four years, I can testify that I finally married a "normal" man!

HOMEWORK:

- Are you going through the battle of being pressured for sex or pressuring another?

- How's that working out for you? Are you willing to try God's way for a change?

- Are you guilty of trying to create intimacy through a physical connection?

- If you've been through a divorce, no matter the years, are you still hurting?

- Will you consider a Divorce Care and Divorce Care for Kids class near you? I would discover much of the "homework" I had to complete is discussed during this thirteen-week class; thus, another factor in helping to potentially shorten your healing time.

No Greater Compliment
– Zechariah 8:23

"Sing, O daughter of Zion: shout, O Israel; be glad and rejoice with all the heart, O daughter of Jerusalem. The Lord hath taken away thy judgments, He hath cast out thy enemy: ...the Lord is in the midst of thee: thou shalt not see evil any more. The Lord thy God in the midst of thee is mighty; he will save, he will rejoice over thee with joy; he will *rest* in his love, he will joy over thee with singing... for I will make you *a name* and a praise among all the people of the earth, *when I turn back your captivity before your eyes,* saith the Lord."

Zephaniah 3:14, 15, 17, 20

During the months while David and I were dating, I attended *two* family reunions on his side of the family, one on his mother's side and one on his father's side, which included all of his siblings, their children, aunts, uncles, cousins, etc. I enjoyed getting to attend these gatherings, as *both* my parents had been only children, thus, we had no aunts and uncles or cousins to join us when we had just started having family reunions in recent years. The second reunion for David's family was always a big affair, lasting four days each year, and they had gotten so big that, during the year before I met David, he laughingly told me, they had to raise a *gigantic tent* to hold everyone in. Now *that* grabbed my attention!

The reunion I would attend that year and the next several for the larger group gathering would be held in Big Sandy, Texas, at the Air Land Emergency Resource Team (ALERT) Academy, which coincidentally is an off-shoot of the Bill Gothard Ministries. It is a very large facility which was formerly Ambassador College, founded by Herbert W. Armstrong,

239

established in 1947 and subsequently closed in 1997. The campus was then sold to the Green family, owners of Hobby Lobby, who donated the facility to Bill Gothard's ministry. The ALERT oversees the property and operates their disaster service ministry there. ALERT is a Christian training program for men that equips them to serve others by deploying them to disaster-stricken areas affected by hurricanes, tornadoes, floods, ice storms, and mudslides. They also conduct lost person searches, crime scene evidence searches, and underwater dive recovery. David's cousin, Janet Tanner, is married to John Tanner, the executive director and commander for ALERT and the facility.

Janet and her mother, Nona, were from the Dallas area and were involved for years in a quilting group. I discovered that weekend that my sister, Julia, was also part of the same quilting group and knew both women, thus it was a "family" reunion for her as well. The facility is set up with a large conference center with a kitchen as well as dorms, making it the perfect place for such a large gathering. We all enjoyed getting to watch some of the training going on as the academy would train year round, even with us in their midst.

When David and I became engaged, we both agreed that, before a date was set, there were some other things we needed to accomplish in order to improve those grim odds for our failure. If we were going to go all the way with God, it was important to do something that I had *not* done previously, before marriage, partly because my father had passed away when I was thirteen, and partly because I didn't realize the significance at the time. At age fifty-three and fifty-four, we both sought to request the parental blessing from both sides of the family as well as the blessing from both of David's children before moving forward. Although both dads had already passed away, it was still intimidating for David to approach both mothers *and* his children. For us, it was all or nothing, and if one person did not offer the blessing, there would be no wedding. I'm sure it was a little disconcerting for David's family to consider a woman who had been married twice before and had been single for over eighteen years, as they probably wondered if I really had completed my "homework" as well as whether I would be able to re-enter marriage after being so independent all those years. I know it was very disconcerting for David to approach *my* mother, who is a dyed-in-the-wool liberal, who has wondered for years how she got such a religious daughter who turned out to be so conservative. Even though David's ex-wife announced she was engaged as well, it would still be difficult to approach your own children, who most likely wondered what happened that their parents were no longer together and how that might affect their own future marriages. We were thrilled to be able to get the blessing from everyone involved.

Another item on our list was to undergo a discussion on money matters. We discovered that we had both been through the Dave Ramsey Financial Peace University[41] video series, which we both felt was important in order to be on the same page financially. Along with this discussion came the issues of where we would live and where we would attend church. As I owned my own home and David had left his home and furnishings for his ex-wife and children so his children would experience the least amount of discomfort due to the divorce as possible, the easy decision would be to stay in Jacksonville. As far as church was concerned, we would be happy at either church, but the final deciding factor was the deaf couple, James and Pamela Johnson. Although there was a teenager from my church who was assisting with the deaf ministry, I had no adult substitute for this service; thus, it would leave James and Pamela with no means of attending a church in their area. To "remember the oppressed" was important for both of us, so we decided to stay at Central in Jacksonville and visit whenever possible to David's church.

David would lose his beloved pastor to a brain aneurysm about eighteen months after we married, and it was a tremendous loss we both deeply felt, as did his church family. It was this pastor who had performed our wedding, as David had known and loved him for so many years, and Central had just recently found our new pastor, whom we both really liked but had not yet formed such an endearing bond with, as David had with his pastor.

The greatest change for the woman in marriage is the *new name* she receives; thus, just as I received a new name spiritually, I would get to exchange a name that was associated with past failure for a new name, one which was associated with God's blessings as well as those from both families.

We decided that, since we had both been married previously, there was no sense in spending an exorbitant amount of money on a wedding. We surmised how fun it would be to "surprise" all of our dance club members, except for a few that would be "in on it," and have the wedding at the first break between dance sets at the May 2010 ballroom dance. We told the band members what we were doing as well as one couple who would be taking photos and a long-time friend whom I had known both through dancing and as an instructor at U.T. Tyler, who both sang at and give me away during the ceremony. Otherwise, none of the sixty other people knew. They knew we were having several special guests attend, but we had previously had guests who usually demonstrated a new dance number, so most assumed we would be doing the same thing again. Unknown to them, the three tables of "guests" were both David's as well as all my family members, including parents, all of our siblings and their spouses, and David's children. I was "camouflaged" in a black and white outfit, with my wedding dress underneath, where I could exit one door in black and white, and walk through the other door in white.

When the wedding began, all of the dancers had been told something special would happen at the end of the first set and to remain in their seats. My friend Tom Fernandez sang one of my favorite Big Band era tunes, "Blue Moon." He then came and escorted me in, and David's pastor asked everyone to stand. When the band starting playing the wedding march, people were gasping everywhere and exclaiming out loud,

"Is this for real?!"

I nodded yes, and there was joyous clapping and then hushed silence as they realized what was unfolding before them. They all knew how long I had been single and the desire of my heart to find Mr. Nice Guy. They had all met David and had voiced their approval during the months we had dated, and now, they would be witness to the great things God had done and to the fulfillment of a long-awaited dream.

Before David's pastor had us recite our wedding vows, he read something I had given to him to read for everyone that night. It was a reminder of some of the verses the Lord had given me over the past two to three years in expectation of this very night:

"Enlarge the place of your tent, stretch your tent curtains wide, *do not hold back*, lengthen your cords, strengthen your stakes, for you will spread out to the right and to the left.

Isaiah 54:2 (NIV)

"'Yet the Lord longs to be gracious to you, He rises to show you compassion. For the Lord is a God of justice. Blessed are all who wait for Him.'

Isaiah 30:18 (NIV)

"'Because you got a double dose of trouble and more than your share of contempt, your inheritance in the land will be doubled and your joy go on forever.'

Isaiah 61:7 (The Message)

"The Lord gave Susan these verses about eighteen months ago, *before she met David,* and the overriding message seemed to be asking, "What are you expecting? Go ahead and start expecting something good, for it's coming.

"Susan has been divorced and single for over eighteen years and has never had children of her own, and she has longed for many years to have a healthy, happy marriage and family with a good and kind Christian man.

"Then she met David and has been privileged to attend a couple of family reunions on David's side of the family, and when she got to meet his children and these wonderful people that are a part of his family, it became apparent what was transpiring.

"What an awesome, grounded, stable, gracious, and inspiring family, full of hilarity and love, that she believed she would be gaining in this relationship with David. She was also to discover that, at the last full family reunion, there were so many of them, they had to have a gigantic tent to make room for all of them. How ironic!

"Susan feels so blessed to know that the desire of her heart – to love God and to love one man and to have that love returned – being fulfilled, and as she and David take their vows before friends and family this evening, that her family, as represented here by her siblings and her mother, will also get the chance to experience the double blessing of meeting the family she is entering into, as promised by God, and represented by David, himself, for, as Susan says, God and David are my *double portion.*"

As a special gift to me, during the cake cutting, David presented a scrapbook he had made for me, documenting *every date* we had been on from the day we met until that very night. It brought me to tears.

One of the last Sunday School classes I taught with that high school class all those years ago began with this question: "What is the greatest compliment you have ever received?" After reviewing all of the nice statements people had made about them, I then asked, "What is the greatest compliment you could ever receive"? When they didn't know for sure, I told them to turn to Zechariah 8:23, where it says, "Let us go with you, because *we have heard that God is with you.*" In saying goodbye to those beloved students, I told them that the greatest compliment in the world would be for others to say about you, "I know God is with you." I knew my captivity of soul had been broken that night as the well wishers exclaimed to us both, "God bless you, we know that God is with you."

HOMEWORK:

- What homework do you need to complete before entering into your next relationship?

- If you are currently in a relationship, is homework there for you to work on to improve your odds of success?

- Would you be willing to get your parents' approval, even at your current age?

- Have you discussed finances, raising children, where you will live, etc.?

- Isn't it time for you to discover freedom from emotional captivity?

Remember Whence Thou Came

More than twenty-five years ago, a sociologist-turned-minister named Anthony Campola shared the results of a social study of fifty people, all over the age of ninety-five, when asked the question: "If you had it to live all over again, what would you do differently?" Campola reported that three responses popped up over and over again:

1. We would *reflect* more: by reflecting on what God has done by probing into the depths of His truth as well as reflecting on life itself by asking ourselves, "Have I really lived?" We would reflect more by redeeming the time.
2. We would *risk* more: Christianity is a call to *not* play it safe but to risk it all on God.
3. We would do more things that would live on after we were dead. Campola questioned his listeners by asking, "Will they stand around your grave and read titles or will they stand around your grave and give testimonies of the difference you made in someone's life for Christ? Campola exclaimed:

Pharaoh had a title...	but Moses had a testimony.
Nebuchadnezzar had a title...	but Daniel had a testimony.
Jezebel had a title...	but Elijah had a testimony.
Herod had a title...	but John the Baptist had a testimony.
Pilate had a title...	but Jesus had a testimony. [42]

Might I ask you the same thing? I pray that, as you have read this book, it has caused you to reflect more by probing into the depths of His truth. Have you really *lived* or are you just *surviving?* Are you redeeming the time that you have or just waiting? What are you waiting for?

As the daughter of a compulsive gambler who was too afraid to take a risk but risked it all on God, have I persuaded you to also take a risk and put it all on the line for God? Does He not say, "Try me, prove Me; taste and see that the Lord is good?" (Malachi 3:10; Psalm 34:8 KJV)

My heart's desire for more than thirty years has been that God might "get a return on His investment" in my life by being able to encourage others who are suffering as well. In writing this true story, I join in with those "older youth" of ninety-five who want to do something that will live on long after they're gone.

If you have never experienced knowing God in a personal way, why not stop right now and ask Him to reveal Himself to you in a way you can understand? It's as simple as saying the following:

"Lord, I want to know you. I know that I'm a sinner and You sent Your Son to die on my behalf so I can live. My life up to now has been one of more surviving than really living. Please forgive me of my sins and come into my heart and save me. Teach me how to really live. Show me how real You are, and show me how You're really my Heavenly 'Dad.'"

Amen

Perhaps you're already a Christian and you're still wondering to yourself, "Why does someone have to go through so much suffering?" Keep in mind I am speaking more about mental, spiritual, and emotional suffering in adults rather than physical suffering, and especially when considering physical suffering in children. With that in mind, may I remind you and suggest that there is always a two-fold reason?

First, as you've seen in the lives of so many Biblical characters, such as Job, Joseph, and David, suffering is often allowed by God to remedy something in that person's life, usually by bringing that person to the awareness of the sin nature within in order to bring that person to victory by entering into the Galatians 2:20 experience, "I am crucified with Christ, nevertheless I still live."

Secondly, Paul reminds us of why God allowed him to suffer so much when he says his life is a "drink offering" for those in the faith (Philippians 2:17; 2 Timothy 4:6). We are to be a "drink offering" for our brothers and sisters in Christ in order that we may "comfort others with the same comfort we ourselves have received of God." (2 Corinthians 1:4, KJV)

The Israelites were instructed by God in Joshua, chapter four, after they had crossed the Jordan River and entered into the Promised Land to do something in order to "remember whence thou came." In other words, they were to remember the way the Lord had led them to tell the coming generations of how great our God is, "That all the people of the earth might know the hand of the Lord, that it is mighty; that ye might fear the Lord your God *forever."* (Joshua 4:24, Complete Jewish Bible)

My brothers and sisters in Christ, this book is for building your stones of remembrance to help you as well to "remember whence thou came," that you might know God's great and mighty hand upon your life! Have you found yourself in God's wilderness? Do you recognize now that it is He who "allures you" to this very place so He can reveal Himself to you, to be your "Ishi," your great and mighty champion? Don't you hear Him calling to you? Be still before Him in order that He, too, may issue you His invitation:

> "Come on in, bring them in,"
> "Come in the Promised Land."

HOMEWORK:

- Haven't you tried it your way long enough?

- What would the "stones of remembrance" say about your life?

- Are you willing to take the "drink offering" of another and pour it onto your own wounded heart?

- Are you ready to come on in to the Promised Land?

Afterword

Susan Brock now lives a quiet and peaceable life with her husband, David, their three-year-old Schnauzer, Hudson, and their ten-year-old cat, Baby, on Lake Jacksonville in Jacksonville, Texas.

Susan's beloved counselor and friend, John Morris, founding pastor of Grace Community Church in Tyler, Texas, passed away July 20, 2013. He is greatly missed.

Susan would love to hear if this book has influenced your life for Christ. You can contact her via email at susanbrock1956@yahoo.com.

Notes

Chapter 4: Shock #3 – Why Is All This Happening to Me?

[1]   Charles R. Solomon, *The Ins and Out of Rejection* (Denver: Heritage House Publications, 1976).

[2]   Solomon, *The Ins and Out of Rejection*, pp. 55,56

[3]   Theodore H. Epp, *Job a man tried as gold* (Lincoln: Back to the Bible, 1967).

[4]   Epp, *Job a man tried as gold*, p. 19.

[5]   D. James Kennedy, *Evangelism Explosion* (Wheaton: Tyndale House Publishers, 1970).

Chapter 5: I Will Bring the Blind by a Way That They Knew Not

[6]   Theodore H. Epp, *Joseph 'God Planned It for Good'* (Lincoln: Back to the Bible, 1971).

[7]   Theodore H. Epp, *David a man after the heart of God* (Lincoln: Back to the Bible, 1965).

[8]   Be Kind to Your Parents (1963). Words by Pete Seeger, Children's' Concert at Town Hall (Columbia/Legacy) Harold Rome.

[9]   More of You (1977) CCLI # 15111, Words by Gary Paxton, music by Bill & Gloria Gaither.

[10]   Watchman Nee, *The Normal Christian Life* (Wheaton: Tyndale House Publishers, 1977)

Chapter 8: War with Amalek – Give Me Liberty or Give Me Death!!

[11]   Theodore H. Epp, *Moses Vol. I God Prepares His Man; Moses Vol. II God Strengthens His Man* (Lincoln: Back to the Bible, 1975).

[12] Epp, *Moses Vol. 1 God Prepares His Man; pp. 30, 31.*

Chapter 10: A Lesson in God's Pursuit of a Relationship with Us

[13] John Ortberg, *If You Want to Walk on Water, You've Got to Get out of the Boat* (Grand Rapids: Zondervan, 2001).

Chapter 11: A Checkup on Motivations

[14] Bill Gothard, *Institute of Basic Youth Conflicts: Research in Principles of Life* (Oakbrook: Institute of Basic Youth Conflicts, 1981).

Chapter 16: Down for the Count

[15] Dr. Susan Forward, *Men Who Hate Women & The Women Who Love Them* (Random House, 1970).

[16] Dr. Margaret J. Rinck, *Christian Men Who Hate Women* (Zondervan, 1990).

Chapter 20: God's Classroom in Assertiveness Training Part II – Going Back to School

[17] Paul Kurtz (editor), *Humanist Manifestos I and II* (Buffalo: Prometheus Books, 1973).

[18] *The Apollo Expeditions and Dust on the Moon*, O'Brien, Brian, South Australian Geographical Journal, Vol. 110, 2011, pp. 77-91.

Paul D. Ackerman, *It's A Young World After All* (Baker Book House, 1986)

[19] *Dyslexia – Contemporary approaches to the teaching of reading.* Snowling, Margaret J. Journal of Child Psychology and Psychiatry, Vol. 37 (2), February 1996. Pp. 139-148

The impact of phonemic processing instruction on the reading achievement of reading-disabled children. Richardson, Ellis. Annals of the New York Academy of Sciences, Vol. 433, December 1984, pp.97-118.

A rescue service for all dyslexic children. Miles, Elaine. Annals of Dyslexia, Vol. 35, 1985, pp. 199-207.

See Dick Flunk: Decades of research shows that kids with reading problems need phonics-based instruction. Why Aren't Educators Listening? Hoover Institution, Policy Review # 86, 2014.

[20] *Parental high concern and adolescent-onset anorexia nervosa: A case-control study to investigate direction of causality,* Shoebridge, Phillip J. British Journal of Psychiatry, Vol. 176 (2), February, 2000, pp. 132-137.

Life events and severe anorexia nervosa in adolescence, Horesh, N.; Apter, Alan; Lepkifher, E.; Ratzoni, G. Acta Psychiatrics Scandinavia, Vol. 91 (1), January, 1995. Pp. 5-9.

Perceived parental rearing practices and eating disorders, Esparon, Janet. British Review of Bulimia and Anorexia Nervosa, Vol. 6 (1), January, 1992. Pp. 39-45.

[21] *Do autistic children come from upper-middle-class parents?* Schopler, Eric; Andrews, Carol E.; Strupp, Karen Journal of Autism and Developmental Disorders, Vol. 9 (2), June, 1979. Pp. 139-152.

[22] *Aluminum and Alzheimer's disease: After a century of controversy, is there a plausible link?* Tonljenovic, Lucija, Journal of Alzheimer's Disease, Vol. 23 (4), April 2011, pp. 567-598

Aluminum ingestion: A risk factor for Alzheimer's disease? McLachlan, D.R.; Massiah, Joan. The vulnerable brain and Environmental risks, Vol. 1: Malnutrition and hazard assessment; Vol. 2: Toxins in food. Isaacson, Robert L. (Ed.); Jenson, Karl F. (Ed.J.). pp. 49-60.

Aluminum and Alzheimer's Disease, Crapper, McLachlan, D.R. Neurobiology of Aging, Vol. 7 (6), Nov. – Dec., 1986, pp. 525-532.

[23] *The effects of shame and parental rejection on homosexual men.* Friedman, Elizabeth S. Dissertation Abstracts International: Section B: The Sciences and Engineering, Vol. 56 (9-B), March, 1996. Pp. 51-69.

Recalled parent-child relations and need for approval of homosexual and heterosexual men, Milic, Johanna H.; Crowne, Douglas P. Archives of Sexual Behavior, Vo. 15 (3), June 1986. Pp. 239-246.

Chapter 21: Taking a Break and Doing "Standup"

[24] Dr. Kevin Leman, *The Birth Order Book, Why You Are The Way You Are* (New York: Bantam Doubleday Dell Publishing Group, 1985).

[25] Walter Toman, *Family Constellation, It's Effects on Personality and Social Behavior* (Springer Publishing Company, 1993.)

Chapter 22: "Feasting on Crumbs"

[26] *Amsel's frustration effect: a pavlovian replication with control for frequency and distribution of rewards.* Dudley, R.T.; Papini, M.R., Physiological Behavior, 1997, April, Vol. 61 (4), pp. 627-629.

[27] *Partial reinforcement, continuous reinforcement, and reinforcement shift effects.* Hulse, Stewart H., Journal of Experimental Psychology, Nov. 1962, Vol. 64 (5), pp. 451-452.

Partial reinforcement effects on learning and extinction of place preferences in the water maze. Jose Prados, Joan Sansa, Antonio A. Artigas, Learning and Behavior, Nov. 2008, Vol. 36 (4), pp. 311-318.

[28] *Transfer of learning, Cognitive Psychology of,* G. Steiner, International Encyclopedia of the Social and Behavioral Sciences, 2001, pp. 15845-15851.

Chapter 23: Why Are We So Attracted to Certain People – What the "Chemistry" Is Based on

[29] Harville Hendrix, Ph.D. *Keeping The Love You Find – A Personal Guide,* (New York, Simon & Schuster Inc., 1992).

[30] Harville Hendrix, Ph.D. *Getting The Love You Want – A Couples Guide,* (New York, Harper & Row Publishers Inc., 1988).

Chapter 24: The Blessing

[31] Rick Warren, *The Purpose Driven Life,* (Grand Rapids, Zondervan, 2002).

[32] PASS IT ON (1969) Kurt Kaiser, Bud John Songs, Inc.

Chapter 25: Rejoicing in Heaven

[33] Don Piper with Cecil Murphey, *90 Minutes In Heaven: A True Story of Death & Life* (Grand Rapids, Revell, 2004).

Chapter 27: The Two-Fold Dream

[34] Beth Moore, *Stepping Up: A Journey Through the Psalms of Ascent* (Lifeway Christian Resources, 2007).

[35] Beth Moore, *Daniel: Lives of Integrity, Words of Prophecy* (Lifeway Press, 2006).

[36] *Rocky Balboa,* Sony Pictures Home Entertainment, (Culver City, 2007).

Chapter 30: There Is No Plan B

[37] Kenny Rogers, *The Gambler* (Sony/ATV Cross Keys Publishing, United Artists Group, 1978).

[38] Steven Wiley Emmett, *Theory and Treatment of Anorexia Nervosa and Bulimia: Biomedical, Sociocultural, and Psychological Perspectives, (Google Ebook, 1985, pp. 115-116.)*

[39] William Thomas Allison, *My Lai: An American Atrocity in the Vietnam War* (John Hopkins University Press, 2012).

[40] Steve Grissom, *Divorce Care, Find Help Discover Hope Experience Healing* (Church Initiative, October 2009).

Chapter 31: No Greater Compliment – Zechariah 8:23

[41] Dave Ramsey, *Financial Peace Revisited* (New York, Viking Penguin, 2003).

Chapter 32: Remember Whence Thou Came

[42] Anthony Campola, If I Had It to Live Over Again *(VHS Tape, Word, Inc. 1988).*

CPSIA information can be obtained at www.ICGtesting.com
Printed in the USA
LVOW11s2141031214

416975LV00003B/3/P

9 781490 856193